THE
National ⚾ Pastime
A REVIEW OF BASEBALL HISTORY

CONTENTS

Editor: James Charlton   Copy Editor: John Paine   Designer: Glenn LeDoux
Designated readers and peer reviewers: Phil Birnbaum, Clifford Blau, Joe Dittmar, Rob Edelman,
Ed Hartig, Cliff Hoyt, Bill Nowlin, Stew Thornley, Lyle Spatz, Dick Thompson

A Note from the Editor

The National Pastime for 2005 has a number of entertaining stories from beginning to end.

At the beginning is Bill Nowlin and Kit Krieger's engaging cover story about discovering a worn and faded commemorative plaque in Havana's La Tropical park. The bronze memorialized a game played there between two teams of American all-stars in 1930. The discovery of the plaque in 2001 came about during a Cubaball trip led by Kit. There were about a dozen SABR members along, including myself, so I was delighted when Kit and Bill wrote up the story. What makes the account even more interesting is the addition of photos from an album given to each of the all-stars who played in the 1930 game by their generous Cuban host Blanco Herrera. Lance Richbourg was one of the touring stars and his son, the artist Lance Richbourg, Jr., graciously lent the album to us.

Tom Altherr and Charlie Metro, the former manager and coach, provide the journal's last article, a short explanation and addition to Richard Puerzer's fine cover story in the last issue of TNP. Puerzer's piece, readers may recall, was on the Kansas City Royals short-lived baseball academy.

One of my favorite writers is Bob Schaefer, a formidable researcher, who has turned his attention to Cap Anson's stage career in *A Runaway Colt*. The play opened in Brooklyn in 1895 at the new 1,700-seat Montauk Theatre, which was later moved around the corner when Flatbush Avenue was expanded as a result of building the Manhattan Bridge. The play moved to Broadway several months later, and then on to Chicago. It appears that Cap Anson was more successful on the diamond than trodding the boards.

There are two articles on foul balls, two that discuss Ole Hoss Radbourn, and two that are interviews with former ball players. The latter includes Jim Smith's article, based on talks with Bobby Doerr, discussing his PCL career as a teenage infielder beginning with the Hollywood Sheiks. When that team shifted to San Diego, Bobby became an original Padre before going on to star for the Boston Red Sox. Jim Sargent shares with us Carl Erskine's reflections on the Boys of Summer. Both former stars come off as remarkable men.

David Vincent takes us on a tour of Arlington National Cemetery and discusses the nearly two dozen baseball notables buried there. From Abner Doubleday to SABR founder Bob Davids (not the only SABR member buried at Arlington), the list includes Lu Blue, Doc Lavan and less-known Major and Negro Leaguers.

Jim Charlton
May 2005

La Tropical Park, Then and Now

by Bill Nowlin and Kit Krieger

In February 2001, more than a dozen members of The Society for American Baseball Research joined the first Cubaball Tours visit to enjoy a week of baseball in Cuba. Most tour participants felt the weeklong tour was one of the best travel experiences they'd ever enjoyed. The group, led by Kit Krieger and Peter Bjarkman, saw five ball games in four stadiums, met with Connie Marrero, visited a baseball academy, joined Havana's daily outdoor baseball discussion group, paid homage at Martin Dihigo's final resting place, and talked a lot of baseball for the whole week.

We didn't get to meet Fidel, but this was a dedicated group of baseball fans, and it amused participant Peggy Engle that we were so wrapped up in talking with Marrero that almost no one but her noticed the topless tourist by the "Havana Libre" hotel swimming pool just on the other side of the plate-glass window from the room in which we were meeting.

At one point, on February 23, on the way back from a seminar on Cuban baseball history at the Institute for Friendship Among the Nations, our *jefes* had the tour bus stop at a former baseball stadium known as La Tropical. This interested Bill Nowlin in particular because he'd visited Havana's Biblioteca Nacional the day before, researching two games that Ted Williams and the Red Sox had played in Cuba in 1946. A visit to La Tropical, initially built in 1930 for the Pan American Games, was not on the original tour itinerary. A Krieger query about the location of the stadium revealed that it was currently used as a track and field facility and was little altered from the days when Martin Dihigo, Oscar Charleston, Josh

Gibson, and Cristobal Torriente roamed the grounds. Our itinerary was adjusted to seize the opportunity to visit this historic site.

We climbed down from our bus and entered La Tropical (now called Pepe Marrero, named after a hero of the revolution) through gates along what had been left field. If the fences are placed as they were in 1930, it was clear that the stadium was a pitcher's park, save for a short porch in right field. The center field fence was well over 500 feet distant from home plate, and left field was more than 400 feet away.

As everyone was looking around, one or two tour members noticed a couple of worn and faded plaques affixed to a wall inside the stadium. They looked like they'd been there a long time, and the heavy patina made the inscriptions difficult to read.

Suddenly, Krieger shouted, "Holy shit!" and we crowded around to see what caused the commotion. Working to make out the wording on the plaque, it became clear that in 1930 a touring group of major league ballplayers had come to Havana and played what was truly an all-star game at Tropical. A commemorative plaque featured the two rosters and facsimile signatures of the stars. As the names of the participants were deciphered and read out loud, it was clear that the game included quite a number of future Hall of Famers.

On Saturday morning, Bill Nowlin returned to the library and flashed his newly acquired library card from the day before, requesting the October 1930 run of the newspaper *Diario de la Marina*. It turned out that this was not just one game, but a seven-game series between Las Estrellas de Davey Bancroft and Las Estrellas de Jewel Ens: Bancroft's Stars versus Ens's Stars. The Ens team won five games, while Bancroft took two.

About 20,000 attended the opening ceremonies at what was then named Stadium Cerveza Tropical.

BILL NOWLIN *has written extensively on the Red Sox, most recently* Blood Feud *(Rounder Books) and is currently Vice President of SABR.* KIT KRIEGER *pitched three innings for the Pacific Coast League Vancouver Mounties in 1968 and currently operates Cubaball Tours.*

In all there were nine future Hall of Famers in the series. They were Davey Bancroft, Heinie Manush, Rabbit Maranville, Paul Waner, Al Lopez, Pie Traynor, Chuck Klein, Carl Hubbell, and Bill Terry. The scores of the games were as follows:

Game 1: Ens 1, Bancroft 0 (this game took only 1 hour and 9 minutes to play—not much time for TV ads in 1930!)
Game 2: Bancroft 4, Ens 2
Game 3: Bancroft 5, Ens 4
Game 4: Ens 3, Bancroft 2
Game 5: Ens 1, Bancroft 0 (a two-hitter thrown by Tiny Chaplin)

In between games 5 and 6, the Bancrofts played a Habana all-star team and beat them, but only by 2-1, winning in the ninth. Ramon Bragana pitched for Habana.

Game 6: Ens 4, Bancroft 1
Game 7: Ens 6, Bancroft 2 (October 19)

Series MVP (actually, the newspaper phrased this as *en nuestra opinion, la figura mas destacada de le serie*) was Larry French, who won three of the five games his team won. Tom Oliver, Lopez, Terry, Maranville, and Chaplin were others noted as standouts.

In game seven, *Diario de la Marina* noted, "El viejo Maranville fue otra sensacion del game. Sus cogidas de balsillo gustaron sobremanera al publico y sus actos comicos aun mas." Maranville was 2-for-5 on the day.

There was an entire page of photos in the rotogravure section, showing fans coming to the game, in the stands, and play on the field.

One of the umpires was Magriñat, who also happened to umpire 16 years later at the Red Sox vs. Senators two-game exhibition there in March 1946, which Bill Nowlin had just researched. This was Jose M. Magriñat, whose box of bones we found later that day inside the 1942 Baseballists Monument in Cementerio Cristobal Colon. That's another story!

The day after this series concluded, on October 20, Luque pitched for the Habanistas Rojas against the Louisville Coroneles. Unfortunately, Cuba's national library lacks a photocopy machine, so the only way to get box scores from there is to copy them by hand. We present the box score for game seven.

Even though our discovery was made in the year 2001, one of the players who participated was still alive and well in Tampa: Al Lopez. Born in 1908, Lopez broke in with the Dodgers in 1929. The receiver hit .309 in his first full season (1930) and was invited to join the touring party.

Soon after returning to the States, Nowlin phoned Lopez and found that he remembered the visit well:

There was a lot of fine ballplayers that went on that tour. We stayed at the Biltmore. It was very nice. It was during the Machado regime and I think there was a lot of rumbling and dissatisfaction among the people there. John McGraw, the manager of the Giants, had some interests, I think, at the Tropical racetrack, the horse track. And he was very friendly with the people in Cuba at that time, and they asked him to bring two all-star teams to go over there. We were there for two weeks.

We played seven games in all. There were some good players on both teams, and we had some real good games at Tropical Stadium. It was a real big ballpark. I don't think there was any home runs hit in the whole seven games we played there. It was big. Yeah, I hit a triple in one of the games.

Then we went back again in 1931, with the Brooklyn club. We formed two teams and played. We had a good time. I like Havana.

Are you going to write about this thing? If you do, mention Blanco Herrera. Went out of his way as a host to treat us very nice. He was the owner of the Tropical Brewery. He did everything he could to be nice to the players and the management.

They were very close ballgames! In fact, some of the fans—because we beat them one game and then they came back and beat us the next day— some of the fans were thinking it was prearranged to go that way.

They were fast ball games. They had tremendous crowds. They didn't have enough capacity in the grandstands, so they roped the field off, on both sides—the left field side and the right field side. We didn't take any Cuban players. They were playing their regular season at Almendares Park.

In a separate interview, Russ Scarritt's grandson Russ shared what he had heard about the tour. He had heard that Blanco Herrera, who obviously had a real love of baseball, traveled to the States "and handpicked a group of men from different teams. Paid them $1,000 per game. He [grandfather] and his wife and other players and their wives traveled down." The $1,000 per game figure seems unlikely, but for the seven-game series it may well have been the pay the players received. They traveled by cruise ship and, grandson Russ heard, played every day and partied every night.

The plaque lists 12 names under the Ens name and 15 under Bancroft. Pretty small rosters by today's standards and, as Al Lopez notes, the rosters were not supplemented by any Cuban players during the tour.

The plaque commemorating the 1930 touring American stars is one of four plaques mounted on the walls of La Tropical. One offers a tribute to Don Julio Blanco Herrera, the owner of the La Tropical Brewery who was remembered so fondly by Al Lopez after nearly seven decades. A date—1956—is inscribed on the plaque, the only one of the four with such an inscription.

Another bronze commemorates the 2nd Central American Games, which took place at La Tropical from March 15 to April 5, 1930, only six months before the American baseball squads arrived in Cuba.

The fourth and final plaque commemorates the Second World Baseball Championships, played at La Tropical, August 12-26, 1939. The inscription reads that this was the "Primero en America." In fact, the first world championship, a competition of amateur teams played from 1938 to 1953, had been hosted by the English and featured only teams from Britain and the United States. In 1939, the host Cubans won the championship, going undefeated in a three-team tournament. Nicaragua split their six games while the Americans went winless!

Because the plaque clearly needed attention, Kit Krieger financed a cleaning and restoration, and was able to return to La Tropical in April 2003 to see that the work had been performed. The four bronzes now gleam and can be easily read by visitors to the historic park. Cubaball has also paid for the cleaning and restoration of two monuments, dated 1942 and 1951, at the Cementario Cristobal Colon. Weathering and neglect had caused many of the inscriptions on the monuments to become nearly illegible.

AMERICAN STARS LISTED ON THE COMMEMORATIVE PLAQUE

Jewel Ens (Pirates)
Don Hurst (Phillies)
Larry French (Pirates)
Heinie Manush (Senators)
Paul Waner (Pirates)
Pinky Whitney (Phillies)
Al Lopez (Dodgers)
Tom Oliver (Red Sox)
Pie Traynor (Pirates)
Steve Swetonic (Pirates)
James Chaplin (Giants)
Rabbit Maranville (Braves)
Dave Bancroft (Giants)
Chuck Klein (Phillies)

Bill Walker (Giants)
Lance Richbourg (Braves)
Tom Zachary (Braves)
Carl Hubbell (Giants)
Eddie Marshall (Giants)
Russell Scarritt (Red Sox)
Wally Gilbert (Dodgers)
Clyde Sukeforth (Reds)
Bob O'Farrell (Giants)
Harry Rice (Giants)
Bill Terry (Giants)
Glenn Wright (Dodgers)
Bobby Smith (Braves)

A Cuban friend of Krieger's has discovered that the artist who designed the plaque commemorating the 1930 series is alive and well on the island. He is Adolfo Gonzales Crespo, now 69. He claims to still have the original molds for the work. On a future visit to Cuba, Krieger hopes to contact Crespo and have a copy made for the Hall of Fame in Cooperstown.

There were no strikeouts in the game.

GAME SEVEN, OCTOBER 19, 1930

ENS	AB	R	H	O	A	E	BANCROFT	AB	R	H	O	A	E
Maranville, ss	5	1	2	6	2	0	Scarritt, lf	4	0	0	4	0	0
Waner, rf	4	1	1	0	1	0	Gilbert, 3b	3	0	0	0	5	0
Oliver, cf	4	0	1	9	0	0	Rice, cf	4	0	1	2	0	0
Traynor, 3b	5	0	1	1	1	0	Terry, 1b	4	1	1	9	0	0
Whitney, 2b	4	1	4	0	2	0	Klein, rf	4	1	2	3	0	0
Manush, lf	5	1	1	2	0	0	Wright, ss	3	0	1	4	5	1
Lopez, C	4	1	1	2	0	0	Marshall, 2b	4	0	1	4	5	0
Hurst, 1b	4	0	1	6	1	0	O'Farrell, c	4	0	0	1	0	0
Chaplin, p	4	1	1	1	1	0	Zachary, p	2	0	1	0	0	0
French, p	0	0	0	0	0	0	Hubbell, p	1	0	1	0	0	0
	39	6	13	27	8	0		33	2	8	27	15	1

```
ENS        000  000  303 - 6
BANCROFT   000  100  001 - 2
```

W - French, L - Zachary

Three base hits: Terry, Lopez. Two base hits: Klein (2), Zachary, Maranville, Waner, Whitney. Sacrifice hit: Wright. Carreras empujadas (RBI): Klein, Lopez, Hurst, Waner (2), Whitney, Marshall. BB: Zachary 3, Chaplin 1. Quedadas en bases (LOB): Ens 9, Bancroft 6. Time of game: 1 hour, 14 minutes. Umpires: McGrew (home), Magriñat, Atan.

Peter Bjarkman, a student of Cuban baseball, says that La Tropical was built by the Machado government for the 1930 Central American Games (the first staged in Havana and second Central American Games overall.) Roberto Gonzalez Echeverria's book *The Pride of Havana* provides further detail. The stadium was built on the Tropical Brewery grounds, and Tropical's Don Julio Blanco Herrera invited the major leaguers to visit Havana and stimulate interest in Cuba and Cuban baseball.

La Tropical was largely abandoned for baseball after the 1946 opening of Cerro Stadium; it has since been used as a soccer stadium and track field under the name of Pepe Marrero Stadium.

Bjarkman adds, "Tropical was used as a Cuban League park for only 15 years; its greatest glories came as a site for Baseball World Cup (Amateur World Series) matches in 1939, 1940, 1941 and 1942. The most famous game in Cuban baseball history (Conrado Marrero and Cuba losing to Daniel Canonico and Venezuela in the 1941, World Cup finals) was played there. Details of that game are available not only in Echeverria's book but also in my own *Elysian Fields Quarterly* story on Marrero."

Images from the Tour

The following photographs have been provided courtesy of SABR member Lance Richbourg, Jr., whose father had saved an album from the tour which was presented to each player.

*Above: Jewel Ens, Don Julio Blanco Herrera,
and Dave Bancroft pose with an umpire.
Below: A group photo; Herrera in white sut
and holding a punama hat.*

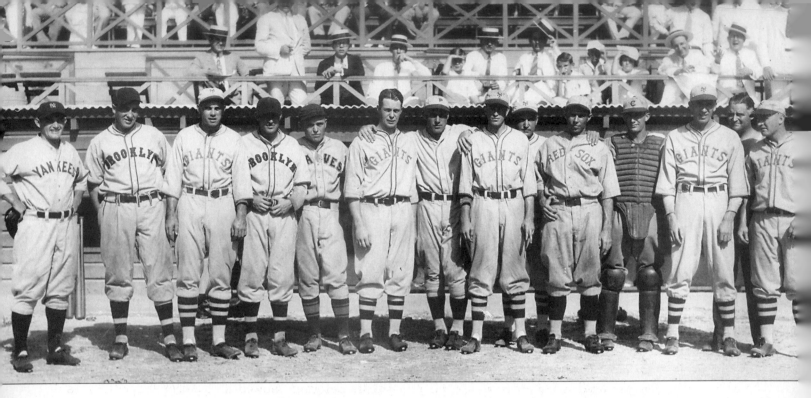

Above: All-Star players pose before the game.
Below: Fans at La Tropical.

THE NATIONAL PASTIME

The Positive Grip Baseball Bat

by Ken Tillman

The Louisville Slugger bat is advertised as "the bat of champions since 1884." Professional players, semi-professionals, and amateur players have used this bat since that date. It has been "the bat" for many major leaguers during the intervening years and, in fact, during the 1940s and 1950s almost every major leaguer used a Louisville Slugger bat. With escalating baseball salaries, major leaguers can now easily afford to have personalized bats made for them. This has resulted in more companies and mom and pop businesses entering the baseball bat manufacturing business. In the early 1900s there were also individuals who became bat manufacturers as baseball expanded and there was an increased demand for bats by amateur teams as well as players in the professional leagues. One of the individuals who manufactured bats during that era was Wellington Stockton Titus.

Titus was not a novice about baseball. He played third base for many years on the Hopewell, NJ town team. However, his greatest claim to fame was the fact that he patented the first portable baseball backstop on April 9, 1907. It is not known when he decided to go into the baseball bat manufacturing business, but he was successful in manufacturing bats that were used extensively by players in the Hopewell area, and some old-timers there insist that his bats were also used by players on the Philadelphia Athletics. There is a certain logic to this claim, since the first major league team to use his portable baseball backstop was the Philadelphia A's.

Titus was a skilled, self-taught engineer who had the ability to design and build many items that were

KEN TILLMAN *grew up in Iowa and became a lifelong Cleveland Indians fan due to the influence of fellow Iowan, Bob Feller. He is a retired physical education professor/coach and currently lives in Virginia.*

not readily available in stores during the late 1800s and early 1900s. He was renowned for his skill as a house mover, and at various times in his life he also served as a postmaster, civil engineer, house builder, and farm foreman. He was characterized as being a person who was always looking for a challenge. The bat he designed showed his perceptive qualities, as it had a special feature which he referred to as the "positive grip." The positive grip consisted of circular grooves, that he had cut into the handle of the bat. He designed a lathe to make these grooves which went from the knob of the bat to about four inches from the trademark. The purpose of these grooves was to provide a firm grip for the hitter. It was common to put various substances or tape on the bat handle to prevent the bat from slipping in the hitter's hand when swinging. Even pine tar wouldn't be needed if the positive groove bat developed by Wellington Stockton Titus had been a business success!

The trademark on his bat had the inscription:

TITUS' POSITIVE GRIP BAT
"MY SPEED"
MANUFACTURED BY W. S. TITUS
GLENMORE, NJ

The town of Glenmore no longer exists, but it was a small village near the current town of Hopewell when Mr. Titus was manufacturing his bats. In fact, Mr. Titus was the postmaster in Glenmore for a brief period.

He later changed his trademark slightly by burning a black diamond into the wood. His bats then became known as the Black Diamond bats and were in high demand by baseball players in the area. There is the theory that his bats were also used by the players on the Philadelphia Athletics' team and other professional teams.

Some of his bats had orange and black rings on them, which gave them the appearance of a tiger's tale. The tiger is the mascot of Princeton University and their colors are orange and black. George Wells, the son of the owner of the farm where Mr. Titus was foreman, was an outstanding baseball player at Princeton University. It is probably this connection that led to the placing of orange and black stripes on some of his bats. He was always the innovator.

Wellington Stockton Titus was not only an innovator, but he was a person who looked forward to new challenges. It was probably this spirit that resulted in the demise of his bat manufacturing business. The company that was seasoning his bats for him tried to speed up the process and either had the ovens too hot or left the bats to cure for too long a period of time. His bats became dry and brittle and broke upon impact with a baseball. At this point he became frustrated, went out of the baseball bat manufacturing business, and moved on to new challenges. He was a proud person, and he knew that the reputation of his baseball bats was ruined.

Mr. Titus was a perceptive person. Maybe he anticipated that the grooves in his bat would eventually become illegal as the baseball equipment rules became more sophisticated and stringent than they were at the time he was manufacturing his "positive grip" bat. His grooves would not be permitted by the current rules of either Major League Baseball or the NCAA.

Major League Baseball Official Rule 1.10.(a) The bat shall be a smooth, round stick not more than . . .

NCAA Rule 1 Section 11. a. Wood bat. The bat must be a smooth, rounded stick not more than . . .

Both the major league rules and the NCAA rules do permit any substance or material up to 18 inches from its end to improve the grip. He designed his bat to improve the grip by making grooves for about 18 inches from the end without the problem of putting on tape or other substances that were commonly used during his era to give a better grip to the batter. Baseball rules requiring a smooth bat made it easier to standardize bats and not give an advantage to batters who had different configurations of their bats. It is also possible that hitting a ball on the grooved part of the handle could change the trajectory of the ball. Although Mr. Titus designed his grooved bat solely to provide a better grip for the batters, batters might get an unnatural bounce or misdirection on the ball when it came off the grooved part of the bat surface. These factors probably led to the smooth bat requirement in baseball rules.

There is an interesting epilogue to the life history of Wellington Stockton Titus. Almost 94 years after he received his patent for the portable baseball backstop, and 60 years after his death, he was inducted into the Inventors' Hall of Fame, where he joined such famous New Jersey inventors as Einstein and Edison.

August 31, 1932: Day of the Ineligible Player

by Lowell Blaisdell

Well-seasoned SABR members will easily recall the days of perusing box scores in which—frequently rather than rarely—the lineups came to nine to a dozen players on each side. In nearly all instances, box scorekeeping was relatively easy. When now and then a box score addict encountered a batting order alteration caused by substitutions, a quick glance at the pinch-hitting notes, clarified how, when, and why this had occurred.[1] For the aficionado, the symmetry, clarity, and certainty that he found in his daily ration of box scores provided a few moments of internal quiescence that seemed constantly to escape him in the otherwise unending turmoil of everyday living.

As an exception to this reassuring tableau, on August 31, 1932, the Chicago Cubs and New York Giants played a game at Wrigley Field that was extraordinary,[2] ending in such a way as to cause two of the most influential newspapers, representing the cities of the rival teams—the *Chicago Tribune* and the *New York Times*—to print discrepant box scores.

In the game the Cubs gradually overcame a four-run deficit, tying it in the ninth and winning it in the tenth. In the tenth inning, a unique batting order entanglement arose that created the newspapers' box score asymmetry. The origins of this snarl began with two substitutions that Cub manager and first baseman Charlie Grimm made in the eighth inning. Having, as number six hitter, doubled, thereby narrowing the Giants lead to 5-4, he then withdrew for a pinch-runner (Stan Hack). The number seven hitter, Gabby Hartnett, though a power at the plate, was slow, so Grimm had Marv Gudat, reserve outfielder and

first baseman, bat for him.[3] After Gudat made out, he stayed in the game as Grimm's replacement at first base. Necessarily, he replaced Hartnett as the number seven hitter. Since there had to be another catcher, Zack Taylor replaced Hartnett, but equally unavoidably, as the number six, not number seven hitter.[4]

In the course of tying the game in the ninth, Frank Demaree, a reserve outfielder, pinch-hit for the relief pitcher, Bob Smith. This entailed no batting order repositioning, so the new Cub pitcher would continue to bat in the ninth spot.

During the Cubs ninth, it began to rain steadily. The umpires would have been justified in declaring the game ended in a 5-5 tie. However, since this was the Giants' last game at Wrigley Field for the season, and it was important for the Cubs, they decided to allow it to continue. From then on, the steady rain had an important bearing on the outcome.

Grimm turned to Guy Bush, a starter, as his next relief pitcher. Unable to grip the wet ball properly, Bush gave up two hits, a walk, hit two batters, and made a wild pitch, while four Giant runs clattered in. Grimm had to replace him with his fifth pitcher, Leroy Herrmann, who had appeared in seven games that year and had a 6.39 ERA. Somehow Herrmann retired the side with no more runs scoring.

As the Cubs' half of the tenth inning started, the rain began to beat down harder. Bill Terry, also a playing manager-first baseman, put in Sam Gibson—like Herrmann, barely a major leaguer—as his new pitcher. Up came the Cubs' first hitter.

Several Cub players gathered around home plate umpire, George Magerkurth, to inform him that Bill Jurges, the injured regular shortstop, would pinch-hit for Leroy Herrmann. Grimm had gotten his number six and nine hitters mixed up. Since, according to the rule book, no manager on offense is permitted

LOWELL BLAISDELL *is Professor of History Emeritus at Texas Tech University. A lifelong Cub fan and SABR member for over 25 years, he has written articles on baseball's past for* The Baseball Research Journal, The National Pastime, *and* Baseball History.

NEW YORK (N.).							CHICAGO (N.).						
	ab.	r.	h.	po.	a.	e.		ab.	r.	h.	po.	a.	e.
Joe Moore, lf.	5	2	1	4	0	0	Herman, 2b...	6	2	3	4	5	0
Critz, 2b....	6	2	4	1	5	0	English, 3b..	6	1	2	0	3	0
Terry, 1b..	6	1	5	13	0	0	Cuyler, rf...	6	2	5	2	1	0
Ott, rf....	6	0	2	2	0	0	Steph'son, lf.	3	1	1	7	2	0
Lindstrom, cf.	5	0	1	2	0	0	J. Moore, cf.	5	0	0	2	0	0
Hogan, c...	5	0	0	3	1	0	Grimm, 1b..	4	0	3	11	1	0
Marshall, ss.	4	1	1	3	5	0	cHack	0	0	0	0	0	0
Vergez, 3b..	4	2	2	1	3	0	Herrmann, p.	0	0	0	0	0	0
Fitzs'mons, p.	2	0	0	0	2	0	eJurges	1	0	0	0	0	0
Bell, p....	0	0	0	0	0	0	Hartnett, c...	2	0	0	1	0	0
aO'Farrell ..	0	1	0	0	0	0	Gudat, 1b...	2	0	0	1	0	0
Gibson, p...	0	0	0	0	0	0	Koenig, ss...	5	2	2	1	3	1
							Warneke, p..	0	0	0	0	0	0
Total...	43	9	16	*29	16	0	Tinning, p...	1	0	0	0	2	1
							bHemsley ...	1	0	0	0	0	0
							Smith, p....	1	0	1	0	3	0
							dDemaree ...	1	1	1	0	0	0
							Bush, p....	0	0	0	0	0	0
							Taylor, c...	1	1	1	1	0	0
							Total...	45	10	19	30	20	2

*Two out when winning run was scored.
aBatted for Bell in tenth.
bBatted for Tinning in fourth.
cRan for Grimm in eighth.
dBatted for Smith in ninth.
eBatted for Herrmann in tenth.

New York ....3 1 0 1 0 0 0 0 0 4—9
Chicago ....0 0 2 1 0 0 0 1 1 5—10

Runs batted in—Terry 3, Ott, Cuyler 5, Stephenson, Hemsley, Grimm, Joe Moore, Critz 2, Koenig, English.
Two-base hits—Critz, Stephenson, Grimm. Three-base hits—Terry, Cuyler, Koenig. Home runs—Koenig, Cuyler. Sacrifices—Fitzsimmons 2. Double plays—Herman, Koenig and Grimm; Critz, Marshall and Terry; Fitzsimmons, Marshall and Terry; Hogan, Marshall and Terry; Stephenson, Koenig and Taylor. Left on bases—New York 10, Chicago 9. Bases on balls—Off Warneke 1, Fitzsimmons 2, Bell 1, Bush 1. Struck out—By Fitzsimmons 3, Smith 1. Hits—Off Warneke 4 in 0 innings (pitched to five men), Fitzsimmons 14 in 8 1-3, Tinning 4 in 4, Bell 0 in 2-3, Smith 5 in 5, Gibson 5 in 2-3, Bush 2 in 0 (pitched to five men), Herrmann 1 in 1. Hit by pitcher—By Bush (Vergez, O'Farrell). Wild pitches—Fitzsimmons, Bush. Winning pitcher—Herrmann. Losing pitcher—Gibson. Umpires—Magerkurth and Quigley. Time of game—2:15.

NEW YORK.							CHICAGO.						
	Ab	R	H	P	A	E		Ab	R	H	P	A	E
Joe Moore, lf	5	2	1	4	0	0	Herman, 2b........	6	2	3	4	5	0
Critz, 2b	6	2	4	1	5	0	English, 3b........	6	1	2	0	3	0
Terry, 1b..............	6	1	5	13	0	0	Cuyler, rf..........	6	2	5	2	1	0
Ott, rf..............	6	0	2	2	0	0	Stephenson, lf......	3	1	1	7	2	0
Lindstrom, cf.......	5	0	1	2	0	0	John Moore, cf......	5	0	0	2	0	0
Hogan, c............	5	0	0	3	1	0	Grimm, 1b..........	4	0	3	11	1	0
Marshall, ss........	4	1	1	3	5	0	‡Hack	0	0	0	0	0	0
Vergez, 3b.........	4	2	2	1	3	0	Taylor, c..........	1	1	1	1	0	0
Fitzsimmons, p......	2	0	0	0	2	0	Hartnett, c........	2	0	0	1	0	0
Bell, p............	0	0	0	0	0	0	Gudat, 1b..........	2	0	0	1	0	0
°O'Farrell	0	1	0	0	0	0	Koenig, ss..........	5	2	2	1	3	1
Gibson, p...........	0	0	0	0	0	0	Warneke, p.........	0	0	0	0	0	0
							Tinning, p........	1	0	0	0	2	1
							‖Hemsley	1	0	0	0	0	0
							Smith, p...........	1	0	1	0	3	0
							‖Demaree	1	1	1	0	0	0
							Bush, p............	0	0	0	0	0	0
							Herrmann, p........	0	0	0	0	0	0
	43	9	16	†29	16	0		45	10	19	30	20	2

°Batted for Bell in the 10th.
†Two out when winning run scored.
¶Hemsley batted for Tinning in the 4th and Jurges for Herrmann in 10th.
‡Ran for Grimm in the 8th.
‖Batted for Smith in the 9th.

NEW YORK ....3 1 0 1 0 0 0 0 0 4— 9
CHICAGO ....0 0 2 1 0 0 0 1 1 5—10

Runs batted in—Terry [3], Ott, Cuyler, [5], Stephenson, Hemsley, Grimm, Joe Moore, Critz [2], Koenig, E. English. Two base hits—Critz, Stephenson, Grimm. Three base hits—Terry, Cuyler, Koenig. Home runs—Koenig, Cuyler. Sacrifices—Fitzsimmons [2]. Double plays—Herman to Koenig to Grimm; Critz to Marshall to Terry; Fitzsimmons to Marshall to Terry; Hogan to Marshall to Terry; Stephenson to Koenig to Taylor. Left on bases—New York, 10; Chicago, 9. Bases on balls—Off Warneke, 1; Fitzsimmons, 2; Bell, 1; Bush, 1. Struck out—Fitzsimmons, 3; Smith, 1. Hits—Off Warneke, 4 in no innings [pitched to five men]; Fitzsimmons, 14 in 8 1-3; Tinning, 4 in 4; Bell, none in 2-3; Smith, 5 in 5; Gibson, 5 in 2-3; Bush, 2 in none [pitched to five men]; Herrmann, 1 in 1. Hit by pitcher—By Bush [Vergez, O'Farrell]. Wild pitches—Fitzsimmons, Bush. Winning pitcher—Herrmann. Losing pitcher—Gibson. Umpires—Magerkurth and Quigley. Time—2:15.

to replace a batter in a fixed batting position with a different player occupying another lineup spot, Jurges—whether Grimm or anybody else understood it or not—was pinch-hitting for Taylor, not Herrmann. It is not an umpire's duty to inform a team that it is about to permit one of its players to bat out of turn, so Magerkurth listened without comment to what the Cubs had to say. The field announcer informed the fans that Jurges would bat for Herrmann.

Jurges made out. Neither before his at-bat nor especially after did the Giants file a protest, since his out had served their purpose. This effectively eliminated Taylor from the game. Gudat, the number seven hitter, easily made out also. The Giants had a four-run lead, there were two outs, and nobody on. How could they possibly lose?

Mark Koenig, the Cubs fill-in shortstop, came up. He drove a home run high into the right field bleachers. This made the score 9-6. Among the players and such rain-drenched fans as remained, this ignited a spark of hope.

Then came the most baffling development of this—or almost any other game. Who batted but Zack Taylor! By rule in the catcher's number six spot, he turned up intending to bat ninth.

In the rule book for 1932, two provisions covered Taylor's situation. First, rule 44, section 1—the usual batting out-of-turn provision—specified that a claim to its application had to be made before the first pitch to the next batter. Second, rule 17, section 2—which almost never was needed—held that any player replaced by another could not return to the game.[5] At this moment Magerkurth should have ordered Taylor back to the bench as no longer eligible to play. That he did not suggests that in the rain and confusion, he too had gotten tangled up.

Taylor singled to right. All that Terry had to do to win the game then and there was, before the next pitch, to remind Magerkurth either that as an illegal batter, Taylor could not possibly be in the correct batting position, or, if Magerkurth's omission had granted him a phantom batting status, then he was still batting out of order because the ninth spot belonged to Herrmann. Magerkurth then would have invoked the "out" penalty for a hitter batting out of turn, and the Giants would have won. In the moment while the great question hung in the rain, Taylor was a hitter who had not only batted out of turn, but was not even in the game, yet had delivered a vital hit.

Terry made no move. It is barely possible that, still enjoying a three-run lead with two out, he felt that it would come more easily through some routine play[6] than to try, in the boggy bedlam, to get the umpire's attention long enough to explain that the Giants had won for as sane a reason as that the rule book said so. Much more likely, however, is that between keeping up with his field position on the field and the chaos on the field, he had become hopelessly entangled in Grimm's substitutions. After all, Grimm himself had. This episode graphically illustrated one reason why playing managers gradually became obsolete. In a sudden, in-game rules crisis a playing manager had too much to do to protect his team on rule book technicalities.

Gibson threw a pitch to the next batter, so Taylor's hit stood. Furthermore, this legitimatized him as a batter hitting in the proper spot. As the game continued, it quickly took an ominous turn for the Giants. The next two batters singled, scoring Taylor and making it 9-7. Up came Kiki Cuyler, the Cubs fine right fielder and years later Hall of Fame electee. He was a valuable clutch hitter. In this game he already had four hits. One was a triple that hit the scoreboard—then at ground level in deep center field—a deed accomplished only thrice before.[7] Another was the two-out single in the ninth inning that had tied the score. Moreover, earlier in the summer, in a last of the ninth tie with Gibson pitching, he had singled to win the game.

Gibson pitched to him this time with it raining harder than ever, and almost unbelievably Cuyler slammed a home run into the bleachers just to the right of the scoreboard. It won the game for the Cubs, 10-9. Such fans as remained all but went berserk. Actually, given the conditions in which Cuyler hit this

Kiki Cuyler

home run, it was a greater feat than Gabby Hartnett's more famous "homer in the gloaming," September 28, 1938.

From the team's standpoint, this was the climactic end of a 12-game winning streak. So inspirational was the finish that it all but ensured that the Cubs would win the 1932 National League pennant. Of its kind, so a rare a feat was it that in more than 70 years since not once has the team won with a five-run rally in the last half of an extra-inning game.

To return to the *Tribune*'s and the *Times*' disparate box synopses, suppose an ardent fan from each city had examined his newspaper's box score and game account. What would he have found? Since the Cubs' victory was a momentous one, the Windy City reader would have been able to pore over several columns devoted to the game, including an elaborate account of the tenth-inning fantasy. However, he would have had to end up shaking his head in disbelief at the *Tribune*'s version of the box score. If, as it insisted in its game account, Jurges had batted for Taylor in the sixth position—where its box listed him as playing—then how could it account for the actual fact that the reserve catcher had batted ninth, without so indicating it? Furthermore, if, as the box conceded in its pinch-hitting footnotes, Jurges had batted for Herrmann, then how did this last pitcher turn up batting sixth, when the only ninth-inning change showed Demaree pinch-hitting for the pitcher, meaning that whoever was the final pitcher had to be batting ninth? There was no possible explanation of the discrepancies.

As for the Giants fan, he would at least have had before him what officially was the correct box score. However, he would have been at a loss to figure out how it possibly could be so. The *Times* account of the game was a lackluster one, so the fan would have obtained no enlightenment from that quarter. But the effect was to leave the fan mystified as to what occurred. This box score addict would have quickly spotted that the only Cub ninth-inning substitution was Demaree batting for the pitcher, meaning that any subsequent Cub pitcher was bound to bat ninth. Yet while Bush was listed in that spot, somehow Herrmann, his successor, appeared in the sixth spot. Furthermore, how could it be that catcher Taylor appeared as batting ninth when his predecessor, Hartnett, was shown as hitting seventh.[8] Whether the box score fancier lived in Chicago or New York, he could only conclude in silent desperation that it was not even safe to assume infallibility in this one small corner of his life where he thought he had found it.

Notes

1. Soon after the end of World War II, the emergence and development of the defensive double switch put an end to easily figuring out how a change in the batting order had come to be. The author desires to express his gratitude to James W. Harper, a longtime friend, former academic colleague, and equally vociferous fan, for his valuable help as advisor, editor, and scribe.

2. The *Chicago Tribune* noted the managers' and umpires' mistakes on September 1, 1932, in an article entitled: "Taylor Bats Out of Turn; Giants Umpires Miss It." As if an omen, players and spectators alike were left agog by a full solar eclipse that occurred immediately prior to the game.

3. In the third inning, a heavy shower had halted play for half an hour, making the infield soft, leading Grimm to feel that if Hartnett hit anything on the ground, he would be a sure out, while Gudat, who was quite fast, might beat out a slowly hit ball.

4. This and subsequent references to game happenings are drawn from the *Chicago Tribune*, September 1, 1932, from the *Chicago Daily News'* "My Biggest Baseball Day" Series, 1940s by John P. Carmichael, which included Charley Grimm's "Greatest Day," as recounted to Hal Totten, and, slightly, from the *New York Times*, September 1, 1932.

5. The two rules from the 1932 rulebook are quoted in the *Chicago Tribune*, September 1, 1932. The author, who listened to the game on the radio as a 12-year-old, recalls that the broadcasters mentioned the batting out of order, but missed the other rule violation

6. This, at least, was what Grimm thought the Giants manager might have had in mind—"Grimm's Biggest Baseball Day," p.15.

7. Previously only Rogers Hornsby, while he was with the St. Louis Cardinals, and Hack Wilson had smashed drives far enough to hit the scoreboard on the fly. A month after Cuyler's hit, Babe Ruth, with his most famous home run, cleared the scoreboard for the only time.

8. Until recent decades it was the scoring custom, when a pinch-hitter stayed in the game, not to list him in the pinch-hitting notes. Ordinarily this made no difference except to leave a certain number of players' pinch-hitting statistics in the record books as fewer than they actually were. However, in a very rare case such as this one wherein Gudat pinch-hit, followed by then staying in the game, produced a lineup alteration, the failure to identify him as a pinch-hitter meant that the *Times* box score left the problem of how the batting order switch had occurred entirely unexplained.

CATCHERS CERTAINLY ARE AT RISK FOR INJURIES, but the Phillies pushed this reality to the limit on May 2, 1970 in San Francisco, when they lost two catchers to broken hands in the same inning! Tim McCarver started behind the plate for Philadelphia that day and in the bottom of the 6th was hit by a foul ball off the bat of Willie Mays, leading off the inning. Mike Ryan came in as McCarver departed for medical attention. The inning continued with Mays collecting a single and scoring on a double by Willie McCovey. Ken Henderson then singled and McCovey was thrown out at the plate by right fielder Bobby Bonds. The play was close and Ryan suffered a broken hand as McCovey spiked him. Amazingly, Mike stayed in the game as Dick Dietz struck out and Alan Gallagher popped up to end the inning. Jim Hutto batted for Ryan in the 7th and stayed in the game as the Phillies third catcher of the day.

—CLEM COMLY

The Nugent Era: Phillies Phlounder in Phutility

by John Rossi

A wag once wrote a history of the Philadelphia Phillies and entitled it "One Hundred Years in the Cellar." He was not far off the mark. In fact, in the first seven decades after the Phillies entered the National League in 1883, save for two brief periods of success in the 1890s and the mid-teens of the twentieth century, the team established a record of futility unmatched in baseball history. Compared to their hometown rivals, Connie Mack's Athletics, the Phillies were orphans in Philadelphia—with just one pennant to their credit in 1915 while playing their games in one of the most outmoded ballparks in baseball, Baker Bowl.

At no time was the Phillies' condition more desperate than during the decade of the team's ownership by Gerald "Gerry" Nugent, 1932-1943. Nugent was born in Philadelphia in 1892. He graduated from Northeast High School and served with distinction in World War 1 with Pennsylvania's 28th Division, twice being cited for bravery. After the war he became a successful leather salesman, but he was restless and wanted a more exciting career. He found one in the professional baseball of the "Roaring Twenties."

In 1925 Nugent went to work for the Phillies. He was named business manager of the team two years later, succeeding longtime Phillies executive William Shettsline. At the time the Phillies were owned by William Baker, a retired New York City police commissioner and a wealthy businessman who bought the team in 1913. During Baker's tenure the Phillies won their first pennant two years later, only to lose the World Series to the Boston Red Sox. The Phillies remained competitive for a few more years

until Baker began a process that became synonymous with the team—he started selling off his best players, beginning with future Hall of Famer Grover Cleveland Alexander in November 1917. Baker pleaded poverty, saying he needed the money. They got $65,000 in cash plus a couple of players, including the legendary "Pickles" Dillhoefer. This was easily the worst trade in franchise history up to that point. Baker had no excuse—he was rich enough to support a major league franchise in those days. In fact, despite a terrible on-field record during the 1920s, the Phillies actually turned a modest profit.

Nugent proved a quick learner and became a keen student of baseball as well as an excellent judge of player potential. In a short time he was indispensable in running the Phillies. Around the same time he joined the Phillies he had married Baker's secretary, Mae Desales Mallon, and the two of them became Baker's surrogate family. When Baker died in 1930 he left Mrs. Nugent 500 of the outstanding 4,800 shares of Phillies stock. Six years later Mrs. Baker died and bequeathed 753 shares to the Nugents. During this time the Nugents gained effective control of the Phillies.

Following Baker's death Lewis Ruch, a former executive with the Phillies, served briefly as president with Nugent handling most of the team's day-to-day work. When poor health forced Ruch to retire, Nugent was elected as his replacement in 1932. From that point Nugent and his wife ran the team, in the process becoming the only husband and wife duo in history to serve as president and vice president of a major league franchise. In reality, Nugent made most of the baseball and financial decisions, but his wife was a key adviser. Aside from them the Phillies had virtually no staff. John Ogden was brought in as a kind of scout and supervisor of player development, but compared to teams like the St. Louis Cardinals

JOHN P. ROSSI, *a professor of history at La Salle University in Philadelphia, has written extensively about baseball history. His most recent book is* The 1964 Phillies: The Story of Baseball's Most Memorable Collapse *(McFarland, 2005).*

or New York Yankees, the Phillies were strictly small-time operators.

Nugent's first great baseball triumph was securing the services of an untried outfielder from Indiana named Charles "Chuck" Klein. In 1928, on the recommendation of Phillies manager Burt Shotton, Nugent bought Klein from the Fort Wayne club for between $5,000 and $7,500. All Klein did for the Phillies over the next five years, 1929-1933, was shatter various National League hitting and fielding records. Twice named league Most Valuable Player—in 1931 by *The Sporting News* and in 1932 by the Baseball Writers Association of America—Klein established himself as one of the greatest sluggers in National League history. His 170 RBI ranks second to Hack Wilson's 191 in NL records while his 158 runs scored remains the top figure. Klein also was a superb outfielder, and he set the major league record for assists in one season with 44. Even today, 60 years after he stopped playing for them, Klein still ranks in the top ten in most Phillies offensive categories.

Nugent had the misfortune to take over as team president just as the Great Depression bottomed out. Philadelphia was among the hardest-hit cities in the nation with an unemployment rate approximating 30 percent. Even Connie Mack's successful A's couldn't prosper in those conditions. After winning three consecutive pennants in 1929-31 and finishing second despite 94 victories in 1932, Mack began to sell off his best players to pay his bills. Over the next three years he would part with the heart of his last dynasty, including future Hall of Famers Jimmie Foxx, Lefty Grove, Al Simmons, and Mickey Cochrane, and recoup over a half million dollars in the process. At this point Philadelphia baseball was in the hands of two men who were in desperate financial straits.

The Phillies, however, were in much worse shape than the Athletics. Unlike the A's, they had not experienced comparable success in the 1920s, then baseball's most prosperous decade. The Phillies finished in the cellar six times during the 1920s and did not have a winning season between 1917 and 1932. Attendance in this so-called "Golden Age of Baseball" was woeful for the Phillies, which averaged just over 225,000 a year, this at a time when just about every team in the majors established new records for attracting fans.

On the day he took over the Phillies, Nugent told the press he would not "trade or sell any of my key players." This is precisely what he was forced to do to keep the Phillies afloat.

Nugent was a shrewd judge of baseball talent, and the Phillies under his stewardship produced some of the best players in the National League in the 1930s; unfortunately, they were unable to keep them. The 1932 team he inherited included several outstanding players, including Klein, shortstop Dick Bartell, third baseman Pinky Whitney, catcher Spud Davis, and first baseman Don Hurst. Klein, Hurst, and Whitney drove in 100 runs that year. Of the five only Whitney failed to hit .300 and he missed by only two points.

Despite Nugent's protestations all five would be traded or sold within two years: Whitney to the Boston Braves, Davis to the Cardinals, Klein and Hurst to the Cubs, and Bartell to the Giants. In return Nugent got some fine players, including catcher Jimmy Wilson and first baseman Dolph Camilli. But the key to all these deals was what came along with the players—cash, $65,000 in the case of Klein alone.

Like Connie Mack, Nugent had a network of friends scattered throughout baseball who alerted him to potential major leaguers. From the early 1930s Nugent bought, developed, or traded for some quality players, such as pitchers Claude Passeau, Kirby Higbe, and Bucky Walters, outfielders Ethan Allen and Danny Litwhiler as well as first baseman Camilli. After a year or two with the Phillies for some polishing Nugent would package them in a deal with an eager National League pennant contender. As Bartell observed, the Phillies "became jobbers of players for the rest of the National League." It worked too, as every one of these ex-Phillies except Allen went on to play for a pennant winner. The cash Nugent got in return in these deals enabled him to keep the Phillies functioning, but just barely.

Some of his deals were ingenious. He sold Klein to the Cubs for $65,000 after the 1933 season and then got him back in 1936 for two players, Ethan Allen and pitcher Curt Davis, plus $50,000 in cash. In other words Nugent realized $115,000 in two deals for the same player. When Larry MacPhail's Dodgers needed a starting pitcher to round out their roster in 1940, Nugent sent them Kirby Higbe and got back three undistinguished players along with $100,000 of MacPhail's money.

Nugent once even got the best of Branch Rickey, no easy mark when it came to money matters. The Phillies drafted pitcher Rube Melton from the

Gerry Nugent and his grandson

Cardinals' minor league system for $7,500 and then turned around and sold him back to Rickey for $15,000. It was a perfect Nugent play: double your investment in a matter of days. Unfortunately for him, Commissioner Landis vetoed the deal, claiming that the Phillies had drafted Melton as a favor to the Cardinals to keep him out of rival hands. Nugent got the last laugh. He kept Melton for two years and then sold him to the Dodgers, where Rickey had moved, for $30,000, a nice increase of 400% on his investment. These moves showed what a clever dealer Nugent was, but they also made the Phillies into a standing joke in the National League.

The reason for Nugent's machinations was simple: he was chronically strapped for cash. Despite taking a salary of around $20,000 for himself and his wife, the Phillies were always in debt throughout his tenure. The team's payroll during the 1930s was approximately $250,000, with Klein drawing the highest salary the team paid, $18,000. Spring training expenses were $20,000, hotels during the season cost $15,000, railroad travel $12,000 while maintaining Baker Bowl in playing condition added another $5,000. On top of those expenses Nugent had to pay an exorbitant rent of $25,000 for Baker Bowl under a bad 99-year lease negotiated by Baker. The team also had to pay taxes of $15,000 a year.

Nugent estimated that it cost him $350,000 to run the Phillies. With attendance in the Depression averaging around 210,000, bringing about one dollar per customer, the team usually ended the year $150,000 in the red. Nugent tried any number of desperate measures to increase income, such as renting Baker Bowl to high school and college football teams, staging boxing matches, including a heavyweight bout featuring the "Ambling Alp," Primo Carnera, which drew a gate of $180,000, almost as much as the Phillies drew in one season. Nugent rented Baker Bowl to the popular local Negro League team, the Hilldale Daisies. Hilldale often drew crowds of 18,000, a turnout that Nugent could only dream about for the Phillies, which averaged around 2,500 to 3,000 throughout the 1930s.

As a way of luring new fans Nugent instigated numerous ladies day games where women paid only 10¢ admission. He set up a Knot Hole Gang system to interest kids in the Phillies, hoping if nothing else to get some money from them for his concessions. Nothing much seemed to work.

Part of Nugent's problem in generating income arose from the existence in Pennsylvania of a strict set of blue laws that banned paid sports events on Sundays. Until the law was changed in 1934 the Phillies and Athletics when they were home had to travel to a nearby city to play a Sunday game. This forced the Phillies and A's to play their doubleheaders, in the Depression the most popular way to see baseball, on either Saturdays or Mondays.

Sunday baseball gave a slight boost to revenue, but the Phillies were such a poor team in the late 1930s that they hardly benefited from increased fan turnout. One innovation that did add some money to Nugent's empty coffers was the beginning of radio broadcasting in 1936. The Phillies got $25,000 for their broadcasting rights, money which Nugent desperately needed.

By the late 1930s Nugent's various expedients were exhausted. Baker Bowl needed a thorough renovation—its stands had collapsed twice in the ballpark's history, most recently in 1927—but Nugent could barely afford minimal repairs. In baseball circles Baker Bowl was considered the worst ballpark in the majors. Its rundown condition generated jokes that were not far off the mark. Red Smith, then writing a sports column for the *Philadelphia Record*, described Baker Bowl in the late 1930s as resembling a seedy men's room. Toward the end of Nugent's tenure a local sportswriter brought some good news to visiting players: "National League will be pleased to learn that the visiting team dressing room at Baker Bowl is being completely refurbished for next season—brand-new nails are installed on which to hang their clothes."

For years Connie Mack had tried to lure the Phillies to Shibe Park, located just a few streets west of Baker Bowl. The idea made sense for both teams. For Mack it would mean doubling the occupancy rate of his ballpark at a time when he needed every nickel. For the Phillies the deal offered them the use of a modern ballpark with the hope that bigger attendance would follow. Mack gave Nugent a good deal. The Phillies would have to pay the A's only a small amount for every ticket sold.

It took Nugent some time to renegotiate his lease for Baker Bowl, but finally in June 1938 it was official—the Phillies would play their last game there and move to Shibe Park beginning in mid-July. Appropriately in their final game at Baker Bowl the Phillies were blown out by the Giants, 14-1. The deep sentiment of Philadelphia fans felt for Baker Bowl was shown by the turnout for the closing of baseball after 51 years of operation. There were 1,500 fans in a park that held 20,000.

Unfortunately for Nugent and the Phillies, the change of venue didn't help. By this time Nugent was running out of players to sell as a way of keeping the Phillies functioning. Attendance rose in 1939, the team's first full season at Shibe Park, but then settled back to Depression levels. Nugent had nothing to build on. The 1938-1942 teams were the worst in the Phillies' history. They lost one hundred games for five consecutive seasons, compiling a ghastly 185-534 record during those years. Even the awful Mets teams of the 1962-1966 era could not match this record for futility.

By this time Nugent was having trouble paying his bills, as his teams in the early 1940s lacked the quality players he could turn into cash. He was forced to borrow money to stay in business and even defer paying Mack his rent. The National League helped out for a few years as a way of keeping baseball alive in Philadelphia, but league president Ford Frick began to press Nugent to sell the team. By this time he wasn't averse to getting out of baseball: "Find me a buyer," he said, "and I'll sell out."

By 1942 it was clear that time had run out for Nugent. Frick and the National League owners refused any more bailouts, and Nugent put the Phillies up for sale. Surprisingly, there were buyers. One syndicate headed by a local millionaire businessman, John B.

Kelly, father of Princess Grace of Monaco, made a serious offer. But a wealthy businessman and Yale graduate, William Cox, who was often referred to as a "sportsman," beat out the local group. Cox paid around $50,000 in cash and assumed all of the team's debts, a deal that totaled $400,000. Later Bill Veeck would say that he tried to buy the Phillies and stock them with players from the negro leagues, thus integrating baseball five years before Branch Rickey and Jackie Robinson. The story sounds good but is basically a figment of Veeck's lively imagination.

In early 1943 the Nugent era of Phillies baseball came to an unlamented conclusion. It was a sad ending and something of a shame. Gerry Nugent had the makings of a skilled baseball executive. Given adequate funds, Nugent could have made the Phillies a success in the 1930s. There were no dynasties in the National League during his years at the helm of the Phillies, just good teams. The personnel that passed through his hands would have over the course of a decade constituted a serious pennant-contending team.

But it wasn't to be. Nugent's limited resources pointed the way to the future for baseball owners. A stable financial situation was necessary for a team to compete. Shoestring operations like Nugent's were a thing of the past.

References

Jordan, David. *Occasional Glory: The History of the Philadelphia Phillies*. Jefferson, NC: McFarland, 2002.

Jordan, David, Larry Gerlach, and John Rossi. "A Baseball Myth Exploded: Bill Veeck and the 1943 Sale of the Phillies," *The National Pastime* 18. SABR, 1998.

Kuklick, Bruce. *To Everything a Season: Shibe Park and Urban Philadelphia, 1909-1976*. Princeton, NJ: Princeton University Press, 1991.

Lewis, Allen and Larry Shenk. *This Date in Phillies History*. New York: Stein and Day, 1979.

Orodenker, Richard, ed. *The Phillies Reader*. Philadelphia: Temple University Press, 1996.

Porter, David L. *Biographical Dictionary of American Sports: Baseball*. Westport, CT: Greenwood Press, 2000.

Ritter, Lawrence S. *Lost Ballparks: A Celebration of Baseball's Legendary Fields*. New York: Studio, 1992.

Seymour. Harold. *Baseball: The Golden Age*. New York: 1971.

Westcott, Rich. *Philadelphia's Old Ballparks*. Philadelphia: Temple University Press, 1996.

Westcott, Rich and Frank Bilovsky. *The New Phillies Encyclopedia*. Philadelphia: Temple University Press, 1993.

White, G. Edward. *Creating the National Pastime: Baseball Transforms Itself*. Princeton, NJ: Princeton University Press, 1996.

Ty Cobb, Master Thief

by Chuck Rosciam

Even though the value of stealing bases can be argued, there is no dispute about the impact on a game's outcome when a runner steals home. And one player, more than any other, can be considered the "Master Thief": Tyrus Raymond Cobb. His record-setting career 54 steals of home (SOH) is a mark that may never be surpassed.

Only two players stole more than half of Cobb's 54 total: Max Carey (33) and George Burns (28). Not even the all-time overall stolen base leader, Rickey Henderson, with his 1,406 thefts, could approach Cobb's SOH total. Henderson stole home only eight times during his career. By comparison, Cobb stole home eight times in just one year alone (1912), setting the single-season major league record. The closest any player has ever come to Cobb's seasonal SOH record is seven, reached by Pete Reiser in 1946 and Rod Carew in 1969.

Although Cobb never stole home twice in a game, a feat accomplished by 11 players, he did steal second, third, and home in one inning on four different occasions to set the major league record (July 22, 1909, July 12, 1911, July 4, 1912, and August 10, 1924). Only Honus Wagner with three such events came close to Cobb's record. During the July 12, 1911, game versus the Athletics, Ty stole second base, third base, and home plate on consecutive pitches by left-handed Harry Krause.

Which teams were the victims most often for Cobb's SOH thievery?

Philadelphia Athletics 11
Cleveland Indians 9
Boston Red Sox 9
Washington Senators 8
New York Yankees......... 6
St. Louis Browns 6
Chicago White Sox 5
Detroit Tigers............. 0

May 4, 1912, Navin Field: Ty Cobb leaps into Browns catcher Paul Krichell in the first inning. The Browns scored five runs in the ninth to win the game, 10-8.

It must have been gratifying to Philadelphia fans for Ty to leave the Detroit Tigers at the end of the 1926 season to join the Athletics, for which he subsequently stole home four times, twice against Boston and once each against Cleveland and Washington. Otherwise the Philly total might have been higher.

Apparently an opponent had to keep an eye on Cobb early on in a game. He was more aggressive in the early innings, stealing home 24 times in 46 attempts in the first three innings. From the seventh inning on, he was more responsible (and successful), swiping home 16 of 19 tries—an amazing 84%. The breakdown by inning for Cobb's steals of home are:

1st	14	6th	6
2nd	0	7th	8
3rd	10	8th	6
4th	3	9th	2
5th	5		

Of Cobb's 98 regular-season dashes for home, two-thirds occurred with two outs. Of these 66 "all-or-nothing" attempts, he was successful half of the time (33). He made 28 attempts with one out; 18 were successful for a decent 64%. Only four of his attempts were with none out, and he was successful the first three times he tried it. His 54 steals of home out of 98 attempts (a 55% success rate) is far above latter-day base stealers, who manage only a 37% success story.

Which backstops suffered the most humiliation? That dubious distinction goes to Val Picinich (Philadelphia, Washington, and Boston) and Muddy Ruel (New York, Boston, and Washington), who were stung three times each. Ruel was the victim with the longest span of time (1917 and 1927) with a third one thrown in the middle years (1922). Cobb used to love taunting the catchers. He would routinely shout at them that he was going on the next pitch, which he usually did. Although Ty never did steal home against Lou Criger, he was a favorite backstop to taunt and run against.

Several pitchers were the victims twice (Jack Coombs, Bob Groom, George Kahler, Ray Caldwell, Vean Gregg, and Fred Blanding). Coombs became a victim just three days apart in 1908. Although it's

CHUCK ROSCIAM *is a retired Navy Captain with 43 years active service. A SABR Member since 1992, he also created www.baseballcatchers.com and www.tripleplays.sabr.org.*

generally believed to be easier to steal home on a southpaw because his back is turned to third base, fewer than one-third (17) of Ty's successful thefts came off left handers.

Throughout his entire career Ty kept the opposition guessing whenever he was on base. He stole home in each month from April to October in almost equal proportion to the number of games he played.

April	8	August	6
May	10	September	8
June	11	October	2
July	9		

Cobb's first steal of home occurred when he was age 20, and his last one was at the ripe old age of 41, during a season in which he stole only five bases. Ty stole home 26 times in a solo effort, 23 times as the front end of a double steal, and six times as the front end of a triple steal. These are records that have never been approached. One of the triple steals resulted in catcher John Henry being spiked on his throwing hand on the play (June 18, 1915), which was a hazard often suffered when Ty stole home.

One of Cobb's most original steals of home took place in a home game on May 12, 1911, against New York. Detroit trailed 5-3 in the seventh with two outs and men on first and second when Ty slammed a two-bagger to left field. The runner at second scored easily, and the man on first dashed toward home. The left fielder threw to the plate to cut down the runner. Cobb stopped on second. The runner slid across the plate and was called safe. The catcher, Ed Sweeney, began a protest with his infield flocking around him and the umpire. Even though it was customary for any base runners remain in place until matters were settled, Cobb trotted to third; no one saw him. He then tiptoed toward the group at the plate; still he remained unobserved. Peering into the cluster of disputants for an opening to slide through, he found one and skated across the plate with the winning run under the noses of almost the entire Yankee team.

The 17th career steal of home by Cobb was the very first run ever scored by Detroit in their new stadium, Navin Field. It happened on April 20, 1912, in the bottom of the first inning when Ty, timing the Cleveland pitcher Vean Gregg's delivery perfectly, took off from third base and hook-slid around the lunging catcher, Ted Easterly.

On July 12, 1911, just after his 40-game hitting streak, Ty was responsible for four runs in a 9-0 win against Philadelphia without even a hit. In the first inning, he walked and stole the next three bases, twice beating perfect throws by catcher Ira Thomas. A fielder's choice and a run scored on Sam Crawford's homer plus a sacrifice fly accounted for two more. In the seventh frame he walked and came all the way around on a Crawford sacrifice to score by knocking the ball from the hands of the new catcher, Paddy Livingston.

Cobb's only theft of home in 1917 came at the end of the season (September 26) when he was tied with Eddie Collins for the overall stolen base leadership with 53 steals. The SOH that day gave him the league lead for the season, which he increased in the next week by swiping one more base, to finish the year with 55 thefts to Collins 53.

Ty was partial to the home field, where he stole home 34 of the 54 times. His thefts occurred in a winning cause 40 times, of which six steals resulted in a one-run victory for his team (Detroit). He was more likely to try to pilfer home with his team ahead (28 steals in 53 attempts) than with his team behind (14 steals in 27 attempts). With the score tied, he was successful on 12 of 18 attempts.

Five of his 14 first-inning thefts came with two outs and the clean-up hitter, Sam Crawford, batting. In three of those five games, the pitcher was so unnerved by the steal of home that he tossed a sitting duck to the batter, who promptly knocked one into the stands. Many times, with Cobb on third base, Sam Crawford would draw a walk, trot down to first base, and then suddenly speed up and round first base as fast as he could toward second. The battery would be watching Cobb and wouldn't know what to do. If they tried to stop Crawford, then Cobb would take off for home. Sometimes they caught Ty and sometimes they'd catch Sam and sometimes they wouldn't get either. Most of the time they were too paralyzed to do anything, and Crawford wound up at second on a base on balls. Such was the threat of Cobb stealing home.

Age did not slow down the Georgia Peach. Thirteen of his 54 SOH's came after the age of 35. As an example, his 52nd robbery at age 40 demonstrated that. He was the whole show during the game as the Athletics overcame a six-run lead to beat the Red Sox. Not only did he steal home, he drove in two runs, scored twice himself, and ended the game with a circus catch and an unassisted double play by coming in from right field to tag the runner at first.

His last steal of home was memorable. Cartoonists of the day depicted Cobb as an aging old man with a gray beard growing down to his waist and walking with a cane. On June 15, 1928, at Cleveland, with crowds estimated as the largest in the game's history—up to 85,000—Ty demonstrated how much he had left. It began in the eighth inning, when he hit a grounder to first base that was bobbled by Lew Fonseca. Cobb went right on past first and on to second safely. On a groundout by Max Bishop he advanced to third. Then he caught pitcher George Grant off guard and a roar from the crowd went up—"There he goes!" Before catcher Luke Sewell could handle Grant's snap throw and apply the tag, Cobb was in safely.

The regular season was not the only time that Cobb performed his derring-do. During game two of the 1909 World Series, Ty stole home in the third inning to break open the game. Pirate pitcher Vic Willis was making his debut, in relief of starter Howie Camnitz, and before he could retire the first batter he faced, Cobb stole home with catcher George Gibson unable to stop him.

Because Cobb mastered all of the tools of the trade he made himself into one of the greatest base runners of the game. By his own admission he was not the fastest runner. He was the smartest and most aggressive thief. During his entire career he studied every pitcher's delivery, and he invented the fall-away slide maneuver, which completely fooled basemen. Furthermore, he tricked his opponents into traps and throwing errors, plus feigned injuries to lull the defense into forgetting about him.

A hundred years ago (September 12, 1905), Ty Cobb stole his very first base, and for the next 24 seasons he proceeded to steal 896 more to set the modern record subsequently broken by Lou Brock (938) and then Rickey Henderson (1,406). However, Cobb's 54 steals of home far overshadow the combined SOH totals of Lou Brock, Rickey Henderson, Rod Carew, and Paul Molitor—all of which are considered premier base stealers. In addition, no one has come close to Cobb's record of stealing three or more bases in a game 37 times. He is undoubtedly the "master thief" of baseball.

TY COBB'S STEALS OF HOME

#	DATE	H/A	INN	W/L	SCORE	OPP	PITCHER	L/R	CATCHER	TYPE
1	6/29/1907	H	6	W	12-2	CLE	Heinie Berger	R	Howard Wakefield	D
2	7/5/1907	H	7	W	9-5	PHI	Rube Waddell	L	Ossee Schreckengost	D
3	6/23/1908	A	1	W	6-1	CHI	Ed Walsh	R	Billy Sullivan Sr.	D
4	9/24/1908	H	1	T	4-4	PHI	Jack Coombs	R	Doc Powers	D
5	9/27/1908	A	3	W	5-2	PHI	Jack Coombs	R	Doc Powers	D
6	5/13/1909	H	7	L	4-6	NY	Rube Manning	R	Red Kleinow	S
7	6/16/1909	A	1	L	4-5	PHI	Chief Bender	R	Ira Thomas	D
8	7/22/1909	H	7	W	6-0	BOS	Harry Wolter	L	Pat Donohue	D
9	5/30/1910G2	H	1	W	9-4	STL	Bill Bailey	L	Jim Stephens	S
10	8/16/1910	A	4	W	8-3	WAS	Bob Groom	R	Eddie Ainsmith	S
11	10/5/1910G2	H	3	W	4-2	CLE	Fred Blanding	R	Grover Land	S
12	4/18/1911	H	1	W	5-1	CLE	George Kahler	R	Syd Smith	D
13	5/1/1911	H	6	W	14-5	CLE	George Kahler	R	Grover Land	S
14	5/12/1911	H	7	W	6-5	NY	Ray Caldwell	R	Ed Sweeney	S
15	7/12/1911	H	1	W	9-0	PHI	Harry Krause	L	Ira Thomas	S
16	8/18/1911	H	1	L	3-9	BOS	Jack Killilay	R	Bill Carrigan	T
17	4/20/1912	H	1	W	6-5	CLE	Vean Gregg	L	Ted Easterly	D
18	5/1/1912	H	1	L	2-5	CHI	Joe Benz	R	Bruno Block	S
19	5/13/1912	H	1	L	4-15	NY	Hippo Vaughn	L	Gabby Street	D
20	6/21/1912	H	6	L	4-9	CLE	Fred Blanding	R	Steve O'Neill	D
21	7/1/1912	H	3	W	8-2	CLE	Vean Gregg	L	Steve O'Neill	D
22	7/4/1912G1	H	5	W	9-3	STL	Geo. Baumgardner	R	Paul Krichell	D
23	8/1/1912	H	6	L	3-6	WAS	Bob Groom	R	Rip Williams	S
24	9/6/1912	H	8	L	2-4	STL	Earl Hamilton	L	Paul Krichell	D
25	4/30/1913	H	8	L	3-8	CHI	Eddie Cicotte	R	Ray Schalk	S
26	5/18/1913	H	7	L	1-2	WAS	Walter Johnson	R	Eddie Ainsmith	S
27	5/20/1913	H	3	W	8-7	PHI	Duke Houck	R	Jack Lapp	S
28	9/15/1913	A	5	W	7-5	NY	Jack Warhop	R	Ed Sweeney	D
29	6/9/1914	H	4	L	3-7	PHI	Bob Shawkey	R	Jack Lapp	D
30	4/28/1915	H	3	W	12-3	STL	Bill James	R	Sam Agnew	T
31	6/4/1915	A	9	W	3-0	NY	Ray Caldwell	R	Les Nunamaker	S
32	6/9/1915	A	3	W	15-0	BOS	Ray Collins	L	Bill Carrigan	S
33	6/18/1915	A	1	W	5-3	WAS	Joe Boehling	L	John Henry	T
34	6/23/1915	H	8	W	4-2	STL	Grover Lowdermilk	R	Sam Agnew	S
35	8/23/1916	A	8	W	10-3	PHI	Tom Sheehan	R	Val Picinich	S
36	9/26/1917	A	3	W	5-1	NY	Jack Enright	R	Muddy Ruel	S
37	7/9/1918G2	A	5	W	5-4	PHI	Scott Perry	R	Cy Perkins	D
38	8/23/1919	H	3	W	8-4	BOS	Waite Hoyt	R	Roxy Walters	T
39	5/18/1920	A	8	W	8-2	PHI	Pat Martin	L	Glenn Myatt	S
40	9/18/1920	H	1	L	4-7	BOS	Elmer Myers	R	Wally Schang	D
41	9/19/1920G1	H	4	W	9-7	WAS	Harry Courtney	L	Patsy Gharrity	S
42	6/9/1921	A	6	W	10-6	WAS	Eric Erickson	R	Patsy Gharrity	D
43	9/16/1921	A	5	W	7-3	PHI	Roy Moore	L	Glenn Myatt	S
44	5/8/1922	A	9	W	6-2	BOS	Allan Russell	R	Muddy Ruel	D
45	7/26/1922	H	3	L	4-5	WAS	George Mogridge	L	Val Picinich	S
46	10/2/1923	A	7	W	7-5	CHI	Paul Castner	L	Buck Crouse	D
47	4/22/1924	H	3	W	8-4	STL	Bill Bayne	L	Pat Collins	D
48	4/27/1924	H	5	W	4-3	CHI	Ted Lyons	R	Buck Crouse	S
49	8/10/1924	H	7	W	13-7	BOS	Buster Ross	L	Val Picinich	S
50	7/3/1926	A	1	L	5-7	CLE	George Uhle	R	Luke Sewell	S
51	4/19/1927	A	6	W	1-3	WAS	General Crowder	R	Muddy Ruel	T
52	4/26/1927	A	7	W	9-8	BOS	Tony Welzer	R	Grover Hartley	D
53	7/6/1927G1	A	1	W	5-1	BOS	Del Lundgren	R	Grover Hartley	T
54	6/15/1928	A	8	W	12-5	CLE	George Grant	R	Luke Sewell	S
WS	10/9/1909	A	3	W	7-2	PIT	Vic Willis	R	George Gibson	S

KEY: G1 = Game 1 and G2 = Game 2 of a double header; H = Home and A = Away; R = Throws Right and L = Throws Left; S = Solo Steal and D = Double Steal and T = Triple Steal on Play

Sources

Identifying and documenting Cobb's steals of home and stealing second, third, and home in an inning is a work in progress, and the research is incomplete. The above list represents the latest research following cumulative efforts of SABR members over the years, most notably Bob Davids. It is the most accurate compilation from available sources.

Stump, Al. *Cobb: A Biography* (Chapel Hill, NC: Algonquin, 1994) pp. 421-422, appendix list of 35 SOHs.

Bak, Richard. *Ty Cobb: His Tumultuous Life and Times* (Dallas, TX: Taylor, 1994) pp.90-91, list of 54 SOHs.

The Sporting News Complete Baseball Record Book, 2003 ed., p.75 and p.179, lists Cobb as having stole home only 50 times. Also p.75 lists Cobb as stealing second, third, and home in a single inning four times with the years: 1909, 1911, 1912 (2). Only 1909 and 1911 have been confirmed by box scores. One 2-3-H feat in 1912 was noted by Charles Alexander in his book on p.107 and in Richard Bak's book p.84.

Joe Reichler's *The Great All-Time Baseball Record Book*, 1991 ed., lists Cobb as stealing second, third, and home in a game six times (not necessarily the same inning): 9/2/1907, 7/23/1909, 7/12/1911, 7/4/1912, 6/18/1917, 8/10/1924. In three of those games (1907, 1909, and 1917) Cobb did *not* do it as confirmed by box scores.

Davids, Bob. "Ty Is Still Stealing Home," *The Baseball Research Journal*, 1991, p. 40.

Retrosheet & David Smith, SABR Member, confirmed by the box score of the game of 7/22/1909.

Palmer, Pete and Gary Gillette, eds. *The Baseball Encyclopedia*, New York: Barnes & Noble Books, 2004. p.1623 identifies Cobb with 897 career stolen bases.

Alexander, Charles. *Ty Cobb* (New York: Oxford University Press, 1984), p. 207, career SOHs 35.

Mouch, Warren. "Ty Cobb Steals Home!" *Baseball Historical Review*, 1981 reprint of 1972 article, pp.48-51.

Washington Post box scores with write-ups for 13 games confirming steals of home.

New York Times box scores with write-ups for 10 games confirming steals of home.

Chicago Tribune box scores with write-ups for nine games confirming steals of home.

Detroit Free Press, April 21, 1912, reporting first run scored at Navin Field by Cobb's steal of home.

www.baseball-reference.com/c/cobbty01.shtml source for Cobb's career stats.

Official scorers during Cobb's time did not record a stolen base of home on a passed ball or a wild pitch when the attempt was made before the pitch was delivered. Had Rule 10.08(a) been in effect, Cobb would have had at least six more steals of home.

Trent McCotter, SABR member, verified or disavowed Cobb's 2-3-H steals in an inning from his database, which contains every game Cobb played in his career, including stolen base totals.

Other SABR members who contributed confirming and/or verifying information: Bill Deane, Steve Hoy, Dennis VanLangen, Jim Charlton, Francis Kinlaw, Bill Dunstone, Joe Murphy.

◇◇◇◇◇◇◇◇◇◇◇◇◇◇◇◇◇◇◇◇◇◇◇◇◇◇◇◇◇◇◇ ⚾ ◇◇◇◇◇◇◇◇◇◇◇◇◇◇◇◇◇◇◇◇◇◇◇◇◇◇◇◇◇◇◇

From GLADLY TEACH: REMINISCENCES *by Bliss Perry (Boston: Houghton Mifflin, 1935)*

DESCRIBING HIS YOUTH in Williamstown, Mass, Perry wrote: "The ingenious Dr. Freud had not, in 1873, invented the term 'inferiority complex,' but that was what ailed me, and my vain struggles with that brute of a beast increased the malady. There was no real reason for it, except in my worrying mind. I was a tall-ish, pale, delicate-looking boy; shy and sensitive, and I hope gentle-mannered; disliking loud noises and violent words; hating the brutality and cruelty of the big boys on the school-ground, and dreading to see, at the Smedley farm, a calf or pig or even a chicken killed. Of course I had killed butterflies with a drop of benzine, and had shot birds and squirrels without remorse. A gun was somehow different! As one of the younger boys in each successive grade of the public school I had endured stoically the hair-pulling and arm-twisting propensities of my elders. Of course one must not cry or tell the teacher, for that would be breaking the unwritten code. The small boy had to keep back the tears, pretend to smile—and hope to God that some day he would be big enough to hit back!

"In the woods and fields I was perfectly happy, and also when I was playing ball. Somehow I had been chosen captain of a nine, at twelve. Two of the players, Clarence and Frank Grant, were colored boys, sons of our 'hired girl.' Clarence became, in time, catcher and captain of the Cuban Giants, and Frank (whose portrait I drew later in a novel called The Plated City) was a famous second baseman for Buffalo before the color line was drawn. Rob Pettit, our left fielder, afterward played for Chicago and went around the world with Pop Anson's team. We called ourselves the 'Rough and Readys.'"

— JOHN THORN

The Odyssey of Carlton Hanta

by Robert K. Fitts

With the recent success of Ichiro Suzuki, Hideki Matsui, and other Japanese nationals in the major leagues, American fans are becoming curious about the history of baseball in Japan. There are several good histories of Japanese baseball published in English, but little compares to listening to a player talk about his own experiences. Oral histories give readers insight on aspects of the game that narrative histories rarely provide. In this article Carlton Hanta, a Hawaiian-born Nisei (second-generation Japanese immigrant) tells about his baseball career in the States and in the Japanese professional leagues during the 1950s through early 1970s.

Born on the island of Oahu in 1931, Carlton Hanta was a standout pitcher and hitter at the Mid-Pacific Institute in Honolulu. Moving to shortstop, Hanta led the University of Houston to the College World Series in 1953, and became the first Japanese American to be named to the All-American College Baseball team. After a stint in the minors, in 1958 Hanta signed with the Nankai Hawks of the Pacific League in Japan. In 1960 he was the only foreigner elected by the Japanese fans to the All-Star teams. He rewarded the fans with a two-run inside-the-park home run. He played five years in Japan and coached for an additional seven seasons.

CARLTON HANTA REMEMBERS

I was born in Hawaii and attended the Mid-Pacific Institute, a boarding school in Honolulu, where I was a pitcher. After graduation, I couldn't find a job. My parents wanted me to go to school, but I rebelled and

ROBERT K. FITTS, PH.D., *is a historian of Japanese baseball and runs RobsJapaneseCards.com. His book,* Remembering Japanese Baseball: An Oral History of the Game, *is now available from Southern Illinois University Press.*

bummed around for about a year and a half. Then somebody asked me if I wanted to go to Alaska and make some money. So I begged my mother relentlessly and she finally gave in. I went to San Francisco and met up with the person who was supposed to take me to Alaska, but it didn't work out. Eventually, I met a Nisei boy from San Fernando Valley who took care of me and helped me become a fruit tramp. We started out in Watsonville in March picking lettuce. That was harsh work! Then we went and picked strawberries. That was harsher! In Watsonville they had a Nisei baseball team. I hooked up with them and pitched a couple games. One game was in Monterey against an all-Nisei team from Fresno. I impressed their coach, Mr. Kenichi Zenimura, whose sons played professionally in Japan. He invited me to come to Fresno if I needed a job. So this Nisei boy and I went to Fresno to prune vines and pick grapes for a winery. This was during the Korean conflict, and the FBI was looking for my friend because he had not fulfilled his military commitment. They caught up with him and took him to the disembarkation center at Fort Lewis, Washington, and shipped him directly to Korea. I never saw him again.

That got me scared, so I decided to go to school. I went to the library, looked up colleges, and picked the University of Houston. I wrote them and, lo and behold, they accepted me. I boarded the Southern Pacific in San Francisco and left for Houston in September 1954.

One day I was playing intramural football and the football team was practicing across the way. The freshman coach saw me and asked if I wanted to play football. It was like a movie script! I said no because I had never played organized football. But the kids around me said that I might be able to get a scholarship, so I turned out. I didn't even know how to put on the football equipment! But the kids were really nice and they taught me. I missed the fall season, so I went to the freshman Spring drills.

The football coach also introduced me to the baseball coach, Lovette Hill. I told him that all I did was pitch, but he said, "You're too little to be a pitcher. Why don't you play second base?" Well, I looked at the roster and noticed that the shortstop was a senior but the second baseman was only a junior. So I told him that I wanted to play shortstop even though I had never played the infield. One of my new teammates, named Foy Boyd, spent 20-30 minutes every day after practice hitting ground balls to me at shortstop. Oh, I got bruises! But I had to learn how to play the spot.

My sophomore year I played JV football. When we were freshman, I could run rings around the other guys—they weren't that fast. But when they came back as sophomores, they were much bigger! I played three-fourths of the season on JV. And boy, I got beaten up so badly! Well, that convinced me to leave football and concentrate on my studies and baseball.

Coach Hill let me play shortstop my sophomore year. I must have really disappointed him, making so many errors and not being able to hit, but he stuck with me. In the summer, I met some Mexican boys and played semi-pro baseball with them. That helped me a lot. When I came back for my junior year in 1953, I ended up being an All-American shortstop. It was a great season and we became the first University of Houston team to go to the College World Series. I also joined the ROTC because if you did, you'd stay out of the service until you graduated.

In 1954, I signed professionally with the AA Beaumont Exporters in the Texas League. They had a working agreement with the Chicago Cubs. So I played with them that summer before I went back to school in September to get my ROTC commission. I returned for spring training with Beaumont in 1955, but they said that I wasn't going to fit into their plans because I was going into the service. So I was optioned to Amarillo in the West Texas-New Mexico League. I played there until May, when I reported to Fort Lee, Virginia, to serve my two-year commitment with the United States Army.

As soon as I got out of the Army, I came back to Houston. The owner of the Beaumont team, Mr. Russell, contacted me and asked, "What kind of shape are you in?" I said, "I just got out of the Army, sir." He said, "Well, join them in San Antonio on Sunday for a doubleheader." So I reported to the stadium.

Ryne Duren, later a relief pitcher for the Yankees, was pitching for San Antonio. I remember him because he wore thick glasses. My teammates tried to scare me by saying that when he pulled his glasses down to wipe his face that he couldn't find them again. He was so fast. I had never seen anything like that.

In the second game, the manager put me in and I got a base hit. After the game, he said, "You lied to me!" I said, "No sir, I haven't had any training because I've been in the service." I followed the team back to Austin and I started practicing by myself. I had the clubhouse boy come out early and hit me ground balls. In those days they didn't have pitching machines, so I couldn't take batting practice. Well, I didn't have confidence in my fielding, so after 30 days I went to the manager and said, "I still have two more options left, could you please option me out?" They shipped me out to El Paso in the West Texas-New Mexico League. I stayed there until June, when El Paso was going to fold. I was hitting a little over .300, and Mr. Russell called and said to join the team in Tulsa. I said, "I'm going to need a raise." He said no. So I said, "Well, I'm not going up there." I drove all the way back to Houston, got my things, and drove back to San Francisco. I have a secondary education degree, so I started teaching. Then I got a letter from the minor league director, saying that I was suspended from Organized Baseball because I had jumped.

At the end of February, I got a phone call from Mr. Angel Maehara. He said, "Do you want to go to Japan and play baseball?" I said, "Wait a minute, who am I talking to? I'm still suspended from Organized Baseball." I called Hawaii and asked my brother about Mr. Maehara. My brother said, "Oh, he was my classmate at the University of Hawaii, and he owns an express company here in Honolulu." He also owned a semi-pro Nisei team in Honolulu called the Asahi. So I called him back, and I asked him about the deal. He said, "I'll pay your way to Honolulu and from Honolulu to Tokyo." I asked him, "What happens if I don't get signed up in Japan?" He said, "I'll give you a job in my company while you look for a teaching job." So I resigned my teaching position and came back to Honolulu, met the boys, and practiced a week. Of course, I didn't know anyone. In those days it took 17 hours to get to Japan, and nobody would talk to me! I spoke like a Texan with a Southern accent, and the boys stayed away from me. We landed in Tokyo and were supposed to play about 10 games. The first game was in Yokohama, and sliding into second base, I sprained my ankle. Well, I was a spectator until the last three or four games.

I came back and started working for Mr. Maehara at his Express shop. Then one day he got word from the Nankai Hawks of the Pacific League that they might sign me. I said, "How come? I only played two or three games." Well, being a businessman, Mr. Maehara knew how to talk to people. I joined the Hawks during the All-Star break and God, I never practiced so hard! They had me taking batting practice for about 30 minutes. I was getting jammed, and I ended up with a swollen right thumb. I found out later that they used their farm team boys to pitch batting practice and the kids threw hard because they wanted to impress the pitching coach.

I didn't get to play the first week because of my thumb, but they expected me to be at the ballpark every night. We were playing the team from Fukuoka called the Nishitetsu Lions, and they had a pitcher named Kazuhisa Inao. My God, he pitched one night and then came back the next night and started again, and then the third night he came in to relieve. I was thinking, how can this guy pitch a full nine-inning game, then a nine-inning game, and then relieve on the third day? That was the way they played baseball. Inao could thread the outside corner with a slider or fastball. He would make you chase a slider outside, come back with a fastball on the corner, then wake you up with a screwball on the inside. He was one of the smartest pitchers I've ever seen.

I roomed with the Japanese players, and that helped me get accustomed to their culture. I didn't have much trouble with the food, but the culture, sleeping on the floor, and using the Japanese-style toilet—that was harsh! In Japan, you had to show respect to the older players, coaches, and managers. For example, when the team went to eat, the older players went in first. I didn't know about these things at the beginning, and I called an older person by his first name. Boy, did I get a scolding! You're not supposed to do that. You're supposed to put "san" after the last name.

By talking with the boys, I picked up the language. I learned all the bad words first and eventually I could carry on a conversation. Actually, that's how I met my wife. She was an usherette at the stadium and had gone to Catholic school in Japan, so she spoke a little English. One of the ballplayers said that he knew somebody who could speak English, so we got hooked up. She helped me get by in the beginning, and we've been together for 43 years.

Although I was the first American on the Nankai Hawks after World War II, they accepted me pretty well. I don't care where you are, or who you are, if you produce nobody says anything. In my first at-bat, I dropped a drag bunt down third base because the third baseman was playing so deep and got on. They thought that it was the most impressive thing. Then in the second or third game, I got lucky. I got fooled on a curveball and hit a home run to right field. That was a big thing because they wanted you to hit to the opposite field.

In those days, they used to say "American Baseball." Anything I did, like breaking up double plays, sliding hard, or hook sliding, was called "American Baseball" because at that time the Japanese didn't do those things. They played a more passive game. For example, if they hit a ground ball to the pitcher or right at an infielder, they never ran hard to first base. They probably thought I was nuts, running as hard as I could.

During my first year I slid into second base to break up a double play against the Daimai Orions, and I broke the second baseman's left shin. I heard the damn thing crack! I didn't mean to do that. The center fielder and the shortstop came charging in and they were going to hang me out to dry! They said it was dirty baseball. That's when my manager, Kazuto Tsuruoka, stepped in. He was like God. Tsuruoka said, "This is American baseball!" And that ended it.

Tsuruoka was one of the smartest managers, bar none. He had a sixth sense. Later, when I was a defensive coach for him, we'd be sitting in the dugout and he'd be picking on his nose and all of a sudden he would say, "Carl, move the third baseman to his left." So I would yell and move him to the left and by God, the batter would hit the ball right there. Once when we were playing Wally Yonamine's Chunichi Dragons in an exhibition game, in the first inning with nobody out and a runner on third, Tsuruoka moved the infield in. I was kind of embarrassed moving in, but the fans didn't understand that you don't do that in the first inning. Then the batter dribbled the ball to the second baseman and the runner on third couldn't score. Wally came to me after the game and said, "Why'd you move your infield in?" I said, "I didn't. The old man did." So I asked Mr. Tsuruoka, "Why did you do that?" He said, "Well, our pitcher was a screwball pitcher." It never dawned on me. He knew all those things without a computer. His mind was a computer! That was exactly what had happened. The screwball came in; the batter got jammed and hit a slow roller to the second baseman. If he was back, the guy on third could have walked home.

Mr. Tsuruoka managed with his feelings and hunches. He never went with the percentage. I distinctly remember one time; the opposing team had a left-handed pitcher and Tsuruoka called time, took out his right-handed hitter and brought in a left-handed pinch-hitter. Joe Stanka looked at me and said, "Boy, this damn old man is something else!" You never do that in American baseball. And lo and behold, this guy comes in and gets a single over shortstop and we won the ballgame. This shut Stanka and me up forever! We felt that this man knew something that we didn't. He was amazing.

The Hawks had a great team, and we won the Japan Series in 1959 and the Pacific League championship in 1961. We had one of the best pitchers in Japan: Tadashi Sugiura. He was a submariner with an easy motion and a good wrist. I tried to hit against him during our inter-squad games and no way! In those days they didn't measure speed like they do today, but I would say that he was sneaky fast. The St. Louis Cardinals came to Japan during my first year there (1958). They had Stan Musial, Ken Boyer, and Don Blasingame. I had played in the Texas League with two of the Cardinals players, and Jim Brosnan had been my roommate. The Cardinals were impressed with Sugiura. He beat them at our stadium 9-to-2 and gave up only six hits in nine innings. I heard that they wanted to sign him for $100,000—at that time that was big money. But Sugiura declined because of his loyalty to Mr. Tsuruoka. I tried to tell him that in the majors you don't have to pitch every day. If you won 10-12 games a year, that was good enough and you could play for 10 years and make a lot of money. But he didn't think like that. He would give the ball team everything he had; whether it was for one, two, or three years, it didn't matter. Then he would have fulfilled his obligation to the manager and the team. That was the way they thought, whereas we Americans think of longevity.

Our catcher was Katsuya Nomura, the best catcher in the history of Japanese baseball. Boy, he could hit! He ended up with 657 home runs, second only to Sadaharu Oh. He was also one of the smartest catchers—he could read every hitter. He always looked half asleep, but he'd go out and catch every game of the season—including doubleheaders. He was a magnificent specimen!

Hirose, the center fielder, was one of the fastest runners I've ever seen. This guy could score from first base on a hit-and-run single if the right fielder dallied the throw. Our third baseman, Shigeyoshi Morishita, was the Ty Cobb of Japan. He'd do anything. If a pitch was close enough, he'd pinch himself to redden his skin and show the umpire to convince him that he was hit. Boy, he was a mean guy! But he was for winning. Then we had Isami Okamoto at second base. I used to call him "ninja" because he was a magician! He would jump up in the air and the ball would be stuck in his glove. At first base was Yosuke Terada. He was the greatest first baseman I've seen. He caught one-handed. In those days the Japanese didn't allow you to catch one-handed, but they didn't say anything to him.

After my first season, a few other Americans joined me. In 1959, John Sardina came over from Maui. He was a submarine pitcher. This was his first fling at professional baseball. He had a good year in 1959, but he didn't know how to pace himself. Japanese pitchers threw every day. They could do it because they had been practicing that way since they were yay high to a grasshopper, through elementary, high school, and college. John tried to keep up with the Japanese pitchers, and he overworked himself. He started out like on a house on fire, but then just before midseason he started tapering down.

In 1960, Joe Stanka and Buddy Peterson came over. In those days we were able to play three foreigners on a team. Pete was at third base, I played shortstop and second base, and Joe pitched. I was also an interpreter for Joe and Buddy. On the road, we stayed at Western-style hotels, while the rest of the team stayed in a Japanese-style inn. Those were great times! The Hawks were a partying team. There was no curfew, but when it came to playing ball, everybody was in there playing hard. I think that this had a lot to do with Joe Stanka. When he pitched, he'd challenge you, and this caught on with everybody.

Joe Stanka really wanted to win. After I retired, the Hawks faced the Hanshin Tigers in the 1964 Japan Series. Stanka won the first game, pitched in the third game, and then pitched a complete game and won the sixth. We didn't have a rested front-line starter for the seventh and final game, so Joe went to Mr. Tsuruoka and volunteered to start with no rest—after pitching a complete game the day before! That popped the eyes of the Japanese. They never believed that an American pitcher would do that. The Japanese pitchers would do it, but they thought that Americans were softies and needed their four days off. So when he volunteered to pitch the following day, I think it changed the minds of many Japanese. Stanka pitched a complete-game shutout and won the Series! That was how much this man was willing to sacrifice to win.

Both times I played in the Japan Series, we faced the Tokyo Yomiuri Giants, who had Sadaharu Oh and Shigeo Nagashima. In 1959, I got hurt in the first inning of the first game. I was stuck in the hospital for the rest of the Series. That was the year that Tadashi Sugiura won all four games in the Series and we swept the Giants! That was an amazing feat.

In 1961, our scouts came up with ways to contain Oh and Nagashima. We did the Ted Williams shift on Oh. The shortstop moved over to second base and the third baseman covered the hole. Also, because he lifted up his front leg, we thought that we could throw him off-speed stuff. But he had a lot of discipline. He would wait on a pitch and he was fast enough to come around anyway. He still hit over .300 against us. During the scouting process on Nagashima, we noticed that he was stepping into the bucket with his left foot. So we thought that we could pitch him outside. But we didn't realize that he waited on the

ball long enough to pick up the outside pitch and would hit it to right-center.

But the thing that I remember most was the fourth game at Korakuen Stadium. We were up 3-2 in the ninth, and a pop fly was hit near the pitcher's mound and Terada called for it. He came underneath it and the ball hits his glove and bounces out! This man had caught thousands of balls one-handed, but he booted it and the Giants turned the game over. We went back to Osaka and the Giants took the Series.

After the 1961 Series, Terada, Shigeo Hasegawa, and I were traded to the Chunichi Dragons. It didn't bother me because in the States your home is where your suitcase is. But the other two players felt insulted because this was just after we had won the pennant. One of the things that I was told before I left was "Go out and taste the food of somebody else." I had eaten Nankai's food—got used to their way. Mr. Tsuruoka said, "Go see what other teams do."

When I was with the Dragons, I decided to quit baseball. God, the way they practiced! It was really different from the Hawks. They got us up about 6:00 to 6:30 in the morning to do calisthenics and run up a mountain. Then we'd come back, have breakfast, rest a little while, and go to the ballpark. At the park, we had our regular practice, but before we finished, we had to field 100 ground balls. They just credited you with balls that you got in your glove, so after about 40 or 50, you don't care what you do. I wouldn't bother going after balls hit to the side, and balls that we should have charged, we'd back up on because we didn't want to get hit. There were no fundamentals. So I said, "You guys are teaching us all these bad habits." But the Japanese players had done the drill since elementary school, so they could close their eyes and pick up balls.

At the end of the 1962 season, the Dragons manager asked me, "Why don't you stay another year and help break in this new second baseman." But I said, "No, thank you. I don't want any part of baseball anymore." Then on a road trip to Tokyo, I got a phone call at the hotel saying that Mr. Tsuruoka wanted to talk to me. So I secretly went out and met him at a restaurant. He asked me if I wanted to come back and coach Nankai's farm team. He said, "We can't pay you much." But he said that there was a future in Japan for me.

So that's how I started my coaching career. I coached for seven seasons. I stayed with the Nankai

Hawks for a few years. I was planning to go back to the States and start my teaching career, but then Chunichi asked me to coach. I coached there for two years, but nothing had changed. It was still practice, practice, practice. I got fed up, came back, and taught half a year of school in Hawaii. Then the Toei Flyers manager, Kenjiro Tamiya, called me from Japan in 1969 and asked me if I wanted to coach. I said, "No, I don't think so." But he called back and I finally said, "Yes, under the condition that you let me run spring training." So I signed a two-year contract. The first year I cut practice sessions shorter. The Japanese thought that if you practice eight hours you accomplish a lot, but the front office and management didn't understand that a player who puts in eight hours on the field is going to pace himself. It's not full force like in a game. I said that those who wanted extra hitting could stay later, but I was surprised that not too many stayed. I think we ended up in fifth place.

The following year at spring training the kids understood that the harder they worked, the shorter practice was going to be. On May 25, 1972, we were a game and a half out of first place. Slowly the kids understood. They were having fun because they didn't have to practice hours and hours. To make a long story short, I got a lymph node growth on my groin and it turned out to be Hodgkins Disease. I went to the International Cancer Center in Tokyo, and the doctor looked at me and said, "I'll give you six months to live." The doctor tried an experimental medicine. Today it's known as chemotherapy. By September, my hair was falling out and my skin was getting dark. They were experimenting with the dosage. The doctor would give it to me on Thursday and I'd go home and not wake up until Saturday. I sort of recovered, and in December the Orions said they were willing to renew my contract if I was strong enough. The doctor said that I could coach but that I couldn't do any physical work. So I explained that to Tamiya-san, and he said, "Okay, don't worry." But he didn't know how to run spring training, and I just didn't have the strength to start it again. So the team didn't hit at all and we were fired in July or August.

So I came back to Hawaii in 1973. My sister was working at a luau and asked me if I wanted to be a bartender. After a few years the owner asked me to be the manager. I said that I didn't have any experience, but she said that I played professional baseball and that you manage and coach people the same way. I stayed there for the next 20 years.

I'm really thankful that I had the opportunity to play in Japan. I don't think I could go over there and play in their leagues today. The players are much bigger now. Forty years ago, they were little. Now they are six footers and they keep up with the modern training tactics. I'm glad to see that they have improved, but at the same time I'm sad that they're losing their good players to the major leagues. It's diminishing the caliber of Japanese baseball. Hopefully, someday they'll have a global World Series and the Japanese stars will stay in Japan.

WHEN A BATTED BALL HITS A RUNNER, the runner is out, the batter is credited with a single, the ball is dead and all runners return to their bases. However, if the runner interferes with the ball intentionally, the umpires have the discretion to rule a double play, retiring both the runner and the batter. As is often the case with interesting rules, this one came about as the result of some specific plays. The key events happened in April 1957. In that month, there were three cases in which runners for the Cincinnati Reds were involved in this kind of interference. The most glaring was one by Don Hoak on April 21 in Milwaukee in which he "fielded" the ground ball and tossed it to shortstop Johnny Logan. George Kell of the Orioles did a similar interference in the same week. As a result, the two leagues issued an emergency directive on April 25 to their umpires directing them to award a double play in these cases of intentional interference. Interestingly, the very day the directive came out Whitey Herzog of the Senators was running at first and was hit by a batted ball, but the umpires ruled that it was not intentional and the batter was credited with a hit, as before.

—DAVID SMITH

The Best (and Worst) St. Louis Cardinal Trades

by Lyle Spatz

Unhappy with the team's contract offer for 2003 and beyond, Philadelphia's All-Star third baseman Scott Rolen was threatening to become a free agent at the end of the 2002 season. Taking those threats seriously, the Phillies chose to get what they could for Rolen and traded him to the Cardinals two days before the July 31 deadline. In return for Rolen, minor league pitcher Doug Nickle, and cash, the Phillies received Placido Polanco, a fine young infielder, Mike Timlin, a veteran reliever, and Bud Smith, a young pitcher who had failed to live up to his early promise. Rolen had an immediate impact on his new team, contributing 14 home runs and 44 runs batted in the second half of the '02 season to help lead St. Louis to the National League East title. He added 28 home runs and 104 RBI in 2003, and did even better in 2004, when he finished fourth in the Most Valuable Player Award voting.

It is not too early to note that this has been a very good trade for the Cardinals, one that may eventually rank with the best they have ever made. While the perspective of time does not yet allow us to judge fully the Scott Rolen trade, it does allow us to rate some others the Cardinals have made in their long and glorious history. Let's begin with a few of the worst.

On November 12, 1903, St. Louis acquired catcher Larry McLean and pitcher Jack Taylor from the Chicago Cubs. Taylor had won more than 20 games two years in a row, and he would make it three in a row in his first year with St. Louis. He was also in the middle of setting a major league record that will never be broken. Between 1901 and 1906, Taylor pitched 187 consecutive complete games.

LYLE SPATZ *is the chairman of SABR's Baseball Records Committee and most recently the author of* Bad Bill Dahlen: The Rollicking Life and Times of an Early Baseball Star *(McFarland & Company).*

To get Taylor, St. Louis sent Chicago catcher Jack O'Neill and a young pitcher who was 9-13 as a rookie. Taylor would win only 42 more big-league games after leaving Chicago, and just 23 of them would be for St. Louis. Meanwhile, that young pitcher, Mordecai "Three Finger" Brown, would go on to a Hall of Fame career, finishing with 239 wins and only 130 losses, making this one of the worst trades, if not the worst, in Cardinals history.

Still, modern-day Cardinal fans might have their own choice for the team's worst trade ever. For many, it would be the February 1972 swap of pitchers that sent Steve Carlton to Philadelphia for Rick Wise. Actually, this trade has an amusing story connected to it. Carlton had been holding out, demanding that the Cardinals pay him a salary of $65,000 for the 1972 season. The Cardinals said no. Wise also had been holding out, demanding that the Phillies pay *him* a salary of $65,000 for the 1972 season. The Phillies said no. So, each team solved their problem by trading the two holdouts. Both pitchers then immediately signed with their new teams. The Cardinals, who refused to pay $65,000 to Carlton, did pay it to Wise. And the Phillies, who refused to pay $65,000 to Wise, did pay it to Carlton.

Not only were they paid the same, but also at the time of the trade, the right-handed Wise and the left-handed Carlton were considered mirror images of each other. Wise was 26, with 75 big league wins. Carlton was 27, with 77 big league wins. And it's not that Wise was a bust in St. Louis. He pitched two years for the Cardinals and was a 16-game winner in each one. In addition, when they later dealt him to Boston, they got a very good player in return, Reggie Smith. Yet, as was the case with Three Finger Brown, when the Cards traded Carlton, they were trading a future

Sam Jones and
Leo Durocher (inset)

AP PHOTO

Hall of Famer. That first season in Philadelphia, he won 27 games, and that was for a last-place team. In all, Carlton would win 252 games and four Cy Young Awards after leaving St. Louis.

———

Paul Derringer was not a Hall of Famer like Mordecai Brown or Steve Carlton, but he was an excellent pitcher, and another one St. Louis let get away. In May 1933, the Cardinals traded Derringer, along with second baseman Sparky Adams and a pitcher named Allyn Stout, to Cincinnati for three players. In return, they got shortstop Leo Durocher, Butch Henline, a catcher who later became a National League umpire, and pitcher Jack Ogden.

The impetus for the trade was a simple one. Cincinnati really needed pitching and St. Louis really needed a shortstop. Charlie Gelbert had been their shortstop for the past four seasons, but had suffered a severe leg injury in a hunting accident that would keep him out of action for two years. Durocher, the most prominent player in the deal, took over at shortstop and did well in his five seasons with St. Louis. His aggressive style of play fit right in with the Gas House Gang, and he was the shortstop on the 1934 world champions.

In Derringer, the Reds were getting a pitcher who had a great rookie year for the Cardinals in 1931. He was 18-8 and led the National League in winning percentage, but he fell off to 11-14 in 1932 and he was 0-2 at the time of the trade in 1933. When Derringer went to Cincinnati he continued to be dreadful. He won seven and lost 25. He lost 21 more in 1934, but then turned it around, winning 20 or more four times and 19 once. In all, Derringer finished with 223 big-league wins.

———

Wayne Granger had been a rookie with the Cardinals in 1968 before they traded him to Cincinnati. Pitching in relief for the Reds, he led the league in games finished in 1969 and in both games finished and saves in 1970. Granger was with Minnesota when in November 1972 St. Louis decided they wanted him back and traded pitcher John Cumberland and outfielder Larry Hisle to the Twins to get him. Unfortunately, for St. Louis, Granger had lost his effectiveness and did not even finish out the 1973 season with them.

Hisle, meanwhile, went on to some very productive years with the Twins and the Milwaukee Brewers. Now, if you don't remember Larry Hisle playing with the Cardinals, it's because he didn't. They had only gotten him from the Dodgers in October for two minor leaguers, and so he belonged to them for only a month, and that during the off-season.

———

In May 1956, St. Louis traded center fielder Bill Virdon to Pittsburgh for outfielder Bobby Del Greco and pitcher Dick Littlefield. The trade greatly upset Cardinals fans at the time and, as it turned out, with good reason. Never, at any time, did General Manager Frank Lane's trading of Virdon to Pittsburgh make any sense. Del Greco had been and always would be strictly a journeyman player. The same was true for Littlefield. He had been and always would be strictly a journeyman pitcher.

By contrast, Virdon was only 24 years old and had been the National League Rookie of the Year in 1955. The Cardinals had gotten him out of the Yankees' farm system in April 1954 in exchange for the popular Enos Slaughter, one of their all-time greats. However, Lane had recently taken over as the Cards' GM, and he was completely overhauling the team. He justified this deal by saying that despite his Rookie of the Year season, Virdon had not hit well in September and that he had started slowly this year. Well, he had started slowly, but he sure recovered quickly after the trade. Virdon batted a combined .319 for the 1956 season and continued to serve as the Pirates center fielder for the next 11 years.

———

Dick Allen was another former Rookie of the Year the Cardinals had for only one season and would have been better off keeping. Allen, who won the award with the 1964 Phillies, went to the Los Angeles Dodgers in October 1970 for second baseman Ted Sizemore and rookie catcher Bob Stinson. Sizemore, himself a one-time Rookie of the Year, with L.A. in 1969, was a serviceable player who spent four years with the Cardinals. Still, he was no Dick Allen, who in his one year in St. Louis hit 34 home runs and had 101 RBI. The Dodgers would also keep Allen for only one season, but later on with the White Sox, he would win a couple of home run titles and the American League's 1972 Most Valuable Player Award.

Bill Virdon

An earlier trade that the Cardinals certainly didn't get the better of took place just four days after the Japanese bombed Pearl Harbor. For those paying attention to baseball during that chaotic time, this was an eye-opening exchange. St. Louis sent first baseman Johnny Mize, one of the game's most feared hitters, to the New York Giants for pitcher Bill Lohrman, catcher Ken O'Dea, and first baseman Johnny McCarthy. Mize had been with the Cardinals for six years and had batted better than .300 in each of those six seasons. He had a career batting average of .336, including highs of .364 in 1937 and .349 in 1939, when he won the batting title. Still only 28, he was a consistent All-Star, and had been in the top ten in voting for the league's Most Valuable Player in five of his six years, twice finishing second.

General Manager Branch Rickey, who made the trade, assured Cardinals fans that he had a satisfactory replacement for Mize. The man Rickey had in mind was Ray Sanders, who'd batted .308 with 14 home runs for St. Louis's American Association Columbus Red Birds in 1941. Furthermore, said Rickey, if Sanders proved unready for the big leagues, manager Billy Southworth had the option of moving outfielder Johnny Hopp to first base. As it turned out, Hopp and Sanders split the first base duties in 1942. Of course, by that time Rickey had left St. Louis to become president of the Dodgers.

The Cardinals got just about nothing out of this trade. McCarthy never played for them, and Lohrman won one game in 1942 before they sold him back to the Giants, where he won 13 and lost four. O'Dea was the only one who stuck around, serving as a backup catcher to Walker Cooper during the war years. Mize, meanwhile, continued to be a leading slugger with the Giants and later with the Yankees, and he too is in the Hall of Fame.

Okay, we've dwelt long enough on the bad trades. Let's look at a few of the good ones the Cardinals have made, beginning with a December 1981 six-player deal with the Padres. Primarily, it was an exchange of shortstops: St. Louis's Gary Templeton for San Diego's Ozzie Smith. Also involved were outfielder Sixto Lezcano and pitcher Jose DeLeon, going from the Cardinals to the Padres, and pitchers Steve Mura and Alan Olmstead going the other way.

It took three distinct stages to complete this transaction. Lezcano and Mura accepted the trade right away; however, Smith, who lived in San Diego, balked at going to St. Louis. Although he had batted just .222 in 1981, he had just won his second Gold Glove and was holding out for more money. Arbitrators finally decided Smith's salary, and the Smith-Templeton part of the deal was done on February 11, 1982, 62 days after the trade was made. The DeLeon for Olmstead part of the deal followed.

Templeton had been a consistent .300 hitter in his five and a half seasons in St. Louis, and at the time seemed a more likely Hall of Fame candidate than Smith. But while he played ten seasons for the Padres, Templeton never quite fulfilled his early promise. Smith, of course, had 15 sensational years with the Cardinals and was a first ballot Hall of Famer.

Another profitable trade the Cardinals made with San Diego was the one on May 26, 1978, that brought them outfielder George Hendrick in exchange for pitcher Eric Rasmussen. Hendrick had been the Padres' MVP in 1977, a year in which he batted .311, with 23 homers and 81 RBI, but he was hitting just .243 at the time of the trade. Rasmussen was also struggling. He was 2-5 this year, and 24-39 in his four years in St. Louis.

Each man picked up following the trade. Rasmussen went 12-10 for San Diego, while Hendrick hit a solid .288 with 17 homers for St. Louis. Yet while the trade was mostly a draw for the rest of the season, from 1979 on the output of the two men was vastly different, and much to the Cardinals' advantage. While Rasmussen won just 14 more games in his career, Hendrick had six first-rate seasons with St. Louis, including twice making the All-Star team. St. Louis later received an additional bonus from this deal. When they finally traded Hendrick, they sent him to Pittsburgh for John Tudor, a pitcher who paid them back with a 44-17 record over the next three years.

———

In December 1957 the Cardinals sent reliever Willard Schmidt and two minor league pitchers, Marty Kutyna and Ted Wieand, to Cincinnati for two young outfielders. One was Joe Taylor, who lasted 18 games with the Cardinals; however, the other one, who'd had only eight games of major league experience, was Curt Flood. This was one of those trades that barely are noticed by the general baseball public. Schmidt was really the only one involved with a recognizable name. A workhorse relief pitcher, he had gone 10-3 in 40 appearances in 1957, but would win only six more games after the trade. Wieand would not win any, and Kutyna won only 14—all in the American League.

While Taylor's career did not amount to much either, the Cardinals hit pay dirt with Curt Flood. He was their center fielder for the next 12 years, leading the league in putouts five times and in fielding average three times. He batted close to .300 over those 12 seasons and made the All-Star team three times. Then, after the 1969 season, St. Louis traded him to Philadelphia. The only problem was that Flood refused to go, and the Cardinals eventually were compelled to send Willie Montanez to the Phillies to complete the deal. Of course, the big story here was Flood's refusal to be traded and his suing baseball to challenge the reserve clause. For better or worse, we all know how that has changed the game.

———

Left to right: Curt Flood, Ray Sadecki, Bill White, Joe Torre, Lou Brock, Ernie Broglio.

When early in the 1966 season the Cardinals traded pitcher Ray Sadecki to the Giants for first baseman Orlando Cepeda, it was considered an even trade, one that filled the needs of both teams. San Francisco needed a left-handed pitcher, and St. Louis needed a long-ball hitter. Sadecki was 28, and like many lefties considered temperamental. He had been a 20-game winner in 1964, but was only 6-15 in 1965 and 2-1 this season. Cepeda, who was also 28, had a .308 career batting average and 233 home runs. However, he'd had a knee operation after the 1964 season and played in only 33 games with just one home run in 1965. Because of his injuries, and because they had Willie McCovey to play first base, the Giants considered him expendable.

Sadecki did well after leaving St. Louis. He pitched for another 11 seasons, for several different teams, and added 68 wins to the 67 he'd had for the Cardinals. Cepeda played only three seasons in St. Louis,

but they were all outstanding. He hit above .300 each year, led the Cardinals into the World Series in 1967 and '68, and was the league's Most Valuable Player in 1967. The ripple effect of trades led to this being one of the best the Cardinals ever made, because when they traded Cepeda, they got an awfully good player named Joe Torre in return.

Torre then went on to have six top-notch years in St. Louis, especially 1971, when he hit .363 to win the NL batting championship and the Most Valuable Player Award. Coincidentally, when the Cardinals traded Torre, to the Mets on October 13, 1974, the player they got in return was Ray Sadecki. (Sadecki lasted only a few months into the 1975 season.)

During spring training 1959, St. Louis made another trade for a Giants first baseman that worked out well, although they had to give up their best pitcher to get him. Going to San Francisco was Sam Jones, along with a minor league pitcher named Don Choate, in exchange for third baseman Ray Jablonski—a former Cardinal—and first baseman Bill White. The Giants needed a fourth starter to go with Johnny Antonelli, Jack Sanford, and Mike McCormick, and Jones was an excellent choice. He was the Cardinals' leading winner in 1958, and had led the league in strikeouts and finished second in earned run average.

Jones paid quick dividends in San Francisco. He had his career year in 1959, leading the league in wins and ERA, and finishing second in strikeouts. Additionally, he finished fifth in the MVP race and second to Early Wynn of the White Sox for the Cy Young Award. At the time, the Cy Young Award covered both leagues, so Jones obviously would have been the National League winner had there been separate awards. In 1960, Jones won 18 more games for San Francisco, but that was it for him. Arm problems limited him to just 12 more big-league wins.

Despite Jones's early success with the Giants, the Jones-for-White trade proved to be a terrific one for St. Louis. Between 1959 and 1965, White had seven stellar seasons with the Cardinals. The future National League president hit .300 or close to it in each of them, knocked in more than 100 runs three times, made five All-Star teams, and won six of his seven Gold Gloves.

––––––––

In yet another trade for a Giants first baseman that turned worked out fairly well for the Cardinals, they traded four players to San Francisco in February 1985 to get Jack Clark. Clark was one of the top sluggers in the National League, but he wanted out of Candlestick Park. The Giants accommodated him, but they didn't get very much in return: pitcher Dave LaPoint, shortstop Jose Uribe, first baseman David Green, and outfielder Dave Rajsich.

In his first season in St. Louis, Clark hit the home run off Dodgers pitcher Tom Niedenfeuer that put the Cardinals in the World Series. He was hurt for a good part of 1986, but came back to have a terrific year in 1987. Clark was on his way to a probable MVP award, but he hurt his ankle in early September and missed the rest of the season. St. Louis lost him in 1988 when he signed as a free agent with the Yankees.

––––––––

And, finally, one more trade for a Bay Area first baseman. On July 31, 1997, the Cardinals traded three nondescript pitchers, Blake Stein, T. J. Mathews, and Eric Ludwick, to the Oakland Athletics for Mark McGwire. McGwire was one of the top sluggers in the game, but he was threatening to become a free agent. Rather than lose him and get nothing, the A's were forced to trade him. He hit 24 home runs after joining the Cardinals to finish with 58 for the year. That was the major league high, but not enough in either league to lead that league for the season. Larry Walker had 49 for Colorado and Ken Griffey Jr. had 56 for Seattle.

Contrary to the predictions of many, McGwire chose to remain with the Cardinals, and the next season he broke Roger Maris's home run record by hitting 70. Though he was with the team for just a few years, Mark McGwire became one of the most popular men ever to play in St. Louis.

Many people in St. Louis and elsewhere believe the best Cardinals trade ever was the one they made on June 15, 1964, the day of the old trading deadline. It was a six-player deal with the Cubs, with the two principals being Cardinals pitcher Ernie Broglio and Cubs outfielder Lou Brock. Coming to St. Louis with Brock were pitchers Paul Toth and Jack Spring. Accompanying Broglio to Chicago were veteran pitcher Bobby Shantz and outfielder Doug Clemens.

Though Broglio was coming off an 18-8 season, his days as a winning pitcher were over. He was 3-5 at the time of the trade, and won only 10 more games in his career, which ended in 1966. The Cubs justified the trade by claiming that getting Shantz was as important as getting Broglio. Now, Shantz had once been an outstanding pitcher, but he was 38 years old and this would be his final season. And he didn't even finish it with the Cubs. Two months after getting him, the Cubs sold him to the Phillies.

Toth and Spring would pitch a combined two games for the Cards, both by Spring. As for Lou Brock, he was a very promising young player, yet it's doubtful that there were very many people who believed St. Louis was getting a future Hall of Famer. But, of course, that's what Brock became while playing for the Cardinals over the next 16 years.

––––––––

We define a one-sided trade as one where the player, or players, on one of the teams goes on to contribute a lot more to his new team than those for whom he was traded contribute to theirs. From that standpoint, that is, what the player the Cardinals gave up did after the trade as opposed to what the player the Cardinals got did, I believe the most one-sided they ever made was Bob Sykes for Willie McGee.

On October 21, 1981, St. Louis traded Sykes, a journeyman left-handed pitcher, to the New York Yankees for McGee, a minor league outfielder. In Sykes, the Yanks got a 36-year-old who would never pitch for them, or for any other big-league team. McGee, on the other hand, batted .293 as a Cardinals rookie in 1982, and became a fixture in center field. He won the batting title and MVP Award in 1985, while also accumulating several Gold Gloves.

McGee was leading the league again in 1990 when on August 29 the Cardinals traded him to Oakland. No one caught him in that last month, and so he won his second National League batting title. In 1996,

Lou Brock and Johnny Bench in a play at the plate.

McGee signed as a free agent with St. Louis and spent his final four seasons with the Cardinals.

I conclude with a trade that doesn't belong with either the best or the worst deals St. Louis ever made. Yet no discussion of Cardinal trades would be complete without the momentous December 1926 swap of the National League's two best second basemen. Rogers Hornsby, the game's best right-handed hitter, went from St. Louis to New York for switch-hitting Frankie Frisch. (The Giants also included Jimmy Ring, a pitcher nearing the end of his career.) Along with their great abilities, both players were very popular in their respective cities. So why did the teams make they trade? They most likely did so because both men were having disagreements with their respective front offices. Hornsby was demanding a three-year contract worth $150,000, and Cardinal owner Sam Breadon would not go for it. Meanwhile, Frisch and Giants manager John McGraw had struggled through several personality clashes during the '26 season.

At the time of the trade, Hornsby was a six-time National League batting champion. On top of that, he had just managed the Cardinals to their first world championship ever. He would spend just a year with the Giants, but continue his great hitting after moving on. Frisch had been a very good second baseman for the Giants, and he would be an even better one in St. Louis. He would eventually become the Cardinals manager and lead them to the 1934 World Series title.

So while the trade did not seem to favor the Cardinals at the time, it turned out very well for them. However, that's not the reason I'm including it here. I think this trade is worth mentioning because of the quality of the players involved and where they stood in their careers when it was made. Throughout baseball history there have been very few trades involving one Hall of Famer for another. When they did occur, they were usually an exchange of one player who was at the beginning of his career for one who was at the end of his. One example would be the Giants trading the washed-up Amos Rusie to Cincinnati for the young Christy Mathewson. But in December 1926, Frisch was 28 and Hornsby 30, and both had many good years in front of them, which makes this, I believe, the only trade that involved two future Hall of Famers who were then at the peak of their careers.

The Face of Baseball

Photo Selections from the Detroit and Cleveland Public Libraries

by Steve Steinberg

Photographs make history come alive, and baseball images enhance books and articles on the national pastime. While there are terrific collections at the National Baseball Hall of Fame and *The Sporting News* in St. Louis, less obvious sources include public libraries. Two of the best are the Detroit Public Library (DPL) and the Cleveland Public Library (CPL).

The Ernie Harwell Collection, a part of the Burton Historical Collection at the DPL, consists of 40,000 photographs, countless newspaper and magazine clippings, books, guides, programs, and scorecards. The veteran broadcaster and SABR member donated them to the DPL, mainly in the mid-1960s, and continued to supplement the collection until recently. The clips are filed both by name and by subject.

The photographs are the heart of the collection. They span from 1901 to the mid-1950s, with excellent coverage of the Deadball Era. They are filed alphabetically by name. The pictures are the work of *Detroit News* photographer William A. Kuenzel, who became the paper's first staff photographer (and one of the nation's first) in 1901 at the age of 17. His exquisite images are both portraits and action shots, including a famous image of Ty Cobb sliding into Frank Baker at third base. Kuenzel developed his "Big Bertha" camera, which the *Detroit News* photo department built and sold to newspapers around the country. He retired in 1953, two years after his 50th anniversary with the *News*, and passed away in 1964.

Ernie Harwell, winner of the prestigious Ford C. Frick Award, bestowed during the annual Hall of Fame induction ceremonies, saw his first ball game in Atlanta in the summer of 1926 and started working for *The Sporting News* in 1934. A sandlot second baseman as a kid, Ernie's favorite ballplayers were infielders Frankie Frisch, Pepper Martin, "Sunny Jim" Bottomley, and Charlie Gehringer. In the early 1930s, when Ernie was making two dollars a week selling newspapers, he responded to an ad offering old baseball guides. When he bought them for $32, his parents were perturbed. When he soon turned a profit by selling them to A. G. Edwards of St. Louis for $75, they were surprised. Ernie was "hooked" on the guides and focused on collecting them rather than baseball cards or photos.

Around 1940, when Ernie started working for WSB radio in Atlanta, he began clipping articles for future reference. He even went back to publications from the 1920s and 1930s (*Baseball Magazine* and *The Sporting News*, for example) in augmenting this database. When he was in the Marines during WWII, his collection continued to grow; his wife clipped articles for him while he was gone.

Ernie acquired the photo collection from the son of a close friend of Kuenzel in the early 1960s, after the Tigers had passed on it. Ernie's entire baseball holdings now took over a large part of his Grosse Pointe home. When the Harwells moved to Florida in 1965 (where they lived until 1981), Ernie decided to donate his collection and make it available for researchers. Recently the Detroit Public Library dedicated a room to the collection, though it is not yet open to the public. Ernie and his wife of 63 years, Lulu, live in the greater Detroit area.

The Harwell Collection is available for research and reproduction, but is not currently available online. The library is embarking on a digitization project. David Poremba, an author of a number of photograph books, is the curator of the Harwell Collection and manager of the Burton Collection.

STEVE STEINBERG'S *book* Baseball in St. Louis: 1900-1925 *was published by Arcadia in 2004. He has a baseball history Web site, www.stevesteinberg.net and lives in Seattle with his wife and three children.*

The CPL has two photograph collections: a general group of 1.3 million images (which includes some baseball) and another 5,000 baseball images. The baseball images are almost all portraits.

The photos come from many sources, including the *Cleveland Plain Dealer*. The largest group came from the Newspaper Enterprise Association when it closed its Cleveland office.

The CPL is home to two remarkable collections, the Charles W. Mears and Eugene C. Murdock collections. Mears (1874-1942) was a well-known advertising executive with a penchant for baseball statistics. He left behind 41 scrapbooks, countless clippings, and hundreds of thousands of box scores.

Murdock was a Marietta College professor who wrote a couple of excellent oral histories and a biography of Ban Johnson, the founder and first president of the American League. Gene was a long-time member of SABR, joining as its 38th member. He left behind hundreds of books, guides, *Who's Whos*, World Series programs, etc. Most of his photos are baseball snapshots and postcards of varying quality. The highlight of his collection is tapes of 88 interviews with ballplayers (one to two hours each; available for lending), which were the basis of his oral histories, some of which were published in the *Baseball Research Journal*. They include sessions with Stan Coveleski, Red Faber, Lefty Gomez, Charlie Grimm, Lefty Grove, Jesse Haines, Waite Hoyt, Fred Lieb, Ted Lyons, Rube Marquard, Joe McCarthy, Bob O'Farrell, Roger Peckinpaugh, Red Ruffing, Ernie Shore, Bob Shawkey, and Smoky Joe Wood.

The following photos are representative of the DPL and CPL collections.

CLEVELAND PUBLIC LIBRARY

Thousands of baseball images are located in several collections. Most of the baseball images are portraits, rather than action photos. They are concentrated on the 1920s to 1940s and later, as opposed to the Deadball Era. Most are 8" x 10" in size, but are not digitized or accessible online. Many of the images—but not all—are considered public domain. Inquiries should be as specific as possible (e.g., subject name, type of image, etc.).

Cleveland Public Library Photograph Collection
325 Superior Avenue, Cleveland, OH 44114
Phone: (216) 623-2871   Fax: (216) 623-2913
Web: www.cpl.org   Email: photos@cpl.org

Open Monday–Saturday 9:00 A.M. to 6:00 P.M.,
and Sunday from 1:00 P.M. to 5:00 P.M.

The CPL's Eugene Murdock Collection is housed in Social Sciences:

Social Sciences (Murdock and Mears Collections)
Phone: (216) 623-2860   Email: socsci@cpl.org
Photoduplication office: (216) 623-2901

Reproductions 8" x 10" or smaller: $21
(+$5.00 per image and $9.00 per order)

Usage Fee: $10.00 per image
(Out of state and for-profit: $20.00)

Pricing is subject to change. The collection may also charge a nominal fee for photocopies.

DETROIT PUBLIC LIBRARY

The Ernie Harwell Collection is part of the Burton Historical Collection. The collection spans the 20th Century, and is particularly rich in Deadball Era material. The collection also contains many classic photos by Charles Conlon, newspaper and magazine clips, and *Sporting Life* and *The Sporting News* on microfilm.

The collection is strong in action and full-figure shots, as well as portraits. They are of varying sizes, with many of the early 20th century shots smaller than 8" x 10". The Harwell Collection also contains newspaper and magazine clips, organized by person and by subject. Many of the images—but not all—are considered public domain.

Detroit Public Library
5201 Woodward Avenue, Detroit, MI 48202
Web: www.detroit.lib.mi.us

Open Tuesday & Wednesday from Noon to 8:00 P.M.,
and Thursday–Saturday 10:00 A.M. to 6:00 P.M.

Contact the Burton Collection at:

Burton Historical Collection
Phone: (313) 833-1480 phone   Fax: (313) 578-8271
Email: dporemba@detroit.lib.mi.us

Reproductions 8" x 10" or smaller: $25
(Nonprofit, $15)

Usage Fee: $50 per image

Pricing is subject to change.

Bill Carrigan

Tony Lazzeri

Gavy Cravath

Zack Wheat

Moe Berg

Germany Schaefer

Gabby Street

Baseball Notables at Arlington National Cemetery

by David Vincent

Arlington National Cemetery (ANC) in Arlington, Virginia, is the most famous burial ground in the United States, if not the world. It is a standard item on tourists' must-see lists when visiting the Washington, D.C. area on vacation as it is the final resting place for presidents, generals, and Supreme Court justices. In addition, there are memorials to other people and events throughout the cemetery.

THE SITE

Arlington National Cemetery is on the site of Arlington House, the home of George Washington's adopted grandson, George Washington Parke Custis. Custis's only child, Mary Anna Custis, married Robert E. Lee and was given control of the house by the terms of her father's will after his death in 1857. The Lees lived there until 1861, when Virginia seceded from the Union.

At that time Federal troops crossed the Potomac and took occupied positions in the area, erecting military installations, one of which later became Fort Myer. The property was eventually confiscated by the federal government when property taxes were not paid in person by Mrs. Lee, the owner.

The commander of the garrison on the grounds, Brigadier General Montgomery C. Meigs, appropriated the land on June 15, 1864, for use as a military cemetery. Meigs' intention was to render the house uninhabitable should the Lees ever decide to return to their home. The remains of 1,800 Bull Run casualties from nearby Manassas, Virginia, were among the first to be buried on the grounds. Their tomb is located in the rose garden of the mansion, a startling sight while walking the immediate grounds of the house.

General and Mrs. Lee never tried to regain control of Arlington House after it was taken by the government. However, after the death of the general in 1870, his son, George Washington Custis Lee, attempted to recover the land in the courts. In December 1882 the U.S. Supreme Court returned the property to Lee, who according to the terms of his grandfather's will was the legal owner on the death of his mother in 1873. The court's decision stated that the property had been confiscated without due process from the Lee family. Congress purchased the property from Lee the following March for $150,000.

The cemetery now welcomes almost four million visitors per year to visit the more than 250,000 military graves. The qualifications to be buried in the nation's number one national cemetery have been raised, but many decades ago it was treated as any other national cemetery. Many veterans from the Washington, D.C. area who were buried there in the past would not qualify now.

The grounds are the final resting place for many famous Americans and foreign nationals as well. However, there are 22 people buried here who may not draw many visitors but are of interest to the baseball world. The following listing of these baseball notables is split by whether or not the person was a professional ballplayer.

THE PLAYERS

Sixteen men who played in the major leagues and two who played in the Negro Leagues are interred at ANC. They represent four branches of the military.

The table at the end of this article has a listing of the location of each person's grave. The Arlington National Cemetery Web site (www.arlingtoncemetery.

DAVID VINCENT, *the Sultan of Swat Stats, drives past Arlington National Cemetery on his way to RFK Stadium.*

org) contains a map that can be used to locate graves. The visitors center at the cemetery also distributes maps. Please note that the map coordinates listed in this article's tables are approximations.

Washington native CHARLIE BECKER pitched in 15 games for his hometown Senators during the second half of the 1911 season and the first half of 1912. Later he was a photographer for the *Washington Post* and then joined the Army. Becker served with the 315th Ambulance Company in World War I and was at the Meuse-Argonne offensive. During his time in France he received a dose of gas which affected his lungs. After returning to the U.S. he spent time in North Carolina and New York fighting the effects of the gas, which eventually caused his death. Clark Griffith paid tribute to Becker after his death, saying: "Mr. Becker was a fine fellow. Everyone in baseball loved him."

WILLARD GAINES, a native of Alexandria, VA, and a 1921 graduate of the Naval Academy, pitched in four games for the 1921 Senators, finishing all four. His time in the majors was limited to 4⅔ innings, but his teammates obviously knew his real calling because his baseball nickname was "Nemo." He returned to the Navy and was U.S. Naval attaché in Peru during World War II. Gaines retired from the military in 1946 at the rank of captain and founded the Gaines Brothers hardware store in Alexandria. He also raised cattle and was a director of the Virginia Hereford Association. Gaines, an avid golfer, was a founding member of the Army and Navy Country Club in Arlington. He attained the highest military rank of any of the players.

DOC MARTEL, a native of Massachusetts, played 34 games for the Phillies and Braves in 1909-10 after graduating from the Georgetown University Medical School in 1908. During World War I, Martel served as a captain in the Army Medical Corps. Dr. Martel was a member of the executive staff and a professor of gynecology at the Georgetown Medical School after his Army career. He was a fellow of the American College of Surgeons and served as president of the Washington Gynecological Society. Martel died unexpectedly at his home in Washington.

GIL GALLAGHER was born and died in Washington and served in the Navy during World War I. He was an electrician's mate first class stationed at the submarine base in New London, CT. A shortstop, he played seven games for the 1922 Boston Braves. After leaving baseball, Gallagher was the plumbers' foreman at the New House Office Building in Washington for 22 years. His son, Lawrence Kirby Gallagher, Jr., was a sergeant first class in the Army in Korea and Vietnam and later joined the Washington, D.C., police force. Father and son are buried together at ANC.

Infielder BOZE BERGER played 343 games for the Indians, White Sox, and Red Sox in six seasons during the 1930s. Upon graduation from the University of Maryland, he received a reserve commission in the Army, which became an active-duty assignment after Pearl Harbor was attacked. During World War II he served as the military police commander for the District of Columbia. In the late 1940s he was a United Nations observer in the Middle East, and during the Korean War he was the commander of Iwakuni Air Force Base, Japan. He finished his 20-year career in the military as a lieutenant colonel in the Air Force. Among his recognitions was a Bronze Star. Berger was a guest at a 1979 meeting of the Bob Davids Chapter. He was cremated and his ashes are located in the columbarium section of the cemetery.

DAVE WILLS played first base in 24 games for the 1899 Louisville Colonels. The native of Charlottesville, VA, served as chief paymaster of the Marine Corps during World War I. He retired from the Corps as a major and directed a real estate business. For many years Wills was the secretary of the Army and Navy Club.

SPOTTSWOOD POLES is one of the more famous veterans of the Negro Leagues. He enlisted in the Army in 1917 at the age of 30 and served in the 369th Infantry. Poles received a Purple Heart in France and left the Army at the rank of sergeant. He returned to his baseball career after the Army but retired in the early 1920s and went into private business.

PORTRAITS COURTESY NATIONAL BASEBALL HALL OF FAME LIBRARY, COOPERSTOWN, NY

Spotswood Poles

Shortstop DOC LAVAN played 12 seasons for the Browns, Athletics, Senators, and Cardinals. The Michigan native was a graduate of the University of Michigan Medical School. He retired from the Navy as a commander after serving in the medical corps during both World Wars.

———

OSCAR BIELASKI, born in Washington, played four years in National Association and 32 games for the Chicago NL team in 1876. He also worked as a substitute umpire in the NA. Bielaski served in the 11th New York Cavalry and later worked at the Washington Navy Yard. While at the Navy Yard he frequently coached baseball teams. Bielaski collapsed on a street corner in D.C. on the way to meet friends after work in 1911.

———

BILL STEARNS played all five years of the National Association for various teams. He died in his native Washington, D.C., at 45 years old. A veteran of the Civil War and a member of the Grand Army of the Republic, Stearns later served in Company H of the Engineer Corps in Puerto Rico. He never recovered from his trip to the island, where he contracted a stomach poison.

———

ERNEST "BOOJUM" WILSON served in the Army during World War I. He was a corporal in the 417th Service Battalion of the Quartermaster Corps. Wilson's nickname came from the sound of his hits striking the outfield wall during his time in the Negro Leagues.

Doc Lavan   Charles Becker   Lu Blue   Boze Berger

DENNIS COUGHLIN was born in New York state and played for the 1872 National Association Washington Nationals. He was a Civil War veteran, having served as a sergeant in the 140th Regiment of the New York Volunteers. He died in Washington in 1913.

———

MIKE CANTWELL pitched two innings in one game for the 1916 Yankees as a 20-year-old. He joined the Marines in World War I and then returned to baseball, pitching in 10 games for the Phillies in 1919 and 1920. He served in the Marines again during World War II, attaining the rank of first sergeant.

———

LU BLUE was born in D.C. and had the longest big-league career of any of these players. He played first base for the Tigers, Browns, White Sox, and Dodgers from 1921 through 1933. Blue was an infantry sergeant during World War I. He entered the Army in 1918 and served at Camp Lee in Virginia until 1919. In the late 1930s, Blue operated a baseball school in northern Virginia, and in the 1940s he operated a chicken farm.

———

Outfielder BILL DEITRICK played for the 1927-28 Phillies. He served in the Navy with a final rank of lieutenant commander and died at the age of 44 in 1946 in Bethesda, MD.

———

Nebraska native DALE JONES pitched eight innings in two games for the 1941 Phillies. The 22-year-old never returned to majors after joining the Navy, but he did work as a scout for 33 years for the Phillies and Dodgers. He was cremated and his ashes are in the columbarium section of ANC along with those of his wife.

NON-PLAYERS

There are also a few non-playing baseball figures buried at ANC.

———

LEONARD "BOB" DAVIDS is well-known as the founder of SABR. He served in the Army Air Corps during World War II and had a long career as a federal civilian employee. A complete biography of Davids is available as part of the SABR web site's BioProject.

———

BOB MUHLBACH was a colonel in the Air Force and a SABR member. In the former position he served in World War II and Korea, receiving the Legion of Merit. Muhlbach is one of two SABR members buried at ANC; he attended meetings of the Bob Davids chapter.

ELWOOD "PETE" QUESADA was a 25-year veteran of the Air Force and its predecessors when he retired in 1951 as a lieutenant general (three stars). In 1929 he was part of a flying team that stayed aloft for days to prove that midair refueling would work. One of his posts during World War II was as the commander of the 9th Tactical Air Command, and his command was moved to Omaha Beach one day after D-Day. As part of his duties in France, Quesada served as General Eisenhower's pilot over the war zone. After the war Quesada was the overall commander of the Tactical Air Command. In 1957 President Eisenhower appointed him as the first head of the FAA, a post he filled until that administration left office in 1961. Quesada was the president of the Washington Senators in 1961-62. In 1963 he became chairman of L'Enfant Properties, which developed L'Enfant Plaza in D.C. He also served on many boards and with other corporations through his life.

WILLIAM "SPIKE" ECKERT also was a lieutenant general in the Air Force and a 1930 graduate of the U.S. Military Academy at West Point. He was a pilot early in his career and commanded the 452nd Bomber Group during World War II. After graduating from the Harvard Graduate School of Business Administration, he became a supply and logistics expert. He retired in 1961 as comptroller of the Air Force. The Illinois native served as the commissioner of baseball from 1965 through 1968. Eckert, Quesada, and Muhlbach are buried less than the distance of one relay throw from each other in the same area as President William Howard Taft, who is credited with being the first president to throw a ceremonial pitch at a major league game.

EARL M. LAWSON served as a first sergeant in the Army during World War II, earning a Bronze Star. As a sportswriter, Lawson covered the Cincinnati Reds for multiple newspapers from 1949 until his retirement in February 1985. He is credited as being one of the first sportswriters to use quotes from players and managers in stories. Lawson was a longtime correspondent for *The Sporting News*, and served as president of the BBWAA in 1977. He was the 1985 recipient of the J. G. Taylor Spink Award at the Hall of Fame induction ceremonies.

ABNER DOUBLEDAY, who had no connection to the game but was named incorrectly as the creator of the sport early in the 20th century, has a large, obelisk-shaped marker on his grave.

A visit to Arlington National Cemetery is a moving experience. Many spots on the grounds offer the visitor a touch of history, such as watching the changing of the guard at the Tomb of the Unknowns or seeing the eternal flame on the grave of John Kennedy. Standing in the middle of a field with straight lines of grave markers that continue to the horizon in every direction helps give some perspective to the cost of the enormous job our military does. It is important to remember that many of our honored dead also had connections to baseball during their lives and can be found in many national cemeteries throughout the United States.

SABR founder L. Robert Davids is interred at Arlington National Cemetery

Grave Locations at ANC

PLAYERS

Name	Branch	Rank	Location*	Map
Charles Schlggel Becker	Army	Sergeant	18/4788	S-11
Louis William "Boze" Berger	Air Force	Lt Colonel	**	MM-19
Oscar Bielaski	Army	Unknown	17/17991	J-21
Luzerne Atwell Blue	Army	Sergeant	15/272	G-26
Michael Joseph Cantwell	Marines	1st Sergeant	31/2373	X-35
Dennis H. Coughlin	Army	Sergeant	17/18235	I-20
William Alexander Deitrick	Navy	Lt Commander	2/871	P-31
Willard Roland "Nemo" Gaines	Navy	Captain	59/813	FF-24
Lawrence Kirby "Gil" Gallagher	Navy	EM1	31/5232	Z-35
Dale Eldon Jones	Navy	CSP	†	LL-20
John Leonard "Doc" Lavan	Navy	Commander	3/1352E	L-19
Leon Alphonse "Doc" Martel	Army	Captain	1/863	K-33
Spottswood Poles	Army	Sergeant	42/2324	X-47
William E. Stearns	Army	Unknown	13/13931	L-26
Davis Bowles Wills	Marines	Major	8/314	BB-12
Ernest Judson "Boojum" Wilson	Army	Corporal	43/1114	U-44

*Location noted as Section/Lot unless otherwise specified
**Columbarium 3, Section T, Stack 26, Niche 5
†Columbarium 1, Section G, Stack 17, Niche 4

NON-PLAYERS

Name	Branch	Rank	Location*	Map
Leonard "Bob" Davids	Army Air Corps	Private	33/8910	BB-30
Abner Doubleday	Army	Major General	1/61	N-32
William Dole "Spike" Eckert	Air Force	Lt General	30/370-2	Y-41
Earl Lawson	Army	1st Sergeant	**	NN-21
Robert Muhlbach	Air Force	Colonel	30/604-6	Y-39
Elwood Richard "Pete" Quesada	Air Force	Lt General	30/439	Z-39

*Location noted as Section/Lot unless otherwise specified
**Columbarium 6, Section KK, Stack 7, Niche 5

Forfeits

by James Forr

Forfeits were relatively commonplace in the early days of baseball. There was at least one forfeit in the major leagues every year from 1883 to 1907, including 13 in 1884. A review of the reasons for these forfeits reveals how "bush league" the major leagues still were. In 1889, St. Louis's American Association team failed to show up for a scheduled game in Brooklyn because they feared for their safety. The next year, the National League's New York Giants lost a game when pitcher Mickey Welch, upset over the work of the home plate umpire, simply stood on the mound and refused to pitch. Brooklyn of the American Association and Louisville of the National League both forfeited home games when they ran out of baseballs. The Baltimore Orioles left a game early because they needed to catch a train.

Many forfeits were the results of bad behavior—brawls, fan violence, outrageous arguments among players, managers, and umpires. As Bill James has written, "Baseball in the 1890s was violent. It was violent in every respect." American society itself, for that matter, was violent in many respects. Three presidents were assassinated within a span of 36 years. In the post-Reconstruction South, lynchings were not uncommon. Labor unions literally battled employers to the death. It was an era when grown men settled common, everyday disagreements by walloping the bejeezus out of one another. Baseball was not immune to the spirit of the times.

As the major leagues became better organized and more professional in their operations—and as society became at least a tad more genteel—forfeits became increasingly rare. By 1920, a forfeit had become a noteworthy event. This article will focus on the 13 forfeits that have occurred since the 1920 season.

SHIBE PARK, AUGUST 20, 1920
Chicago White Sox defeat Philadelphia Athletics

A forfeit triggered by a mass misunderstanding and some good old-fashioned stubbornness. Chicago led Philadelphia 5-2 in the second game of a doubleheader. With two outs in the bottom of the ninth, pinch-hitter Lena Styles tapped a weak ground ball, which White Sox pitcher Dickie Kerr scooped up near the first base line. Kerr tagged Styles, apparently ending the game, but umpire Ollie Chill ruled the ball had rolled foul just before Kerr picked it up. At the time it was common practice for fans to walk across field at the conclusion of a game, so once Kerr applied the tag, fans from the bleachers streamed onto the diamond, not realizing that Chill had ruled a foul ball. Philadelphia police corralled the onrushing rabble and herded them back toward the outfield fence, but the fans decided that, since the game was just about over anyway, they would just wait it out there in the nether reaches of the field rather than return to their seats. The outnumbered police figured they had done enough and didn't want to force the issue. Umpire Brick Owens strolled out to see if he could coax the fans off the field, but only succeeded in getting himself pelted with garbage. Next, Chill asked Connie Mack for help, but the Athletics manager merely turned his palms upward as if to say, "What am I supposed to do?" Chill had no choice but to forfeit the game to Chicago. In disgust, fans who remained in the stands cast a plague of seat cushions upon their brethren down on the field.

JAMES FORR *is a long-suffering Pirate fan who lives in State College, Pennsylvania and studies consumer behavior. This is his first contribution to* The National Pastime.

NAVIN FIELD, JUNE 13, 1924

New York Yankees defeat Detroit Tigers

Just a few weeks earlier these clubs had brawled at Yankee Stadium, so neither of them was in the mood to take much from the other on this Friday the 13th. With his team ahead 10-6 as he led off the ninth inning, Babe Ruth had to duck away from a head-high fastball from Tigers reliever Bert Cole. On his way back to the dugout after fouling out, Ruth warned the next hitter, Bob Meusel, that he had spied Cobb in center field signaling Cole to throw at Meusel. Then as Meusel stepped in, catcher Johnny Bassler barked out to Cole, "Come on now, don't be afraid to get it close to his head." Cole settled for the ribs instead, plunking Meusel with his first pitch. Meusel headed for the mound—albeit apparently not very quickly or purposefully, because home plate umpire Billy Evans managed to restrain him before he was able to get to Cole.

The fun was only starting. Ruth was irate, perhaps even more so than Meusel. As the benches cleared, Ruth raced out and began screaming at Cobb. Cobb and Ruth had long resented one another, and it appeared that they were going to mix it up until umpire Red Ormsby and Yankee manager Miller Huggins got between them. In the middle of the whole mess was Wally Pipp, the on-deck hitter, wielding his bat. Cobb said Pipp was just asking for more trouble by waving his bat around, but Pipp claimed that was ridiculous. "Nobody did more to pacify the scrappers as I did," he was quoted as saying.

Ruth, Meusel, and Cole all were ejected. In order to get to the Yankee clubhouse, though, Meusel and Ruth had to walk through the Detroit dugout. The Tigers couldn't help themselves. They began shouting at the two Yankees, whereupon Meusel snapped again, taking a swing at infielder Fred Haney. Within seconds both teams were engaged in hand-to-hand combat on the Tiger bench. According to one account, Pipp fired his bat into the middle of the scrum, which leads one to question his skills as a peacemaker. At this point fans rushed the field, some throwing chairs at the Yankee players. There was no way for the game to continue. Evans declared a forfeit, and ordered police to clear a path for the Yankees to escape to their clubhouse. American League president Ban Johnson suspended Meusel and Cole, and slapped Ruth with a $50 fine.

COMISKEY PARK, APRIL 26, 1925

Cleveland Indians defeat Chicago White Sox

Lots of fans at this game probably made it home not realizing they had just seen (and, in some cases, caused) a forfeit. A record crowd of more than 44,000 crammed into Comiskey Park, forcing the team to rope off part of the outfield to accommodate the overflow. In the first inning, a throng broke through the ropes in the outfield and assumed stations in foul territory behind third base. James Crusinberry of the *Chicago Tribune* estimated about 7,500-8,000 fans stood in roped-off sections on the field. The Indians led 7-2 with two outs in the bottom of the ninth when Chicago's Willie Kamm hit a routine ground ball to shortstop Joe Sewell. As the ball settled in Sewell's glove, fans had already begun to pour onto the field. First baseman Ray Knode took Sewell's throw in front of the base and was unable to locate the bag with his foot. Billy Evans ruled Kamm safe, so the White Sox were still alive, but the crowd had overrun the field. Umpire in chief Pants Rowland, who had managed Chicago to a World Series championship eight seasons earlier, forfeited the game to Cleveland.

BAKER BOWL, JUNE 6, 1937

St. Louis Cardinals defeat Philadelphia Phillies

In the days of the Sunday curfew, prior to the advent of lights in major league stadiums, teams occasionally sank to absurd lows as they schemed to beat the clock. This game was one of the most ridiculous examples. St. Louis defeated Philadelphia 7-2 in the first game of a doubleheader—a game that was delayed by rain for an hour and 28 minutes. The second game began at 5:36 P.M., less than 90 minutes away from Philadelphia's 6:59 Sunday curfew. The Gashouse Gang Cardinals pounced on Hugh "Losing Pitcher" Mulcahy for five runs in the top of the first inning, and with Jesse Haines looking strong after coming out of the bullpen for St. Louis in the first, the Phillies decided their only chance was to drag things out so that the clock struck 7:00 before the game became official.

The fourth inning resembled a scene from *The Bad News Bears*. The Cards' Pepper Martin loped toward second in a halfhearted stolen base "attempt." He was able to reach second only because of a "particularly leisurely" throw by catcher Earl Grace. Joe Medwick, who had homered in the first inning, drove in Martin when his shot eluded the grasp of an indifferent Leo Norris at shortstop. Medwick barreled toward second, hoping to be retired. The throw from the outfield did, in fact, beat Medwick to the bag, but Norris just stood there with the ball as a steaming mad Medwick reluctantly inched into second base. Phillies manager Jimmie Wilson then was thrown out after engineering an interminable pitching change. In the fifth inning, Leo Durocher grounded to Norris, who, completely lacking subtlety, rocketed his throw directly into the Philadelphia dugout. Then came another pitching change, as the Phillies brought in Syl Johnson. Meanwhile, umpire Bill Klem was going nuts. According to the *Philadelphia Inquirer*, Klem was "frothing at the mouth like a mad dog, running from player to player, shaking his finger at their noses and spouting words of liquid fire." Johnson, normally an excellent control pitcher, sailed his first pitch over Martin's head, but Martin swung anyway. Johnson's next pitch was nowhere near home plate, with Durocher scoring on the wild pitch. With that, Klem marched in and ordered home plate umpire Ziggy Sears to declare a forfeit.

Afterward, Wilson was asked if he had ordered his players to stall. "I ain't sayin' nothin'," he explained. But he allowed, "If we were guilty of stalling, then the Cardinals were equally culpable. They started swinging at every pitch from the second inning on and refused to run out balls to the infield." National League president Ford Frick wasn't buying it; he fined Wilson $100. The individual hitting statistics didn't count because the game was forfeited before becoming official, so Medwick didn't get credit for his home run. Because of that, he had to share the National League home run title with Mel Ott.

FENWAY PARK, SEPTEMBER 3, 1939

New York Yankees vs. Boston Red Sox (overturned)

A forfeit that wasn't. The Yankees had long since turned the American League pennant race into a joke. Despite losing the first game of this doubleheader, they still had a 12½ game lead over Boston. The nightcap was tied at 5-5 as the clock ticked toward Massachusetts' 6:30 P.M. Sunday curfew. Under state law, no inning could begin after 6:15 and no play at all was permitted after 6:30. The Yankees began their half of the eighth inning at around 6:10 and quickly scored two runs to take a 7-5 lead. For those runs to hold up, however, New York had to make some outs in very short order, then retire the Red Sox before 6:30. Otherwise the game would revert to a 5-5 tie, the score at the end of the seventh. The problem for the Yankees was that after scoring the tie-breaking runs they still had a couple of men on base with only one out. Everyone knew the deal. The Red Sox had time on their side, while the Yankees wanted to make outs as quickly as possible.

With George Selkirk at third base and Joe Gordon at second, Red Sox manager Joe Cronin ordered Eldon Auker to intentionally walk Babe Dahlgren. In an effort to make a hasty out, Selkirk swung at Auker's first wide pitch. Cronin immediately declared that he was playing the game under protest, and home plate umpire Cal Hubbard warned Dahlgren to knock it off. So the Yankees switched to Plan B. On the next pitch, manager Joe McCarthy ordered a double steal "attempt," with Selkirk jogging toward the plate as the pitch was released. He strolled right into the waiting tag of Boston catcher Johnny Peacock for the second out. Next pitch, same thing. This time Gordon sauntered toward the plate, where Peacock, obviously having none of this nonsense, again applied the tag. This was more than Cronin and the Red Sox faithful could tolerate. While Cronin argued with Hubbard, fans littered the field with hot dogs, pop bottles, straw hats, and just about anything else that would fly. By the time the grounds crew could clean up the mess, the curfew time was past. Hubbard forfeited the game to the Yankees. But five days later, American League president Will Harridge overruled Hubbard, declared the game a tie, and ordered it replayed later in September. He also fined Dahlgren, Gordon, and Selkirk $100 apiece for their "reprehensible conduct." Barrow publicly defended his players, asserting that they were just following McCarthy's orders, and that it really was all Cronin's fault anyway because he tried to delay the game with an intentional walk. Barrow lost that fight—but it likely didn't much matter much to him a month later, when his Yankees swept the Reds in the World Series.

GRIFFITH STADIUM, AUGUST 15, 1941

Boston Red Sox defeat Washington Senators

Again, Joe Cronin is the victim of shenanigans—this time from his former team. A steady drizzle began falling at Griffith Stadium in the fifth inning, but it wasn't until the eighth, with Washington leading 6-3, that the rain became heavy enough for umpire George Pipgras to order a delay. However, when Pipgras requested that the field be covered, he found the Griffith Stadium grounds crew had gone AWOL; the umpires could not find them anywhere. Soon the rain let up enough that Senators pitcher Alex Carrasquel returned to the mound to warm up, but the rain picked up again and Pipgras ordered the teams back to their dugouts. After 40 minutes, Pipgras re-emerged, stuck his toe in the muddy baseline, and declared the field unplayable. It was an official game, with Washington the winner, but Cronin wasn't going to stand for it. He filed a protest, claiming that the Senators were negligent in not covering the field during the rain delay.

Once more Will Harridge came down on the side of Cronin. On August 27, Harridge overturned Pipgras' decision and ruled the game forfeited to Boston. He said the rules stipulated that the home team grounds crew must be available at all times. As expected, Senators' owner (and Cronin's father-in-law) Calvin Griffith disagreed vehemently. "The Washington club got a bad deal from the umpires," Griffith argued. "Their report to Harridge said that (Senators' manager) Bucky Harris refused to order the groundskeeper to cover the field when the game was stopped on account of rain. The umpires never ordered Harris to get the field covered, so how could he refuse?" Griffith was also peeved that Harridge had not consulted with anyone from the Senators' organization before issuing his ruling. No matter, despite the appeals of Griffith and the Cleveland Indians (who were fighting the Red Sox for second place in the AL), Harridge refused to reconsider, and on September 6 declared the issue closed.

THE POLO GROUNDS, SEPTEMBER 26, 1942

Boston Braves defeat New York Giants

A look at the stats from Warren Spahn's debut season of 1942 reveals something weird. No wins, no losses, one complete game. It's not a typo. Spahn, making just his second career start, faced the Giants in a meaningless game on the next-to-last day of the season. Fewer than 3,000 people paid their way into the Polo Grounds that afternoon, but 11,000 kids got into the game free by contributing to the Giants' scrap metal drive in support of the allied war effort. Spahn didn't pitch very well, allowing five runs and ten hits, while walking five over the first seven innings. As Spahn and his Boston teammates emerged from the dugout for the bottom of the eighth, hordes of children, for no discernible reason, poured out of the stands and onto the field. James P. Dawson of the *New York Times* described the scene as a "maelstrom—a hopeless, tangled, confused mass running helter-skelter all over the field." Umpires Ziggy Sears and Tommy Dunn waded into the Giants dugout, called the press box, and ordered an announcement be made that the game was in danger of being forfeited, but the warning was barely audible above the din. What had been a 5-2 New York lead turned into a forfeit loss. All statistics counted, except that there was no winning or losing pitcher; thus, the quirk in Spahn's record. Piled high outside the Polo Grounds was 56 tons of scrap metal—including the hulk of a broken-down car.

SHIBE PARK, AUGUST 21, 1949

New York Giants defeat Philadephia Phillies

In the second game of a doubleheader, the Giants led the Phillies 4-2 in the ninth inning. New York's Joe Lafata hit a line drive to center field, where Richie Ashburn made a tumbling attempt at a shoestring catch. Ashburn thought he made a clean catch. Phillies pitcher Schoolboy Rowe insisted that third base umpire Lee Ballanfant made an out call. But second base umpire George Barr ruled a trap. Willard Marshall scored, Lafata ended up with a double, and Ashburn flipped out. As "Whitey" raced in to argue, Phillie fans in the bleachers showered the field with bottles and assorted produce items. Although pleas from the public address announcer to stop the barrage were answered with boos, the fans seemed to run out of both ammunition and anger after about 10 minutes. For a moment peace and sanity threatened Shibe Park. But as Bill Rigney stepped into the batter's box to resume play, the fusillade began anew; one deadeye splattered home plate umpire Al Barlick's leg with a tomato, while two other fans took aim at Ballanfant with a bottle and a piece of fruit. After a short conference with his crewmates, Barlick waived his arms, forfeiting the game to the Giants. "I had to think of the safety of everyone," Barlick insisted. "There was nothing else for me to do." Philadelphia manager Eddie Sawyer didn't see it quite that way. "It was a stupid decision by the umpire. But they're the boss on the field, so there's nothing we can do about it." Sawyer, who later called it the worst day of his baseball career, said the whole mess could have been avoided had the umpires just gotten it right in the first place. He couldn't understand why neither Barlick nor Ballanfant stepped forward to overrule the call. "Barr was the only one in the park who didn't see Ashburn catch the ball."

Philadelphia's finest arrested two men for their part in the riot. One was fined $25; the other—a 54-year-old man—had his case dismissed for lack of evidence. Police were unable to track down one rubber-armed miscreant who, according to witnesses, launched at least 100 bottles relayed to him by a small but industrious group of young women. The following day, Philadelphia Athletics' assistant treasurer Connie Mack, Jr. announced that Shibe Park vendors would follow the custom observed at most other major league parks and pour all bottled drinks into cups before serving them to fans.

SPORTSMAN'S PARK, JULY 19, 1954

Philadelphia Phillies defeat St. Louis Cardinals

Terry Moore had spent most of his adult life as a St. Louis Cardinal—first as a smooth, graceful center fielder from 1935 to 1948, then as a coach in 1949-52. So when Cardinal manager Eddie Stanky fired Moore following the 1952 season, it was understandable that Moore didn't take it well. "When he loses a ball game he acts more like a nine-year-old than a man," Moore said of Stanky. Moore's resentment festered until the two met as opposing managers a year and a half later. Moore, a scout for the Phillies following his exile from St. Louis, had been named Philadephia's skipper just a few days earlier. A photograph in the *Philadelphia Inquirer* that showed the two men cordially discussing the ground rules prior to the series opener belied the lingering ill will between them. "If there is one man in baseball I want to beat, it is Stanky," Moore confessed. Phillies general manager Roy Hamey razzed Moore, requesting, "If you are going to sock Stanky, at least wait until the game is over." Unfortunately, that was too much to ask.

The Cardinals-Phillies doubleheader on July 19, 1954, was a long, hot one played in 100-degree heat. A thunderstorm delayed the first game for almost 90 minutes, but didn't do much to cool either temperature or tempers. The Phillies led St. Louis 8-1 in the fifth inning of game two with dusk approaching. The Cardinal organization believed NL rules prohibited teams from turning on the lights after a game had already begun, but that was a misinterpretation. They could have turned the lights on; but apparently no one realized it, including the umpires. So Stanky began to stall, hoping darkness would arrive before it became an official game. Cardinal pitcher Cot Deal, in an apparent attempt to drag things out, began to miss the strike zone by a suspiciously wide margin. After one pitch came high and tight on Philadelphia's combustible first baseman, Earl Torgeson, umpire Babe Pinelli walked to the mound to warn Deal about any further delaying tactics. Pinelli returned to home plate to find Torgeson nose to nose with St. Louis catcher Sal Yvars. (Torgeson and Yvars had a history. In 1952, Torgeson accused Yvars of smashing one of his bats. So to even things up, he smashed Yvars' face, opening a gash above the catcher's right eye.) Fists were flying within seconds.

As the benches cleared, Moore was one of the first to reach the home plate area. "I thought it looked like trouble," Moore said, "and I tried to get in there to stop it." He grabbed Yvars and pulled him away from Torgeson. Stanky then sneaked up on Moore and wrestled him to ground. Bad idea. This just gave Moore the opportunity to pummel his nemesis at close range. Stanky emerged from the brawl with a scratch on his neck and a mouse under his eye. In the meantime, though, the clock was ticking. After the umpires and local police restored order, Stanky reemerged from the dugout, walked ever so slowly to the mound, and called in Tom Poholsky to relieve Deal. As Poholsky moseyed his way in from the bullpen, Pinelli decided he had seen enough of the delay tactics and declared the game forfeited to Philadelphia. The St. Louis fans, already fed up with Stanky because of the team's poor record, actually cheered Pinelli's decision.

National League president Warren Giles suspended Stanky for five days and fined him $100. Moore escaped without punishment. Although he initially blamed the fight on Moore's inflammatory pre-game remarks, Stanky was repentant after a tongue-lashing from Giles. "I know I have embarrassed and hurt the St. Louis people, baseball nationally, my reputation as a baseball man . . . and Gussie Busch and the St. Louis Cardinals front office. I know that I owe all concerned a public apology."

RFK STADIUM, SEPTEMBER 30, 1971

New York Yankees defeat Washington Senators

A crowd of nearly 15,000 paid (and 4,000 more crashed the gates) to say good bye to baseball in Washington and good riddance to Bob Short. Short purchased the Senators for $8 million in 1969, whereupon the fortunes of the team (and eventually the team itself) went south. The 1969 Senators excited the city, going 86-76 under rookie manager Ted Williams. But trades for washed-up veterans Denny McLain and Curt Flood were disastrous, and by 1971 the team was headed for a 96-loss season. All this, and the league's highest ticket prices to boot. Then in September of '71, Short announced that he was deserting Washington and moving his franchise to Arlington, Texas.

Dozens of anti-Short banners appeared (and disappeared) throughout the night. One sign reading "Bob Short Fan Club" hung in front of an empty section of the stands. Fans in the left field upper deck dangled two long, thin sheets, upon which were scrawled the words "Short Stinks." Soon after security confiscated that banner, another one sprang up which read "Short Still Stinks," much to the delight of the crowd. Fans who hung Short in effigy from the upper deck earned a standing ovation. A grieving 14-year-old boy lugged a homemade dummy of Short through the stands. "I've been coming out here most of my life," he sobbed to a reporter.

Despite the palpable bitterness, the crowd was generally well behaved, and they enjoyed an exciting game. Washington trailed 5-1 in the sixth inning when Frank Howard, the lone superstar in the history of this second incarnation of the Senators, hammered a Mike Kekich pitch for a home run. It was his 26th home run of the season and his 237th as a Senator.

As he crossed home plate, Howard, suspecting that Kekich had been grooving hittable fastballs to him all evening, thanked catcher Thurman Munson, who replied, "You still had to hit it." The crowd cheered for three minutes as Howard, who had once vowed to never tip his cap to RFK Stadium fans, made two tearful curtain calls. "This is utopia," Howard declared. "This is the greatest thrill of my life."

Howard's home run sparked a big Senators' rally. Washington took a 7-5 lead in the seventh inning, but that's when people started to get loopy. The start of the eighth was delayed when three fans ran onto the field to shake the players' hands. Once those fans were removed, 50 or 60 more followed, while chants of "We Want Short" rang out. By the ninth inning, Williams was concerned for his players' safety. He removed Howard from the game, and ordered his relievers to abandon the bullpen and head for the dugout. After Joe Grzenda retired the first two hitters in the top of the ninth, fans stormed the field en masse, running the bases, digging up home plate, and ravaging the scoreboard for souvenirs. Howard didn't really blame them. "This was their night," he insisted. "They've been hurt. They're disillusioned. They're the greatest fans in the world." Umpire Jim Honochick waited three minutes, saw that the situation was hopeless, and declared the forfeit, ending nearly a century of baseball in the nation's capital.

CLEVELAND MUNICIPAL STADIUM, JUNE 4, 1974

Texas Rangers defeat Cleveland Indians

By the mid 1970s, boorish fan behavior had become increasingly commonplace, mirroring the increased tension and violence in American society at large. Houston outfielder Bob Gallagher observed, "It seems like everybody in the outfield stands is either young kids or drunk old men." Strangely, many major league teams seemed to be OK with that; ridiculously cheap beer promotions were not uncommon during this era, as clubs tried to give blue-collar fans an incentive to spend some money at the ballpark at a time when many of those folks were having their pocketbooks squeezed by inflation and unemployment. Cleveland's "Ten Cent Beer Night" in 1974 was one such promotion that degenerated into a Hobbesian nightmare of drunkenness and violence.

The game between the Rangers and Indians would

have been intense even if everyone in the park had been drinking tea. A week earlier, the two teams had brawled in Texas. Cleveland players had to be restrained from going into the stands after fans who were pelting them with beer and screaming obscenities. Prior to the June 4 game, Cleveland fans booed Texas manager Billy Martin, who antagonized the crowd further by doffing his cap and blowing kisses.

The crowd of 25,134 was double what Indians management was expecting. The team had more security on hand than usual, but the size of that force—two city police officers and 50 stadium security personnel—still was nowhere near enough to keep things under control. Fans started running onto the field in the third inning. One woman tried to kiss home plate umpire Larry McCoy. A streaker dashed through the outfield in the sixth inning. But as the game wore on and more alcohol was consumed (the Indians sold 60-65,000 10-ounce cups of beer that night) the mood of the stadium changed from somewhat goofy to downright nasty. In the seventh inning, someone threw a string of firecrackers in front of the Rangers' bullpen, prompting the relievers to flee for the safety of the dugout. The Indians' relievers did the same the next half-inning.

In the ninth inning, the Indians rallied from a 5-3 deficit and had the winning run on third base with two outs. Martin figured his team was in trouble. "My pitcher [Steve Foucault] was scared stiff and I couldn't warm up anybody in the bullpen." It was at that point that a couple of fans jumped the fence and attacked Texas right fielder Jeff Burroughs. Burroughs tried to run away, then fought them off. But by that time more fans had surrounded Burroughs. Players from both teams, some armed with bats, rushed to Burroughs' aid as hundreds of fans streamed onto the field.

The scene resembled a giant street fight. Once Burroughs was out of immediate danger, the players and umpires raced for their clubhouses amidst a hailstorm of debris and waves of angry drunks. One fan lobbed a metal chair from the stands, knocking Cleveland pitcher Tom Hilgendorf silly. Umpire Nestor Chylak suffered a lacerated hand when someone else threw a chair at him. Texas pitching coach Art Fowler, sightless in his left eye, was punched in the right eye and tumbled blindly down the dugout steps. Someone also punched Foucault in the face.

Chylak and Martin both claimed they saw people with knives. Cleveland's Dick Bosman, who was with Washington in 1971 during that season-ending forfeit, said the two crowds were very different. "The fans in Washington were not mean . . . they were only looking for momentos. This was a mean, ugly, frightening crowd." Martin concurred, predicting, "That's probably the closest we'll come to seeing someone get killed in the game of baseball." Martin telephoned Cleveland manager Ken Aspromonte in the clubhouse to thank him for his team's help, just days after their players were at each other's throats. A security guard summed it up best, "Just about everyone that came out on the field seemed drunk or out of his mind." Nine people were arrested; seven were hospitalized.

Indians executive Ted Bonda perhaps was the only person who was not completely appalled. He criticized Chylak for forfeiting the game without warning the fans first, and declared that future ten cent beer nights would go on as scheduled. "They are our fans," Bonda insisted. "I'm not going to chase them away." Bonda explained that at one point before things got out of hand, he was thinking about asking Gaylord Perry to address the fans and urge them to behave themselves, but instead he did nothing and left the park before the ninth-inning riot (or, as Bonda called it, the "public demonstration") began.

EXHIBITION STADIUM, SEPTEMBER 15, 1977

Toronto Blue Jays defeat Baltimore Orioles

With his history of umpire baiting, dirt kicking, and cap throwing, it is only fitting that Baltimore manager Earl Weaver would eventually find himself at the center of a forfeit. The Orioles, just 2½ games behind New York in the American League East, trailed the Blue Jays 4-0 in the bottom of the fifth inning when Weaver decided to make an issue of a tarpaulin covering the Blue Jays' bullpen mound outside the left field line. The night before, his left fielder Andres Mora had stumbled on the tarp as he went into foul territory to make a catch. Weaver, purportedly concerned about the safety of his players, wanted umpire Marty Springstead's crew to order the Jays to remove the tarp, despite the steady rain that was falling. "That is part of the playing field," contended Weaver. "Whoever heard of covering up part of the field while the game is going on? If a guy slips out there and hurts his leg, how am I gonna feel?" Springstead requested that the grounds crew take away the cinder blocks that were holding down the tarp, and fold back the tarp a bit, but he claimed he lacked the authority to tell them to completely remove it. "There is nothing in the rulebook that says such a thing is illegal," said Springstead. Not satisfied, Weaver waved his arm and ordered his team off the field. The Orioles hastily convened in the clubhouse and decided to stand behind their manager. "I think Earl did the right thing," said shortstop Mark Belanger. "I'd say we were just about unanimous in our decision." After a five-minute wait, Springstead, whose crew had had two major rows with Weaver earlier in the year, forfeited the game to the Blue Jays.

The Orioles were indignant. General manager Hank Peters said he would make his opinion known to American League president Lee MacPhail. "They order banners and pieces of clothing removed from the railings all the time. It appears that they went out of their way to find a reason [to forfeit the game]." Losing pitcher Ross Grimsley called the forfeit "a big bunch of garbage. The umpires have got it in for Weaver." "Marty's just trying to stick it to Earl," echoed Belanger. The Blue Jays were a bit huffy themselves. "I don't understand [Weaver's] thinking," said manager Roy Hartsfield. "What about the 25 guys who have a chance to win the championship? Was he thinking about them?"

Actually, yes, he was. The next day Weaver admitted that he thought his team would have a better chance to win if the American League would overrule the umpires and order the teams to finish the game the following week, when the Blue Jays were scheduled to come to Baltimore. "We might not have gotten to bat again, it was raining so hard. Their pitcher [Jim Clancy] was throwing BBs and the wind was blowing in at 30 miles per hour. A chance is all we've got, but it's a better chance than we had of winning last night." Something else that Weaver might have been kicking around in his head was Toronto's airport curfew; no planes could depart after 11:00 P.M. Had they missed that deadline, the team would have been forced to bus to Niagara Falls, NY, and from there fly back to Baltimore for the start of a key series against Boston the next day. Ultimately, MacPhail upheld the forfeit, and the Orioles finished the year 97-64, tied for

second with the Red Sox but still 2½ games behind the Yankees.

COMISKEY PARK, JULY 12, 1979

Detroit Tigers defeat Chicago White Sox

The mother of all forfeits. Disco Demolition Night was the brainchild of Mike Veeck, son of White Sox owner Bill Veeck, and Steve Dahl, a pudgy, bespectacled 25-year-old Chicago disc jockey. All summer Dahl had been pretending to blow up disco records on the air at WLUP, and his listeners loved it. So on this night, between games of a twi-night doubleheader, he would do it for real. Fans could get into the park for 98¢ (WLUP was at 97.9 FM) if they brought along a disco record for Dahl to use as kindling. Why so much hatred for disco? Dahl despised "the whole white three-piece suit thing. It was about 18-24 year-old disenfranchised rock guys like myself not wanting to have to look like that to get laid." A 17-year-old girl at the game echoed those feelings with an amazing observation. "This is our generation's cause," she squealed. Nonetheless, Dahl initially was worried about how Disco Demolition Night would go over. "I was dreading the whole thing," he recalled. "It seemed to me if I drew 5,000 people I would be parading around in a helmet and blowing up records in what looked like an empty stadium."

Not to worry. As game time neared, *Chicago Sun-Times* columnist Bill Gleason could barely believe his eyes. "I saw the tremendous surge of people coming from the north on Shields Avenue and I realized this was going to be a very, very large crowd. I have become convinced that other than the night that Satchel Paige made his [first major league] pitching appearance that this was the largest crowd at Comiskey Park [history]." It is impossible to get an accurate read on that because so many people sneaked into the park. According to White Sox reliever Ed Farmer, "I remember outside the park someone had parked a Camaro, and people were jumping on the roof and hood of the Camaro to jump through some ventilation holes in the outfield wall behind the ballpark and they would come in that way." A fan said, "It looked like medieval times when they go after a castle, pouring over a wall." Conservative estimates put attendance at 50,000, with maybe another 10,000 people milling around outside. It didn't look like the typical baseball crowd. "I thought, most of these people have never seen a baseball game before and probably will never see one again," said Gleason. It didn't smell like the typical baseball crowd, either. "Marijuana was all over the place," remembered announcer Jimmy Piersall.

Apparently it never occurred to anyone that record albums could be used as missiles. "The first problem," Dahl said, "is that they stopped collecting the albums when they had enough to fill the bin [to be blown up on the field]." Throughout the first game, fans sailed the records onto the field like Frisbees. "Each inning I went out to pitch, the disco records were being thrown from different parts of the upper deck and lower deck," said Farmer. "One flew by me and landed over toward third; another one rolled to me and I caught it with my glove on the mound." Although according to Chicago's Rusty Torres, who was a member of the Indians during the Municipal Stadium forfeit five years earlier, "This wasn't as bad. In Cleveland, they were throwing lighters and bottles."

The Tigers won the opener 4-1. Then Dahl took the field and blew up his records amidst a downpour of cherry bombs and beer. "It was like nothing you ever saw," marveled one fan. "Bottle rockets, M-80s, all sorts of [stuff] whizzing over your head." Then, with the records blown to smithereens, about 5,000-7,000 fans spilled out of the stands. The people on the field weren't especially violent. They dislodged home plate, tore up a patch of grass in front of the mound, and one guy drenched the fans who remained in their seats with an industrial-size hose, but the worst injury was a broken ankle. It was about a half hour before helmeted police arrived, but by that time most of the people had gotten bored and had left on their own. About 1,000 people remained on the field, and the cops cleared them away in about five minutes. Thirty-nine people were arrested.

The condition of the field wasn't that bad, all things considered. But Tiger manager Sparky Anderson refused to play the second game because of the excessive delay. Umpire Dave Phillips conferred with player representatives Torres and John Hiller, then called the second game. Initially there was talk that the game would be made up later that weekend as part of a doubleheader, but MacPhail jumped in and awarded the Tigers the victory via forfeit. Bill Veeck declared that he was, "amazed, shocked, and chagrined. I think the grounds for forfeiting are specious at best. . . . It's true there was some sod missing. Otherwise nothing was wrong."

Gleason's postmortem column made it sound as if Disco Demolition Night was one of the lesser-known signs of the Apocalypse. But time has provided him with some perspective. "As the years pass, it becomes remembered less with bitterness and more with laughter. It really was one of the epic events of baseball history. It will be remembered forever."

DODGER STADIUM, AUGUST 10, 1995

St. Louis Cardinals defeat Los Angeles Dodgers

A year removed from the player strike that wiped out the 1994 season, the relationship between players and fans was still sour. Fans in both Pittsburgh and Detroit sent their teams running for cover on Opening Day, showering the field with debris; a loudmouthed Yankee fan almost came to blows with the Angels' Chili Davis; and Milwaukee fans and Toronto third baseman Ed Sprague, in a kindergarten flashback, threw chunks of tobacco at one another. But it was the normally mellow fans of Los Angeles who were responsible for their team forfeiting a game. A sellout crowd of 53,361 came out to watch the Dodgers try to move into a first-place tie with Colorado in the National League West. It was also a promotional night for the Dodgers; fans were handed souvenir baseballs as they passed through the turnstiles. That would turn out to be a big problem.

Everything was cool until the seventh inning, when some fans began throwing their baseballs onto the field. Play resumed after a six-minute delay, but that was just a taste of what was to come. In the bottom of the eighth, with St. Louis leading 2-1, home plate umpire and crew chief Jim Quick ejected Eric Karros after the Dodger first baseman protested a called third strike that ended the inning. In the bottom of the ninth, leadoff hitter Raul Mondesi struck out thanks to two borderline calls by Quick. Mondesi griped and he, too, was ejected. Quick was on a roll. Next to get the heave-ho was Dodger manager Tom Lasorda, who rushed to home plate to defend Mondesi. Dodger fans lost it, firing baseballs (and other stuff) from all corners of the stadium. L.A.'s Chris Gwynn, standing in the on-deck circle, was hit in the head with an apple. Cardinals right fielder John Mabry said, "I wasn't too worried until a bottle of Southern Comfort flew out of the stands and hit me." Then after Mabry was hit with a bottle of rum, "I finally asked the batboy if I could trade my hat for his helmet, but he said no, because he was in danger, too." The Cardinals retreated to the dugout while the fans settled down and stadium personnel cleared the field. But as the players returned to their positions and the game was set to resume, another baseball landed in center field, and Quick immediately forfeited the game to St. Louis.

As usual, fingers of blame pointed in all directions. The Cardinals blamed the Dodger fans. Reliever Tom Henke claimed the fans threw 200-300 balls onto the field in the seventh inning alone—although Dodgers' officials countered that it was only about 200 for the entire game. The Dodgers blamed the umpires. "I don't know how you can [forfeit the game] without giving a warning over the P.A.," argued general manager Fred Claire. The umpires blamed Lasorda. According to first base ump Bob Davidson, "Lasorda instigated the whole damn thing by running out there, waving his fat little arms."

Dodgers' catcher Mike Piazza said, "I just hope and pray that forfeit doesn't cost us." It almost did, but the Dodgers held on and won the division by one game. Perhaps the happiest man in the whole situation? Mike Veeck. "I'll forever be the godfather of the forfeiture," Veeck declared. "But I finally got it off my back. [I'm] a free man."

References

Akron Beacon Journal (online edition), November 3, 2003.

Alexander, Charles. *Ty Cobb*. New York: Oxford University Press, 1984, p. 172.

Barthel, Thomas. *The Fierce Fun of Ducky Medwick*. Lanham, MD: Scarecrow Press, 2003, pp. 122-23.

Boston Globe. September 3, 1939, p. 26; August 28, 1941, p. 25.

Chicago Tribune. August 21, 1920, p. 7; April 27, 1925, p. 17; November 12, 1952, p. B4; July 13, 1979, section 5, p. 1, 3.

Cleveland Plain Dealer. June 5, 1974, p. 1-A, 6-A, 8-B, 1-G, 2-G; June 6, 1974, p. 4-F.

Deveaux, Tom. *The Washington Senators, 1901-1971*. Jefferson, NC: McFarland, 2001, pp. 257-58.

James, Bill. *This Time Let's Not Eat the Bones*. New York: Villard, 1989; p. 272.

Los Angeles Times. June 14, 1924, p. B1; August 11, 1995, p. C1, C4; August 12, 1995, p. C8.

New York Herald Tribune. June 14, 1924, p. 1, 10; September 27, 1942, section 3, p. 2.

New York Times. June 14, 1924, p. 1; June 7, 1937, p. 23; September 4, 1939, p. 26; September 27, 1942, p. S3; August 22, 1949, p. 1; October 1, 1971, p. 49-50; September 16, 1977, p. 93.

Philadelphia Inquirer. August 21, 1920, p. 6; June 7, 1937, p. 19, 21; June 8, 1937, p. 25, 28; August 28, 1941, p. 25; August 22, 1949, p. 1, 24, 26; August 23, 1949, p. 1, 23; July 19, 1954, p. 1, 19; July 20, 1954, pp. 21-22.

Pittsburgh Post-Gazette (online edition), July 11, 2004.

Pittsburgh Tribune-Review (online edition), July 27, 2003.

Roberts, Robin and Rogers, C. Paul III. *Whiz Kids*. Philadelphia: Temple University Press, 1996; pp. 186-87.

Sports Illustrated. October 4, 1971, p. 17; June 17, 1974, pp. 10-13; September 26, 1977, p. 64; August 21, 1995, pp. 72-73.

The Sporting News. June 10, 1937, Pg. 3, 10; September 14, 1939, pg. 2-3, 10; August 31, 1949, pg. 7; July 28, 1954, pg. 2, 5; June 22, 1974, pg. 5, 14; June 29, 1974, pg. 4; October 16, 1971, pg. 34, 38; July 28, 1979, pg. 20, 36; August 21, 1995, pg. 15.

Toronto Globe and Mail. September 16, 1977, p. 1, 27.

Washington Post. June 14, 1924, p. 25; September 4, 1939, p. 13; September 9, 1939, p. 16; August 16, 1941, p. 12; August 31, 1941, p. X1; September 3, 1941, p. 19; September 7, 1941, p. S1; August 22, 1949, p. 8; July 19, 1954, p. 10; July 21, 1954, p. 23; October 1, 1971, p. A1, D1.

www.dahl.com/memories/dd_audio.asp

www.retrosheet.org/forfeits.htm

www.rollingstone.com/news/archive

◇◇◇◇◇◇◇◇◇◇◇◇◇◇◇◇◇◇◇◇◇◇◇◇◇◇◇◇◇◇◇◇◇◇ ⬭ ◇◇◇◇◇◇◇◇◇◇◇◇◇◇◇◇◇◇◇◇◇◇◇◇◇◇◇◇◇◇◇◇◇

ON JUNE 24, 1958 (first game) with the Dodgers in Cincinnati, Johnny Temple hit eight consecutive foul balls on hit-and-run attempts with Jeffcoat (a pitcher) going from first base. Temple then doubled to center, scoring Jeffcoat, who was not going on that pitch.   –DAVID SMITH

World Series Final Plays

by Joseph Elinich

As Edgar Renteria bounced the final out of the 2004 World Series to Boston's Keith Foulke, the thought immediately popped into my mind that Renteria had also ended the 1997 World Series with a winning single to center field against Cleveland's Charles Nagy. Wondering if that had ever happened before, I began to do a little research.

2004 marked the one hundredth playing of the World Series. With the help of Retrosheet I compiled a table of the final plays for each of those one hundred World Series. Not unexpectedly, the final play was generally an out recorded by the winning team (89 times). However, as I looked further I found an interesting pattern of pairs within those one hundred results.

As it turned out, Edgar Renteria was one of *two* men to end two World Series, once with the winning hit and once with the final out. The other was Goose Goslin who ended the 1925 series for Washington by striking out and ended the 1935 series with a single to drive Mickey Cochrane home with the winning run for Detroit. The 1925 series marked the first series in which a team (the Pirates) rallied from a 3-1 deficit to win. Walter Johnson took the loss after he had won two games earlier in the series as Washington lost in its second World Series appearance. Remy Kremer notched his second win for the Pirates with four innings of one-hit relief as the Pirates rallied from a four-run deficit to win by two. In 1935, Goslin's two-out single brought Detroit its first World Championship and notched Tommy Bridges' second victory of the series.

There were also *two* men who ended *two* World

JOE ELINICH, *a member since 1979, is a retired government employee who stays active by broadcasting Pirate games over the Internet for MLB.com. He has been married for 32 years and has a daughter in college. He is Secretary/Treasurer of the Forbes Field Chapter.*

Series by making the final out. Furthermore, both men did it in successive World Series. Detroit's Boss Schmidt ended both the 1907 and 1908 World Series by making an out. In 1907, Schmidt popped out to shortstop notching George Mullin's second loss of the series as the Tigers lost to the Cubs by a score of 2-0. In 1908, it was a ground out, catcher to first, which sent Bill Donovan to his second loss of the series as the Cubs again defeated the Tigers, 2-0. In 1921 the Yankees' Aaron Ward ended the Series by making the final out at third base as the second out of a double play and then ended the 1922 World Series with a fly out as Bullet Joe Bush lost his second game for the Yanks by two runs, 5-3. Fortunately for both men, they each got to play in a third World Series although only Ward would be with a winner.

Speaking of double plays, there have been *two* occasions in which the World Series has ended with a double play. The first was in 1921 when Frank Baker hit into a 4-3-5 double play with Ward being put out attempting to advance to third. An interesting side note was that the Yankees trailed 1-0 and had Ward stayed at second; he would have been the tying run with Wally Schang coming to the plate. It was only the second time that Baker was involved in a double play in a World Series; the other time being in the 1914 series against the Braves. The winner was Art Nehf, who had already lost two games in the series, while the loser was Waite Hoyt, who had already won two. The second World Series to end with a double play was in 1947 when Brooklyn's Bruce Edwards bounced into a 6-4-3 double play retiring Eddie Miksis at second on the play. The Yankees won the game 5-2 as Joe Page pitched five innings of one hit relief for the victory. Edwards batted .222 for the series and would only get two more at bats in the second of two World Series in which he participated. Miksis and Page would also play in only two World

Series. This game also marked the first of Page's two World Series victories.

As for *doubles*, there have been *two* World Series that ended on a double. Washington's Earl McNeely was the first to do it when his infamous "pebble bounce" over New York's Freddie Lindstrom's head in 1924 scored Muddy Ruel in the bottom of the twelfth inning for Washington's only World Series crown. It was the second double of the inning as Muddy Ruel reached on a double of his own after Giants' catcher Hank Gowdy dropped Ruel's foul pop-up. It would have been the second out of the inning. Jack Bentley took the loss for the Giants, which was his second loss of the series and his final appearance in the two series in which he played. For McNeely, it was his final hit in World Series play. He would play in only two World Series and would finish with a .222 batting average. The second time was five years later when Bing Miller of the Philadelphia Athletics capped a comeback three-run rally in the bottom of the ninth inning against the Chicago Cubs by doubling Al Simmons home from second base. This was the second comeback win for the Athletics in as many games. The game before, the Athletics rallied for 10 runs in the bottom of the seventh to overcome an 8-0 deficit in what is the largest deficit any team has overcome in World Series play. The victim was the Cubs' Pat Malone and marked his second loss of the series in his second start. Miller had two hits off Malone that day and may have been especially satisfied with the hit as two days earlier, when the Athletics staged their famous comeback, Malone entered the game in the seventh inning and hit Miller, the first batter he faced.

Most will easily remember that there has been *two* times in which the World Series has ended on a home run. Pittsburgh's Bill Mazeroski brought the Yankees low in the bottom of the ninth inning in 1960 with a home run in the seventh game. It was Mazeroski's second home run of the series and would be his final home run in the two World Series in which he participated. It was also Ralph Terry's second appearance and second loss of the series although he would go on to win two and lose two in the remaining four series in which he appeared. The second occurrence was when Toronto's Joe Carter ended the 1993 series and dashed the Phillies' hopes of forcing a seventh game as he hit a three-run home run in the bottom of the ninth off reliever Mitch Williams. As with Mazeroski, it was Carter's second home run of the series and was the second time in which he hit two home runs in the two World Series in which he played. As with Terry, it was also Williams' second loss of the series.

Finally, there have been *two* World Series that have ended on base-running plays, and they occurred in successive seasons. New York's Babe Ruth ended the 1926 World Series by being caught stealing second base with the Yankees trailing by one run and Bob Meusel at bat. It netted Jesse Haines his second win of the series. Grover Cleveland Alexander saved the game with his famous relief appearance entering the seventh inning with two out and the bases loaded to strike Tony Lazzeri out. He too registered two victories in the series. The very next year, the Yankees' Earle Combs scored the winning run of the series on a wild pitch by Pittsburgh's Johnny Miljus with the bases loaded, two outs and Tony Lazzeri at bat. It was also Miljus' *second* wild pitch of an inning he almost escaped without a run. Combs had walked to open the inning and after Koenig singled him to second Miljus made his first errant toss. Ruth was walked intentionally to load the bases. Miljus then recorded two strikeouts against Gehrig and Meusel. Tony Lazzeri next strode to the plate. Just as in 1926 against Alexander, he pulled the first pitch just foul into the left field stands. Miljus then delivered a ball, and on the next pitch one of his curves eluded Johnny Gooch and Combs scampered home.

No World Series has ended on a triple.

Baseball has always been a game of symmetry and harmonies; batter and pitcher; winner and loser. So it was both surprising and yet not so to see that through the first one hundred playing of the World Series such dualities would exist. I've included a table with the results of the final play of the first one hundred World Series. Let's see what the next one hundred bring.

WORLD SERIES FINAL PLAYS, 1903-2004

YEAR	TEAM	INN	PLAYER	SCORING, ETC.	YEAR	TEAM	INN	PLAYER	SCORING, ETC.
1903	PIT-NL	9	Honus Wagner	K	1951	NY-NL	9	Sal Yvars	9, line out
1905	PHI-AL	9	Lave Cross	6-3	1952	BKN-NL	9	Pee Wee Reese	7, fly out
1906	CHI-NL	9	Fred Schulte	3, unassisted ground out	1953	NY-AL	9	Billy Martin	1B to CF: Hank Bauer scored
1907	DET-AL	9	Boss Schmidt	6, pop out	1954	CLE-AL	9	Dale Mitchell	5, pop out
1908	DET-AL	9	Boss Schmidt	2-3	1955	NY-AL	9	Elston Howard	6-3
1909	DET-AL	9	Tom Jones	7, fly out	1956	BKN-NL	9	Jackie Robinson	2-3 K
1910	CHI-NL	9	Jimmy Archer	6-4 FC, John Kling batting	1957	NY-AL	9	Jerry Coleman	5 FC, unassisted, Skowron batting
1911	NY-NL	9	Art Wilson	5-3, ground out	1958	MIL-NL	9	Red Schoendienst	8, line out
1912	BOS-AL	10	Larry Gardner	9, sacrifice fly, Yerkes scored	1959	CHI-AL	9	Luis Aparicio	7, fly out
					1960	PIT-NL	9	Bill Mazeroski	HR to left field
1913	NY-NL	9	Larry Doyle	9, fly out	1961	CIN-NL	9	Vada Pinson	7, fly out
1914	PHI-AL	9	Stuffy McInnis	5-3	1962	SF-NL	9	Willie McCovey	4, line out
1915	PHI-NL	9	Bill Killefer	6-3	1963	NY-AL	9	Hector Lopez	6-3
1916	BKN-NL	9	Mike Mowrey	6, pop out	1964	NY-AL	9	Bobby Richardson	4, pop out
1917	NY-NL	9	Lew McCarty	4-3	1965	MIN-AL	9	Bob Allison	K
1918	CHI-NL	9	Les Mann	4-3	1966	LA-NL	9	Lou Johnson	8, fly out
1919	CHI-AL	9	Joe Jackson	4-3	1967	BOS-AL	9	George Scott	K
1920	BKN-NL	9	Hi Myers	6-4 FC, Ed Konetchy batting	1968	STL-NL	9	Tim McCarver	2, pop out
1921	NY-AL	9	Aaron Ward	4-3-5 DP, Frank Baker batting	1969	BAL-AL	9	Dave Johnson	7, fly out
					1970	CIN-NL	9	Pat Corrales	5-3
1922	NY-AL	9	Aaron Ward	9, fly out	1971	BAL-AL	9	Merv Rettenmund	6-3
1923	NY-NL	9	Jack Bentley	4-3	1972	CIN-NL	9	Pete Rose	7, fly out
1924	WAS-AL	12	Earl McNeely	2B, Ruel scored	1973	NY-NL	9	Red Garrett	6, pop out
1925	WAS-AL	9	Leon Goslin	K	1974	LA-NL	9	Von Joshua	1-3
1926	NY-AL	9	Babe Ruth	2-4 CS, Bob Meusel batting	1975	BOS-AL	9	Carl Yastrzemski	8, fly out
1927	NY-AL	9	Earle Combs	WP by Miljus, Lazzeri batting	1976	NY-AL	9	Roy White	7, fly out
					1977	LA-NL	9	Lee Lacy	1, pop out
1928	STL-NL	9	Frank Frisch	7, fly out	1978	LA-NL	9	Ron Cey	2, pop out
1929	PHI-AL	9	Bing Miller	Double: Al Simmons scored	1979	BAL-AL	9	Pat Kelly	8, fly out
					1980	KC-AL	9	Willie Wilson	K
1930	STL-NL	9	Jimmy Wilson	9, fly out	1981	NY-AL	9	Bob Watson	8, fly out
1931	PHI-AL	9	Max Bishop	8, fly out	1982	MIL-AL	9	Gorman Thomas	K
1932	CHI-NL	9	Riggs Stephenson	9, fly out	1983	PHI-NL	9	Gary Maddox	6, line out
1933	WAS-AL	10	Joe Kuhel	K	1984	SD-NL	9	Tony Gwynn	7, fly out
1934	DET-AL	9	Bill Rogell	6-4 FC, Marv Owen batting	1985	STL-NL	9	Andy Van Slyke	9, fly out
1935	DET-AL	9	Leon Goslin	1B to RF: Mickey Cochrane scored	1986	BOS-AL	9	Marty Barrett	K
					1987	STL-NL	9	Willie McGee	5-3
1936	NY-NL	9	Harry Danning	3, unassisted ground out	1988	OAK-AL	9	Tony Phillips	K
					1989	SF-NL	9	Brett Butler	4-1
1937	NY-NL	9	Jo-Jo Moore	3-1	1990	OAK-AL	9	Carney Lansford	3, pop out
1938	CHI-NL	9	Billy Herman	1-3	1991	MIN-AL	10	Gene Larkin	1B, Gladden scored
1939	CIN-NL	10	Wally Berger	6, line out					
1940	DET-AL	9	Earl Averill	4-3	1992	ATL-NL	11	Otis Nixon	1-3
1941	BKN-NL	9	Jimmy Wasdell	8, fly out	1993	TOR-AL	9	Joe Carter	HR, Henderson & Molitor scored
1942	NY-AL	9	George Selkirk	4-3	1995	CLE-AL	9	Carlos Baerga	8, fly out
1943	STL-NL	9	Deb Garms	4-3	1996	ATL-NL	9	Mark Lemke	5, pop out
1944	STL-AL	9	Mike Chartak	K	1997	FLA-NL	11	Edgar Renteria	1B to CF, Counsel scored
1945	CHI-NL	9	Roy Hughes	6-4 FC, Don Johnson batting	1998	SD-NL	9	Mark Sweeney	5-3
1946	BOS-AL	9	Pinky Higgins	4-6 FC, Tom McBride batting	1999	AZ-NL	9	Keith Lockhart	7, fly out
					2000	NY-NL	9	Mike Piazza	8, fly out
1947	BKN-NL	9	Bruce Edwards	6-4-3 DP, Miksis out at second	2001	AZ-NL	9	Luis Gonzalez	1B to CF: Bell scored
1948	BOS-NL	9	Tommy Holmes	7, fly out	2002	SF-NL	9	Kenny Lofton	8, fly out
1949	BKN-NL	9	Gil Hodges	K	2003	NY-AL	9	Jorge Posada	1, unassisted ground out
1950	PHI-NL	9	Stan Lopata	K	2004	STL-NL	9	Edgar Renteria	1-3

Carl Erskine
Ace Right-Hander for the Boys of Summer

by Jim Sargent

arl Daniel Erskine, born and raised in Anderson, Indiana, but famed for his twelve seasons as a stellar right hander for the Brooklyn Dodgers in baseball's postwar era, proved not only to be talented pitcher but also an exceptional teammate and person.

One of the Dodgers of 1952-53 portrayed in Roger Kahn's 1971 baseball classic, *The Boys of Summer*, Erskine pitched for a Dodger team that he still loves—a ball club featuring exceptional players like Jackie Robinson, Duke Snider, Pee Wee Reese, Roy Campanella, Carl Furillo, Billy Cox, Preacher Roe, Joe Black, Clem Labine, George "Shotgun" Shuba, and Erskine himself.

After the cheering stopped, the Erskines had a fourth child, Jimmy, who was born with a genetic abnormality now called Down's syndrome. Rather than keep an executive position with a men's shirt firm in the New York area, Carl and Betty moved Dan, Gary, Susan, and the baby back home. In Anderson, Kahn observed, Erskine believed he could help give Jimmy the chance to be "fully human," a motive which suggests a measure of Carl's compassion.

Erskine had a 122-78 big-league record and a 4.00 ERA over 12 seasons. He posted double-digit winning years for Brooklyn from 1951 through 1956. But his greatest season came in 1953, when he led the National League in won-lost percentage at .769, while fashioning a 20-6 mark.

Erskine began showing his talent, skill, and fortitude by winning his first five games as a rookie for the Dodgers in 1948. Despite a sore arm caused by a shoulder injury in his first start, he came through

with an 8-1 ledger in 1949. But as an indicator of the competitiveness in the majors during the postwar era, Carl spent half of his first three seasons in the minors attempting to rehab a shoulder muscle tear.

"Oisk," as Dodger fans often called him, also rose to the challenge in the World Series. Carl played in five October classics for the Dodgers, winning two games, losing twice, and setting a World Series record of 14 strikeouts on October 2, 1953, against the New York Yankees, a standard that lasted exactly ten years— until southpaw Sandy Koufax fanned 15 Yankees en route to a 5-2 victory on October 2, 1963.

As a further mark of his ability to pitch big games, Erskine hurled two no-hitters, one in 1952 against the Cubs and one in 1956 against the archrival New York Giants. He also pitched his last complete game in the majors on May 26, 1958. Erskine stopped Robin Roberts and the Phillies the day after visiting his longtime battery mate and friend Roy Campanella, who was lying paralyzed in a New York hospital.

"They had Roy strapped in a special bed facedown when I visited him in New York," Erskine remembered in 2003. "We talked, and he said they had a TV rigged so he could watch ball games. It was the first time I saw him after his auto accident in January 1958.

"It sounds corny to say it, but seeing Roy gave me some sort of weird inspiration. The next day I went out and pitched my last complete game in the majors, and we beat the Phillies, 2-1."

Born on December 13, 1926, in Anderson, Carl grew up playing catch with his two brothers. Later, he played sandlot, park league, and American Legion ball. The high school coach, Charles Cummings, asked the hard-throwing youth to play baseball. In the spring of 1941 as a freshman, Carl threw batting practice and made trips with the team. But as a midterm student, he ended up playing four varsity seasons for Anderson High.

JIM SARGENT *is a professor of history and Dean of the Social Sciences Division at Virginia Western Community College in Roanoke. He has written more than 50 profile articles about former major leaguers and players from the All-American Girls Professional Baseball League.*

While Carl blossomed as a high school hurler, World War II formed the backdrop of his teenage years. The Dodgers scouted the 5'10" right hander, sending Stanley Feezle to keep in touch with Erskine's development. Carl graduated in June 1945, and, with the war winding down, he was drafted into the Navy. Three weeks into boot camp, as he was training for carrier duty, the war ended after the United State dropped two atomic bombs on Japan.

His orders changed, and Erskine spent the rest of his service time at the Boston Navy Yard. In the summer of 1945, the Navy wouldn't let him try out for the base team. But one Sunday in August he went to see a semi-pro team practice in Milton, a suburb of Boston. At first the coach, Ernest Sorgi, said they didn't need any pitchers, but then he gave the sailor a tryout.

"He was being nice," Erskine explained in 2003. "When he said I could throw to a catcher, I pulled off my Navy jumper, they gave me a glove and a ball, and I pitched in my bell bottoms.

"I threw the first one past the catcher! I threw a few more fastballs, and the coach wanted me to throw curves. I threw my curve, and the catcher couldn't handle it either.

"After a few more pitches, Ernie Sorgi came over to me, put his hand on my shoulder, and said, 'Son, what are you doing next Sunday?' I pitched the rest of the season for him."

Sorgi was a "bird dog" for Billy Southworth, manager of the Boston Braves. As a result, Carl pitched batting practice for the Braves in the spring of 1946. The Braves wanted to sign him, and they offered a $2,500 bonus.

Because the Dodgers had scouted Erskine in high school, Carl and his high school catcher, Jack Rector, traveled to Brooklyn and spent a week working out at Ebbets Field in the summer of 1945. The young men enjoyed the adventure after graduation, and before the Navy took Erskine.

"When I was being pushed hard by the Braves," Erskine recollected, "I already decided I wanted to play for the Dodgers, because they treated me great with the New York experience.

"I called the Dodgers and said, 'Hey, I'm getting pushed by the Braves, and they are offering a bonus.' They offered $2,500, which is probably what my dad made all year in 1945.

"Mr. [Branch] Rickey said, 'Don't do anything.

Just sit tight.' My parents did come to Boston, but the Dodgers brought them to town, not the Braves. Mr. Rickey signed me, and when I was discharged a few weeks later, they sent me to Danville, Illinois, in the Three Eye League. I reported on July 25, and I finished the season with Danville."

Erskine lost his first three games at Danville. But after thinking about quitting pro ball, he came back to win his last three contests. The right hander threw a good overhand fastball and a sharp-breaking overhand curve. He also threw a changeup, and he changed speeds on his curve.

After the season was over, Happy Chandler, the commissioner of baseball, declared Erskine a free agent. The Dodgers had violated baseball's directive not to sign players until they were formally discharged from the service.

NATIONAL BASEBALL HALL OF FAME LIBRARY, COOPERSTOWN, NY

Carl recalled, "Mr. Rickey had paid me a bonus of $3,500. Nobody got cash money for signing. They might give you a car if you were a hot prospect, and you could buy a Chevrolet or a Ford for under $1,000. But cash was unheard of in those days.

"The commissioner said the directive had wording that could have been misunderstood, so they allowed me to sign with any team, including resigning with the Dodgers. The Phillies, the Pirates, the Cubs, the Red Sox, and the Braves all made me offers. But I agreed to resign with the Dodgers for another $5,000. That was big money in those days!

"Ten years later, in 1956, I pitched a no-hitter against the Giants. Dizzy Dean interviewed me after the game, and he said, 'Who signed you, son?'

"I said, 'Branch Rickey.'

"Dizzy said, 'He's the stingiest man ever lived. I played for him in St. Louis and he starved me. I'll bet he starved you too, didn't he?'

"I said, 'Actually, Mr. Rickey gave me *two* bonuses,' and I told him the story.

"Dizzy turned to the cameras, 'Folks, this here young fella deserves to be in the Hall of Fame, not because he's pitched two no-hitters, but because he got two bonuses out of Branch Rickey!'"

Carl added, "That's how I signed with the Dodgers, and by a stroke of luck, that's one of the smartest moves I ever made, because I got to play with this great team for twelve seasons."

In 1947 Erskine spent the season with Danville and pitched well, notching a 19-9 record and a 2.94 ERA in a league-high 233 innings. That winter he pitched in Havana, Cuba. Carl started the 1948 season with Fort Worth in the Double-A Texas League. He went 15-7 in 23 games before being called up by the Dodgers in late July.

Erskine recalled, "I joined the Dodgers in Pittsburgh. I first saw action in the big leagues on July 25, two years to the day after I reported to Danville in 1946. They put me in the bullpen. Late in the game, in the seventh inning, Hugh Casey, the experienced old relief pitcher—they didn't call them 'stopper' in those days—got in trouble.

"I came in and got through the inning. The Dodgers used a pinch-hitter for me in the ninth, and they scored some runs. We won, 7-6, and I got the win on my first day in the big leagues.

Talking to sportswriter Charlie Park on July 23, 1948, Carl said about his first game:

"I was shaking in my shoes. Johnny Hopp was on first base and there was one out. The batter was Ralph Kiner. He lined a ball to left field that looked like extra bases, but George Shuba made a sensational catch and then threw to first to double Hopp, who was clear around to second. We went on to win and I picked up my first victory for pitching in that one inning." Carl added that several years later he ran across Shuba. They rehashed Erskine's first game, and Shuba remembered that he *trapped* the ball hit by Kiner.

Reflecting on his 1948 season in 2003, Erskine said, "Next I pitched in relief against the Cardinals for two innings with the score tied 1-1. We scored in the ninth, and I got another win."

On August 7 Erskine made his first start against the Cubs in Chicago:

"It drizzled the whole day, and I pitched into the seventh inning, and I did well.

"I remember the pitch to Bill Nicholson, a left-handed-hitting power hitter for the Cubs. I struck him out on a high fastball, and I felt this sharp, hot stab in the back of my shoulder, and I'd pulled a muscle. I'm a kid in my first start. I finished the game, but I was uncomfortable.

"Now I'm 3-0 with a complete game. The Dodgers hadn't had a complete game in a long time, but the next day I could hardly lift my arm.

"You know, you don't go in the trainer's room when you're a rookie, and I didn't say much to anybody, but my arm was killing me. On the second day I just kind of loosened up. The third day you rested, and the fourth day you pitched again."

Erskine took the mound against the Phillies at Ebbets Field on August 9:

"I started against the Phillies in Brooklyn. By the sixth inning, I am hurting so bad that my stomach is nauseous. I'm pitching with this muscle tear.

"When I went to the bench, I spoke to Burt Shotton, our interim manager. Mr. Shotton, who was a real gentleman, was the interim because they had suspended and fired Leo Durocher.

"I said, 'Mr. Shotton, I hurt my shoulder pitching in the rain the other day. It's killing me, and I'm really in bad pain.'

"He looked at me with surprise on his face, and said, 'Son, you're pitching a shutout. Just go right ahead. You're doing fine.' He didn't want to hear that I hurt my shoulder.

"I finished the game, and we beat the Phillies, 2-1, and now my record was 4-0. Nobody is going to believe this kid has a bad arm."

On August 17 Erskine, saying nothing about his arm, started in Philadelphia:

"A few days later I pitched against the Phillies, and I had a shutout until the eighth inning. We beat them, 10-1. Now I'm 5-0 with three complete games, but I've really been pushing this arm. From that point until the end of the season, I was 1-3. I ended that half-season at 6-3, but I did a lot of damage to my shoulder.

"I went home that winter, not knowing what to do, so I didn't do anything. When I went to spring training in 1949, I could hardly throw. I was really struggling.

"With a bad spring and a very competitive pitching staff, I lost one game and the Dodgers sent me back to Fort Worth. It wasn't to rehab. They sent me back there because I wasn't pitching well. Pitching in the good sunshine in Fort Worth in 1949, I won 10 games. My arm was feeling a little better, and they recalled me.

"For the rest of the '49 season, I went 8-1 for the Dodgers, and we won the pennant by seven percentage points. I started and relieved down the stretch, and I think I won eight straight.

"I go home again at the end of the '49 season, and I don't know what to do. I'm just struggling to get by and trying to do my best. But there's no rehab or no attention given to any problem I might have.

"So I go to spring training in 1950, and I experience the same thing—a real hard spring, very difficult. I don't know if there's scar tissue, or what. I'm just having a real hard time."

Carl's high school coach saw him pitch on TV and called to say his delivery had changed:

"I said, 'Well, I've had some tenderness in my shoulder. I guess I'm overcompensating.'

"Remember that even though I was 8-1 at the end of the 1949 season, when I had a bad spring, they sent me back to the minors again, to triple-A Montreal."

But pitching in Canada turned out to be good medicine for Erskine:

"I met a doctor in Montreal, Charles LeTourneau. He was head of the Veterans Hospital in Montreal. He took me under his wing and had me do physical therapy at his hospital. They did a study on my arm motion and tried to decide which muscles were affected. He gave me a weight training program. With that program, I kept on pitching regularly and won 10 games in Montreal.

"The Dodgers finally brought me back, after Mr. Rickey came and watched me pitch *three* times. I pitched and gave up one run in three games. They finally brought me back, and I stayed.

"The Dodgers said to me, 'Look, you tell us when you're ready in the spring. You tell us when your arm feels like you can pitch.' From then on for the rest of my career, I was able to pace myself in the spring and get ready.

"But to this day I never got rid of that muscle problem in the back of my shoulder. I am semi-disabled in my right arm. Apparently the muscle I damaged must have atrophied. But I don't have any strength to do certain things over my head or reaching behind me. I just can't do it. I can't even pick up a briefcase in the back seat of my car with my right arm.

"Somehow I was able to pitch around that injury. But I had a frustrating career in warming up to see if I could get loose. Some days I couldn't get loose. But I took my turn anyway, and I just didn't pitch well.

"Duke Snider was my roommate for ten seasons, and he knew I was fighting this problem all the time. But the trainers, the front office people, the managers, I don't think any of them ever had a clue what I was battling!"

Erskine chuckled and said, "But in all fairness, I didn't say much at the time. It was so competitive in those days. The Dodgers had 26 farm teams and almost 800 players under contract. They had a bunch of pitchers, hard-throwing young guys in the minors. When you faltered, as I did in those first couple of years, you're gone. You're back in the minor leagues.

"When they gave you the ball, you pitched. You had to be productive, or you didn't stay. That's the way it was for everybody.

"But I never wanted to be known as a sore-armed pitcher. I never wanted to read that. So I never said much. I gutted it out. I'm not the only guy who's ever done that. But in my case, I got to be a starting pitcher for a number of years, and I pitched for some great teams."

Putting his experience into perspective, Erskine observed:

"In all of my experience until the mid-1950s, the coaching staffs and managers were non-pitchers.

You will hardly ever find a pitcher who was a coach or a manager. They say 70 percent of winning or losing is pitching, but all the managers and coaches were infielders, outfielders, or catchers. Most of the pitching coaches were catchers.

"They couldn't help a pitcher. The only thing a catcher could tell you was whether your stuff was good when he caught it. But he couldn't come out to the mound and say, 'Look, you're over-striding,' or 'You're releasing too soon.' He couldn't help with mechanics.

"My first pitching coach was Clyde Sukeforth. He's a catcher. My second was Bobby Bragan. He's a catcher. My third was Joe Becker. He was a catcher.

"Later, the Dodgers hired Ted Lyons, who was an outstanding pitcher in the American League. Ted Lyons got discouraged because Charlie Dressen, the manager, wouldn't even talk to him. Dressen didn't want any advice about pitching.

"The manager could tell when the pitcher was tired, or when he could start. And Dressen was a good manager. But he did not accept advice from a pitching coach, and that was typical."

Erskine, a 165-pounder with black hair, brown eyes, and a positive personality, struggled throughout his major league career. Despite pitching with ongoing pain, he accomplished more than most hurlers—and as Carl pointed out, he played on some great Dodger teams.

Brooklyn won the 1949 pennant by one game over the Cardinals. But the Yankees won the World Series in five games. Erskine pitched one shutout inning in relief in game four, a 6-1 Yankee win. He also worked two-thirds of the sixth inning in game six, yielding three runs, as the Yankees closed out the series with a 10-6 victory.

In 1950, when Erskine compiled a 7-6 mark after spending the first half of the season in Montreal, the Dodgers ranked second, two games behind the Philadelphia's "Whiz Kids." But the Phillies lost the World Series to the Yankees in four straight.

The Dodgers enjoyed a stellar year in 1951, but the Giants, winning 37 of their last 45 games, tied Brooklyn on the final day. Erskine enjoyed his first full

Preacher Roe, Clem Labine, Carl Erskine, and Ralph Branca.

season as a Dodger, fashioning a 16-12 record based on 19 starts, nine relief wins, and seven complete games. But New York won the finale of a three-game playoff when Bobby Thomson homered off Ralph Branca on October 3, 1951, breaking the hearts of Brooklyn's players and fans.

Erskine and Clem Labine shared the bullpen that October afternoon with Ralph Branca. But Labine had pitched the day before and won, 10-0, and Clyde Sukeforth, warming up Erskine, had to tell Charlie Dressen, "They're both ready. However, Erskine is bouncing his overhand curve." Dressen said, "Let me have Branca," and Thomson hit the "shot heard 'round the world."

Kahn's *Boys of Summer* covers in detail the 1952 and 1953 Dodgers. During those seasons, Erskine produced records of 14-6 and 20-6, pitching around his arm problem. The Yankees, however, won the World Series both years, despite heroic efforts by the Dodgers.

Erskine's single best effort in 1952 came when he no-hit the Cubs at Ebbets Field on June 19. Only pitcher Willie Ramsdell, who walked on four pitches in the third inning, prevented Erskine from pitching a perfect game. In the first inning, Carl Furillo blasted a bases-empty homer and Roy Campanella hit a two-run shot. Andy Pafko hit a solo homer in the second. After sitting out a 44-minute rain delay in the fourth, Erskine completed the no-hitter and won, 5-0, improving his record to 6-1 for the first-place Dodgers.

When Erskine no-hit the Giants at Ebbets Field on May 12, 1956, he allowed two base runners. Willie Mays walked with two outs in the first inning, and Alvin Dark opened the fourth by drawing a base on balls. Mays followed with a screaming liner toward left field, but Jackie Robinson dived and made a sensational catch, rescuing the no-hitter.

Erskine held the Giants at bay until the ninth, when left-handed batting Whitey Lockman hit an apparent home run to right field, but the ball curved foul at the last instant. Erskine then retired Lockman on a grounder to the mound. Carl polished off the gem by inducing Dark to bounce another one to the mound. The Dodgers won, 3-0, thanks to a bases-loaded walk to Jackie Robinson in the third and RBI hits by Duke Snider and Gil Hodges in the seventh.

Those three runs allowed the slow-starting Erskine to improve his record to 2-2, following his 11-win

season in 1955. For his sterling effort, Carl received a $500 check from Dodger president Walter O'Malley after the game.

When reminded by a reporter that bonuses weren't allowed for special feats, O'Malley told Erskine to consider his contract amended.

Replied Carl, "You got off cheap, Mr. O'Malley. I was about to ask for a $1,000 raise!"

Talking about his second no-hitter in the clubhouse afterward, the modest Hoosier explained, "I don't think I had overpowering stuff. Matter of fact, I didn't have overpowering stuff in either of my no-hitters. Just a good fastball and my control was all right. I used more changeup pitches today than the last time."

In the 1952 World Series, Brooklyn won the opener at Ebbets Field, 4-2, behind the dominating hurling of rookie Joe Black and homers off the bats of Jackie Robinson, Duke Snider, and Pee Wee Reese.

But the series seesawed as the Yankees won the second game, 7-1, behind a fine performance by Vic Raschi. Erskine started the second game, worked five-plus innings, allowed six hits and four runs, and took the loss.

In game three Brooklyn took the lead as Preacher Roe pitched the route, yielding three runs on six hits. Yogi Berra and Johnny Mize homered for New York, but the Dodgers collected 11 hits and won, 5-3. The Yankees won game four, 2-0, as Allie Reynolds threw a four-hit shutout.

Rising to the occasion at Yankee Stadium, Erskine pitched one of his greatest games, winning game five in 11 innings, 6-5. After giving up five Yankee runs in the fifth inning, including a three-run blast by "Old Jawn" Mize, the gritty Brooklyn right hander—hurling on his fifth wedding anniversary—blanked New York for six innings, retiring 19 straight batters.

In the top of the eleventh, Duke Snider gave the Dodgers a 6-5 lead, doubling off the right field wall to score Billy Cox. Mize scared Dodger fans when he launched an Erskine pitch deep to right in the eleventh, but, sportswriter Joe Williams noted, Carl Furillo "went up like the price of sirloin to make a one-handed catch, just as the ball was dropping into the stands."

Undaunted by playing the final two games at Ebbets, the Yankees won both. Raschi, with relief from Reynolds, won game six, 3-2. New York's Eddie Lopat pitched the first three innings of game seven, and Reynolds worked the next three, picking up the win. Raschi got one out in the seventh, and Bob Kuzava blanked the Dodgers the rest of the way.

Joe Black started and lost the seventh game, Roe pitched 1⅔ innings and gave up one run, and Erskine hurled two shutout innings. New York got single runs in the fourth through the seventh innings, before Carl took the mound. Billy Martin made a game-saving catch of Jackie Robinson's bases-loaded infield popup with two outs in the seventh. Kuzava slammed the door, and the Yankees collected their winning World Series checks for the fourth straight season.

In 1953 Erskine, in his third full season with Brooklyn, enjoyed his best year, going 20-6, leading the NL with a winning percentage of .769, and helping the Dodgers win their second straight pennant.

The '53 Dodgers were one of the best teams ever. They led the NL with a 105-49 ledger, topping the second-place Milwaukee Braves by 13 games. Brooklyn paced the league in runs scored with 955, home runs with 208, team batting average at .285, team slugging percentage at .474, and stolen bases with 90 (the Cubs ranked second with 49). While the pitchers staff ranked third in ERA with 4.10 (the Braves were first with 3.30), they ranked first with 819 strikeouts.

Many Dodger hitters enjoyed fine seasons. Catcher Roy Campanella, Erskine's receiver and friend, was voted the senior circuit's MVP, as Campy crashed 41 home runs and produced 141 RBI. Duke Snider hit .336 with 42 homers and 26 RBI, first baseman Gil Hodges had 31 homers and 122 RBI, right fielder Carl Furillo won the NL batting title with a .344 average while hitting 21 homers and driving in 92 runners, Jackie Robinson hit .329 with 12 homers and 95 RBI, Pee Wee Reese enjoyed a fine year at shortstop and also hit 13 home runs, Billy Cox proved to be the league's best third baseman, and Jim Gilliam, hitting .278 and playing second base, won NL Rookie of the Year honors.

Erskine led a fine mound staff with his 20-6 mark and 3.54 ERA. But Russ Meyer went 15-5, Billy Loes was 14-8, Preacher Roe had an 11-3 season (Roe was a combined 44-8 from 1951 through 1953), and Clem Labine was 11-6, thanks to a league-high 10 wins in relief.

During the season Erskine, the Dodgers' player representative, who didn't drink, swear, or carouse, and who read his Bible on road trips, lived with his family in an apartment in the Bay Ridge section of Brooklyn. The right hander was popular on and off the diamond.

Describing the hurler when he was named on September 29, 1953, to start the opener of the World Series, sportswriter Bill Roeder observed, "Erskine is the small boy's concept of a model big leaguer. Besides being a success, he is handsome, intelligent, pleasant-spoken, clean-living. And also a sharp dresser."

In the 1953 World Series, however, the Yankees won the title in six games, again seeming to get a clutch hit or make a big play when the chips were down. Erskine started the opener, but it wasn't his day. He worked only one inning, yielding four runs—fueled by Billy Martin's bases-loaded triple. Gilliam, Hodges, and pinch-hitter George Shuba all slugged homers for the Dodgers. But behind Allie Reynolds and John Sain, the Yankees won, 9-5.

Eddie Lopat outdueled Preacher Roe in game two, 4-2, boosted by a solo homer by Martin and a two-run shot by Mickey Mantle. Martin, the Yankees' hitting star, collected 12 hits, a record for a six-game series.

Still, Erskine helped Brooklyn get back on track by winning game three, 3-2, setting a World Series strikeout record with 14, including four whiffs each of Joe Collins and Mickey Mantle. Two days after a pitched ball broke a knuckle on his right hand, Campanella gave Brooklyn the lead with a remarkable homer in the eighth. Carl closed the game by getting Collins, who feared a fifth strikeout, to tap one back to the mound on a nasty curve that almost hit the dirt.

The Dodgers tied the series in game four behind Billy Loes, 7-3, but New York came back to win games five and six. In the finale at Yankee Stadium, Erskine started and hurled four innings, giving up six hits and three runs. Carl Furillo tied the game at three-all in the top of the ninth with a dramatic two-run homer. But in the bottom of the ninth, Billy Martin's hit off Clem Labine won it for the Yankees, 4-3.

Erskine enjoyed three more good seasons, notching records of 18-15, 11-8, and 13-11 from 1954 through 1956. Led by Willie Mays, the Giants won the pennant in 1954 and swept the Cleveland Indians in four straight. But the Dodgers won pennants in 1955 and 1956, finally outlasting the Yankees in the '55 World Series.

Brooklyn's team was changing by 1955. In the fall

classic, Erskine made one appearance. He started game five and worked three-plus innings, allowing three runs on three hits. The Dodgers came from behind to win, 8-5, and Clem Labine got the victory with 4⅓ innings of solid relief. In the climactic seventh game, Johnny Podres, a southpaw in his third season, won a 2-0 thriller, scattering eight Yankee hits.

In Brooklyn's final pennant summer, 1956, Erskine was cut to $26,000 (his salary peaked at $30,000 in 1954), Jackie Robinson played his final season, and the Dodgers lost a seven-game World Series to the Yankees. *Oisk* started and lost the fourth game, giving up three runs on four hits. Don Drysdale, a future Dodger star, pitched the last two innings. With the clubs tied at three games each, Carl finished his World Series career by pitching a scoreless ninth inning in game seven. But the Yankees crushed Dodger hopes that afternoon with a 9-0 victory.

Erskine's life off the field—he was a lay minister who earned the nickname "Deacon" in his first Dodger season—caused the U.S. Junior Chambers of Commerce to name him on the organization's list of America's "Outstanding Young Men for 1956." Reputed never to say no to a worthy cause, Carl often worked in youth camps and taught baseball to Little Leaguers.

On January 10, 1957, Red Smith observed that among the Jaycees' top young men, Reverend Bob Richards, the Olympic pole vaulter, was "an amateur athlete and a professional clergyman, the other [Erskine] a professional athlete and an amateur parson."

Erskine pitched three more seasons, the Dodger finale in Brooklyn in 1957, when he struggled with shoulder pain but produced his last winning record, 5-3, and the first two seasons in Los Angeles. After going 0-3 in the early part of 1959, Erskine walked away from the game he loved on June 15. Under Walt Alston's shrewd management, the Dodgers, pitching younger stars like Don Drysdale, Roger Craig, and Sandy Koufax, regrouped and won the pennant and World Series—a victory that netted each Dodger a check for $11,231.

On June 28, 1959, sportswriter Melvin Durslag wrote, "Throughout his time in the majors, Carl has been one of baseball's noblemen, a remarkably high-type individual. Off his recent form, the Dodgers won't miss him as a pitcher, but they will miss him as a gentleman."

Speaking to Bill Roeder during spring training in April 1957, Pee Wee Reese said, "I'd rate Erskine right next to Whitlow Wyatt as one of my all-time pitchers on the Brooklyn ball club. Carl's a real competitor for as nice a guy as he is. You know him, he's a nicey nice guy, but he wants to beat you. Like with me, he'll work the pickoff play any time I want to try it. Some pitchers never bother looking around."

Returning with his family to Anderson, Indiana, Erskine launched a second career running an insurance business. Later, he served as president and director of Star Financial Bank. For 12 years he also coached baseball at Anderson College, where his teams won four Hoosier College Conference titles. In 1997 he was inducted into the university's Sports Hall of Fame. Retired from banking, Carl still participates in Dodger fantasy camps at Vero Beach, Florida.

Involved in a variety of community activities and charitable concerns, including the Special Olympics, Babe Ruth Baseball, and the Fellowship of Christian Athletes, Carl kept his family first. He always managed to find plenty of time for Jimmy, reported Roger Kahn, who interviewed Carl and Betty at their home in Anderson in 1969.

Looking back in 2003, Carl said, "Aside from the special days you would expect to be highlights, I think the most rewarding feeling is for me to be respected by other players on my team and on the opponents' teams as a *quality major league player*—to have fellow players know I *belonged* there. I was good enough to stay for 12 years as a major leaguer. It answered my dream as a kid, to be able to grow up and have people say, 'He played in the big leagues.'"

An exceptional person who was a clutch big-league pitcher, Erskine left an indelible mark on one of the greatest teams in baseball history.

The Dodger hero epitomizes the kind of ballplayer that boys and fathers dream about when they travel to a ballpark, watch clubs like Brooklyn perform, and—in the irrational daydreams of the fan's mind—make the mental leap from being a *spectator* to being a *major leaguer*, good enough to put on uniform number 17, take the mound, and pitch in the big time, just like Carl Erskine.

Anson on Broadway
The Failure of *A Runaway Colt*

by Robert H. Schaefer

Adrian C. Anson, who rose to national prominence as captain of the Chicago White Stockings, was the first of what is now a long list of baseball players who succumbed to the lure of the footlights. Anson made his theatrical debut in 1895 in a production called A Runaway Colt. Arguably the most famous baseball player of his day, the play was written expressly for him by the leading playwright of his day. It was performed on Broadway, as well as theatres in Brooklyn, Buffalo, Syracuse, Troy, Chicago, Minneapolis, and Duluth. Despite its sterling pedigree, the play and its star were universally judged to be an utter catastrophe. The failure was so colossal that it echoes across decades to this day, and Pop Anson was haunted by its specter for the rest of his life.

The popularity of baseball had enjoyed a continual expansion since its inception in the 1840s, transitioning from an innocent amateur pastime to a serious professional business. Concurrently, live entertainments in theaters also rapidly gained in popularity. Sooner or later it would occur to some enterprising theatrical producer to bring the two together and star a famous baseball player in a stage performance. With this goal in mind Charlie Hoyt met with Anson in June 1895 in Chicago. Born in Concord, NH in 1859, Charles H. Hoyt was perhaps the leading playwright of the late 19th century.

After graduating from the Latin school in Boston, he worked as reporter on the *Boston Post*. Later Hoyt was assigned to do dramatic reviews for that paper. At the suggestion of Willie Edouin he wrote his first play, *A Bunch of Keys*, and it became a smash hit. Hoyt specialized in comical farces and satires, and

enjoyed a huge success as a humorist. By the late 1880s his career was in full flower. One drama critic remarked, "Charles H. Hoyt writes a great deal of rot, to be sure, but it is immensely popular rot and he is growing rich."[1]

At this first meeting, Hoyt outlined a play about baseball and suggested that Anson star in it.[2] Anson pointed out that he was not an actor. Hoyt assured him that baseball would be central to the production, and one act would actually present a game in progress on the stage. On that basis, and the generous financial arrangement offered by Hoyt, Anson accepted. Hoyt immediately started working in earnest on his new play.

As the summer of 1895 drew to a close, Hoyt announced his new play, *A Runaway Colt*.[3] The title was derived from the popular name of the Chicago team that Anson captained. This once formidable team of the 1880s had now fallen on hard times. By 1890 star players Michael "King" Kelly and pitcher John Clarkson had been sold.

Other key veterans of Anson's pennant winners had also departed. Anson was forced to desperately try to build a competitive team from a collection of untested youngsters. Reflecting their tender years and lack of experience, his new players were called "colts." Consequently, the sportswriters hung the label "Anson's Colts" on the team.

A Runaway Colt is a farce in four acts. The exemplary character of Captain Anson and the glories of the American game are the theme of the whole piece.[4] The first act is set in the home of the Reverend Manners. His son, Manley, the "colt" of the title, is a pitching phenomenon Anson desires to recruit for his Chicago club. Manley has been offered a salary of $800 a year for a position with a bank. Anson offers him $2,000. Initially, Manley's parents are against his playing baseball. Throughout the play Hoyt uses

BOB SCHAEFER *has authored a number of essays that deal with 19th-century baseball. Three of his works have been honored with the annual McFarland-SABR award.*

double meanings in baseball to good advantage. Manley's sister, Dolly, for example, denounces the wickedness of baseball as it encourages stealing bases. Fortune smiles on Manley when the local bishop recognizes Anson and greets him warmly. This endorsement converts Manley's parents. They consent to their son joining Anson.

The second act is set at the Colts' spring training camp, the Ponce de Leon Hotel in St. Augustine, Florida. The main action involves Anson being pursued by an old maid who is unaware that he is married. Anson exhorts Manley, "Don't leave me alone with her, or I'll sell you to Louisville," clearly a fate worse than death for an aspiring player. Anson, as the colt's mentor, writes a letter to Rev. Manley vowing that he will not allow the boy to associate with disreputable members of the fraternity—and here Anson (or rather, Hoyt) names the most notorious diamond growlers justly famous for their chin music—Dad Clarke, Pat Tebeau, Scrappy Joyce, and Muggsy McGraw. This prohibition was extended to any other player who used vile language such as "damn."

The third act presents the Colts, overweight and out of shape, working out in the club's gymnasium. The cast was selected to deliberately impersonate certain members of the real Colts. The scene set in the gymnasium gives the actors a chance to demonstrate athletic feats of jumping and the like. The India club swinging by Messrs. Alburtus and Bartram was judged to be remarkably good.

The plot revolves around an implausible scheme. Manley Manners is enamored of the adopted daughter of Rev. Manley, Merey Given. His rival for the fair lass, Rankin Haight, is characterized as "a doer of dirt." Anson learns that Rankin and his brother are conspiring to ruin Manley's brother, Dolton. The Haight brothers induce Dolton to wager $2,000, which he embezzles from his employer, on Anson's team, believing that they can bribe Anson to throw the game. Loss of the bet will force Merey Given to marry Rankin Haight. But Anson is incorruptible and the attempt at bribery fails.

The fourth act is the dramatic climax. It takes place on a ball field as the Colts face the Baltimores. The stage set is a grandstand viewed from behind the seats. The ball players are unseen by the audience. Every ball, strike, and decision by the umpire is heard plainly. An offstage voice announces every hit, error, or stolen base. McMahon is pitching for

Cap Anson circa 1895   *Playwright Charlie Hoyt*

Baltimore and the score stands 1 to 0 in the bottom of the ninth. Dahlen gets on base and Captain Anson comes to the bat. Three balls and two strikes are called. The realistic crack of the bat represented a great triumph in stage devices, and the sound of a ball and bat meeting squarely is heard. This is Anson's great moment, as he hits a game-winning home run. Curtain.[5]

Julian Mitchell, a theatrical manager and producer, told a story about Anson's conduct during rehearsal. Anson and the others in the 40-member cast apparently had their lines down pat, and the piece seemed to be getting smoother. On this day, during the scene where the umpire is almost mobbed in the center of the stage, Anson stunned the cast by snarling to the umpire, "You blank robber, I'll cave your face in!" It's worth noting that Anson in his prime stood 6'1" and was a muscular 200-pounder frequently called "The Blond Giant," among other nicknames. He routinely used his size to intimidate umpires. After the cast recovered from their shock, Anson explained that he had forgotten his lines and reverted to type with this realistic ad lib.[6]

Anson was full of optimism, but when the play opened on November 11 at the Wieting Opera House in Syracuse, NY he had an all too obvious case of stage fright. He muffed several lines and appeared jittery. The audience forgave him and at the play's end both Captain Anson and Mr. Hoyt were called before the curtain. The critics were enthusiastic, based on the witty dialogue and clever situations. They predicted success for the play and proclaimed the last act to be one of the best things ever done by Hoyt.

Of Anson's debut performance, a *New York Times* reporter wrote on November 13 that he ". . . acquitted himself very well. He is scarcely an actor, but he was thoroughly in earnest."

At this time Hoyt's play *A Milk White Flag* was

playing in New York City. Its manager, John Hogarty, met with John M. Ward and discussed Captain Anson's acting debut. Ward, a baseball star in his own right, had intimate knowledge of the theater, as his former wife, Helen Dauvray, was a famous actress. Ward was less than sanguine about Anson's ability to make the transition from ball field to theater:

"The boys who patronize the bleachers during the baseball season will be in the galleries to watch Anson act and to 'guy' him. When they were in the bleachers they were too far away from Anson for the old man to hear the *bon mots* they cracked at his expense, but up in the gloaming next to the roof they are within earshot of him, and he can hear every word."

On November 17 the *Brooklyn Daily Eagle* predicted a great success for the play: "The wonder is that the base ball craze has not been put upon the stage before, but now that it has waited for the humor and satire of Charles H. Hoyt, it is almost certain to be well done. *A Runaway Colt*, which comes to the Montauk next week, has more claim on the interest of the sporting fraternity than even its base ball atmosphere because Anson, the famous Chicago baby, will play himself in it."

From Syracuse *A Runaway Colt* went to Buffalo, then to Troy, where it had a profitable stand at the Star Theatre. Anson arrived in Brooklyn on November 24, accompanied by his wife, Virginia. "Pop," as Virginia loved to call him, spent the day quietly at his hotel, declining to be interviewed about either the play or baseball matters.

Anson opened his play at Colonel Sinn's Montauk Theatre in Brooklyn on November 25. The advertisements boasted that Hoyt's newest production was his "most laughable hit" and would provide the audience with "three hours of incessant laughter." The ads further stated that the play was presented with elaborate scenic effects, a monster cast of prominent comedy celebrities, and proudly proclaimed, INTRODUCING CAPT. ADRIAN C. ANSON OF THE CHICAGO BASE BALL CLUB.

Anson was the only cast member whose name was featured in the advertisements. General admission tickets were priced at 25 and 50¢. Reserved seating for evening performances were scaled at 35¢, 50¢, 75¢, $1.00, and $1.50. Matinees were given on Wednesday and Saturday, with a special matinee on Thanksgiving Day. The prices for reserved seats at matinee performances were 35, 50, 75¢, and $1.00.[7]

The Montauk Theatre provided accommodations for Anson that were appropriate to his star status. His dressing room was brilliantly illuminated with electric lights, while three mirrors flanked the dressing table. His costumes for the play were hung on a row of pegs: a dress suit, a white duck suit, an ordinary business suit, and two baseball uniforms.

Virginia had needed only one lesson to learn the art of theatrical makeup. In preparation for going on stage, Pop sat quietly with a towel draped across his chest while she applied his makeup, turning his face the color of a healthy schoolboy's. Virginia shaded his eyes with a black substance that was first heated over a gas jet to soften it. Next she darkened Pop's flaxen eyebrows. Finally, she applied a few dabs of makeup to his lips to make them redder, and the transformation was complete.

Pop Anson confessed to being a little nervous in Syracuse. Not only was there very little opportunity for preparation before the show, but his part required him to appear in every act and make six costume changes. Though accused of forgetting his lines, Anson said the applause was so great when he made his initial appearance on stage that he had to wait for it to die down so he could be heard. Other times it appeared that his lines were late only because he had to wait for his cue from the other actors. Pop readily admitted he had no pretensions as an actor, but felt he could not pass up Mr. Hoyt's lucrative offer.[8]

Despite miserable weather the Montauk Theatre was packed on opening night. When Captain Anson came on stage early in the first act the applause lasted for more than a minute—and he hadn't even spoken a word. It was obvious from their generous applause that the audience had come to see their old friend. Many cranks were present and they cheered Anson.

Charles Hoyt gave Anson some clever lines that demonstrate inside knowledge of the game. In the scene where Anson is attempting to recruit the colt for his club, Mrs. Manley listens to their conversation and inquires what type of work her son will be required to do. Aware that Mrs. Manley is opposed to baseball, Anson says:

"To travel more or less, to handle leather goods, and in certain cities to deal with strikers."

"I suppose that would be out west," she replies, thinking the strikers referred to dissatisfied workers and protestors.

"In the west, and in the south."

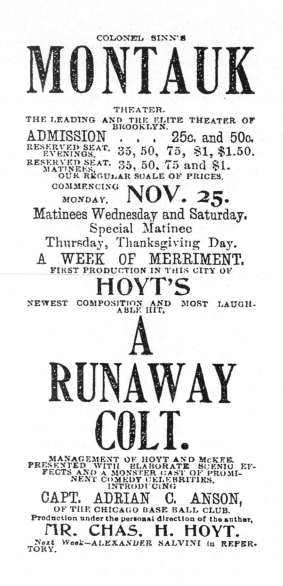

"There are no strikers in New York, are there?" Mrs. Manley's straight line sets up one of the cleverest comebacks in the show.

"There haven't been any this year in my business," a sarcastic reference to the New York Giants' weak hitting. The audience howled.

Anson had a curtain call after the play ended. President Byrnes and Dr. McLean of the Brooklyn club and their guests, Robert Russell and John T. French, had occupied the lower left-hand box. Directly opposite them were Albert G. Spalding, William T. Redding, and Henry Chadwick. President Byrnes and his party entertained the veteran ballplayer after the performance was concluded.

The play's popularity derived solely from Anson's presence. Critics initially were kind to the old man, but faulted Hoyt for not providing a more lively and witty vehicle. Once the novelty of seeing Anson on

stage diminished, the drama critic of the *Brooklyn Daily Eagle* rendered this cutting verdict of the evening's entertainment:

"The comedy is not up to the Hoyt level. It goes by bits and starts, ending with a bump at the end of every act; that is after the first, which is flat from the start to finish. Pop Anson is lumbering and good natured throughout, but his ability to make a hit is now, and must for some time to come, be confined to the ball field. The company which is called on to support the big ball playing should be taken in hand by Mr. Hoyt. It is with them either a case of natural inability or insufficient training, for Pop at times rose to the level of several of his alleged support. Those who were not painfully unaccustomed to being on the stage were Aubrey Bouchnit, Alice Evans and Jennie Weathersby. Hoyt got considerable fun out of the great game of base ball, but when he exhausted the supply of base ball humor he had recourse to some old and familiar material. So long as the public wants to see Anson in the winter, however, this piece will no doubt do just as well as any other, and the old man will be applauded to the echo."

It is clear from this critic's comments that the major weakness of the play lay not at Anson's feet, but rather with the distinguished playwright, Charlie Hoyt. It is equally clear that Anson was painfully unaccustomed to being on stage.

The *New York Times* provided this appraisal of Anson's acting: "The 'Pop' of the 'White Stockings' carries himself well in the scenes, where he has to talk to other persons, and from his mild and often meek demeanor one would suspect that in summer months its supporter is one of the greatest men who talks under, over, across, and about things that happen on baseball diamonds."[9]

Was this "mild and often meek" man in the play the same Pop Anson renowned as the greatest kicker in the game, a man who had no peer when it came to buffaloing umpires, and a man who relished an argument on the diamond? Surely Anson displayed considerable acting ability if he could convince the drama critic that he was "mild and meek." Remarkably, this pugnacious and autocratic ruler of the diamond was able to mold himself to the part created by Hoyt.

The play ran at the Montauk Theatre over the Thanksgiving weekend. It then moved across the East River to New York City, where it opened at the

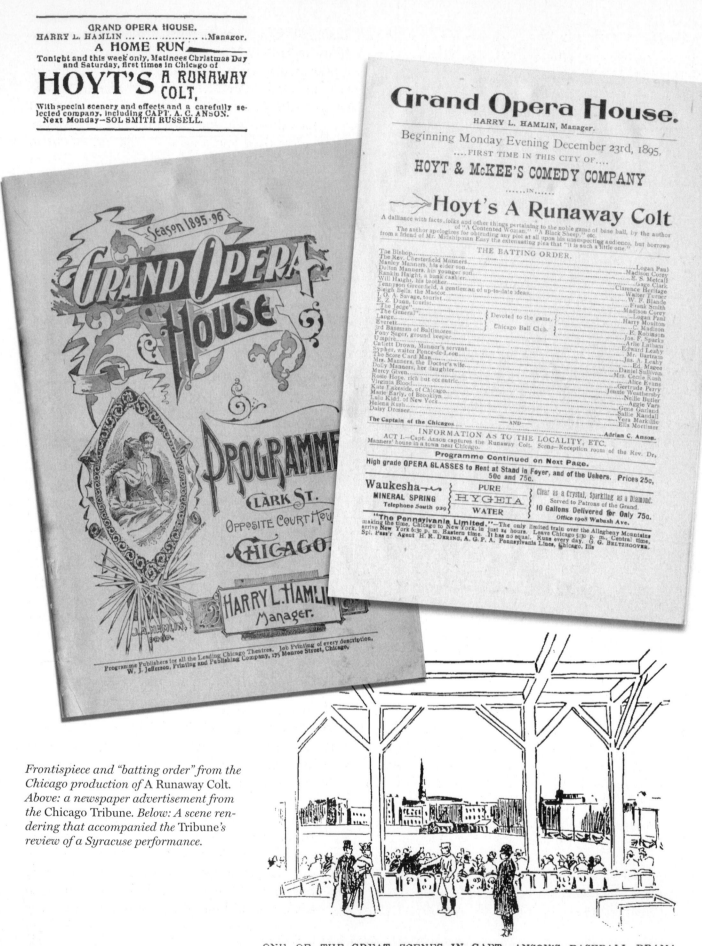

Frontispiece and "batting order" from the Chicago production of A Runaway Colt. *Above: a newspaper advertisement from the* Chicago Tribune. *Below: A scene rendering that accompanied the* Tribune's *review of a Syracuse performance.*

ONE OF THE GREAT SCENES IN CAPT. ANSON'S BASEBALL DRAMA.

American Theatre on December 2. Based on the experience at the Montauk Theatre, several changes were made. The author improved some of the lines, and specialties were added to the second and third acts. The most important change completely revised the final act. Formerly, Anson's time at bat was played offstage and the action described to the audience. This sensational scene was now moved out front where it belonged, so the umpire, the battery, and most important, Anson at the bat were seen by the audience.

In the revised final act, Anson hits the ball out of sight, literally, and runs offstage himself as he tears around the bases. The ball reappears at the same moment Anson runs thunderously for home plate and slides across it The catcher makes the tag, and after a dramatic pause, the umpire calls Anson safe, the game is won and Anson is the hero.

On December 3 the *New York Times* reported, "Adrian Constantine Anson, colt, Chicago baseball player, and kicker for the amusement of a public that likes vocal prize fights, made a home run in the American Theatre last night . . . convinced the public of New York last night that he was many measures better than the pugilists who have been breaking theatrical boards lately."

The production quickly grew in popular favor, and *A Runaway Colt* played at the American Theatre for two full weeks.[10] During the play's run on Broadway Anson enlisted several big-league umpires to appear in the play. Big Tim Keefe got almost as much advance publicity as Anson himself. Keefe strode on stage dressed in his old blue uniform, lugging his mask and little whisk broom. He was ably assisted by the vociferous cheers of the "rooters" in the grandstand. The enthusiasm of the actors rapidly spread to the members of the audience, who spontaneously broke out in uproarious applause. The entire theatre rocked and Keefe was a huge success.

The next genuine umpire to appear on stage with Anson was Tim Hurst. At the climactic moment, Anson slid across the plate as the catcher put the tag on him. Hurst, a consummate professional, called the play just as he saw it. His voiced boomed throughout the theatre, "*Yer out!*" Anson flew into a rage and the theater was ripped by pandemonium. The theatre manager T. H. French was forced to appear before the footlights to restore order.

These successes prompted French to orchestrate a "base ball night." The National League meeting was in session in New York, and he invited many stars to appear as players in the great home run scene. The cast included John McGraw, Hugh Jennings, Joe Kelley, Willie Keeler, Wilbur Robinson, and featured Arlie Latham in the role of umpire. The show was widely advertised and a great throng turned out to see these men on stage. But the blackguard Latham altered the script, unbeknownst to Pop. He fixed it up with Keeler, who would play third base that night. After Anson walloped the ball he tore around the bases. As he rounded third, Keeler stuck out his foot and tripped him.

Poor old Pop sprawled on the floor. Before he could regain his feet, the ball was thrown to catcher Robinson, who tagged Anson and Latham called him out. The audience went wild. Anson went wild. He roared so deafeningly the house shook.

"I'm *not* out!" Pop yelled. "Yer *out*!" Latham yelled back, "Get off the field or I'll send yer to the clubhouse!" In desperation Mr. French rang down the curtain and then announced to the audience that trickery had been involved. He told them that the ball used by Robinson to tag out Anson had been hidden in Kelley's shirt and the ball Anson actually hit was yet to be found. Several seasons on the diamond passed before Anson would speak to any of the culprits.

Following this success in New York, *A Runaway Colt* went to Chicago. Grand Opera House manager Hamlin announced the play as a distinct novelty for his Christmas holiday attraction. Naturally, its appeal was increased considerably because it starred Chicago's own Adrian C. Anson. The play was scheduled to start its run on December 22. All of Chicago awaited the opening of *A Runaway Colt* with great anticipation, as the play had earned the approval of those who had already seen it.

Following its opening, the *Chicago Daily Tribune* pronounced the play a hit, if the auditors in attendance were fair umpires. Anson's initial appearance on stage brought forth a full minute's worth of applause. At the close of the first act Anson had to come before the curtain "clothed in a white chrysanthemum and a large smile." By the third act, bouquets were plenty and nothing would do but a speech—and a speech Anson gave them. Of Anson's work, the critic said, "Mr. Hoyt has done judicious work in constructing the play so as to use Mr. Anson's fine form to good advantage without giving him too much heavy batting. He is a good deal on the stage and doesn't say too much. The ornamental yet important part he plays is done with spirit if not with polish."[11]

Yet only a week after this encouraging if not glowing review the drama critic of the *Chicago Daily Tribune* effectively killed *A Runaway Colt.*

"Every day we hear that the people do not want clean and intelligible wit, honest humor, or plays that demand serious and sustained attention, but will have and force the managers to provide them with coarse and dirty farces, idiotic farce-comedies, and bur-lesques that haven't a leg to stand on but the chorus girls'. The experience of the Grand Opera House during the last fortnight is sufficient refutation of this depressing theory. Week before last Charles H. Hoyt presented to the patrons of that theatre a drama (may heaven forgive us for calling it thus) designed solely to exploit a dull and uneducated professional athlete. Its language was slangy, its fun was the fun of the tavern, its plot was preposterous, its actors were mostly variety performers. Mr. Hoyt has put together some entertainments that were really clever, but *A Runaway Colt* was driveling stupidity."[12]

Arlie Latham, blackguard

William A. Phelon Jr., in *The Sporting Life* of January 4, 1896, provided this review of Anson's performance and Hoyt's endeavor: "Well, we have seen him [Anson]. We looked upon the new star of the legitimate theatre and bowed our knee in worship at his shrine. And he is a corker. . . . Hoyt has written better plays than the one in which he has selected Adrian C. Anson as a star. There are few, painfully few, of the delightful Hoytean situations and absurdities. . . . the bubbling Hoytic humor is absent almost all through the play. Almost any writer of even average merit could have taken Anson for the central figure and woven around him a better play than the one perpetrated for him by Charlie Hoyt. In fact, Anson carries the play, and is even the leading point of interest—the polar star round which the fun revolves."

The critic's reviews are a mixed bag, alternately condemning Hoyt's work and praising Anson. The play disbanded on January 11, 1896, while in Minneapolis. Charles Hoyt acknowledged it as a failure, the first one of his career, and pinned the blame squarely on Anson. According to Hoyt: "The business was poor from the time the play was produced and playgoers seemed to take no interest in the appearance of Adrian C. Anson, the baseball player, about whom the sensation was supposed to attach."

In the light of the initial favorable critical reviews—there were no unfavorable ones when the play first opened—it is difficult to comprehend its sudden demise. It is truly said that success has a thousand fathers while failure is an orphan. Surely, a failure of this magnitude was a bitter experience for both Hoyt and Anson. As neither man had previously been personally acquainted with failure, each one very publicly blamed the other, and even threatened lawsuits to recover their financial losses. Anson demanded $10,000 for damages. Anson had a one-eighth interest in the play, and so McKee and Hoyt threatened to file a cross petition against Anson for $1,500, which they claimed was one-eighth of their losses.[13]

That notorious spinner of baseball fables, Ted Sullivan, reported this conversation with Charlie Hoyt in New York: "Ted, tell you how 'tis, b' gosh. Anson wanted me to write a play for him and I did, I'm sorry to say. It was killed by Anson, and I gave it a burial without flowers. I called it *A Runaway Colt.* It was a case, b' gosh, of a runaway audience after the first night. Anson used to boast to me what a magnetic chap he was; how he could draw thousands to see him play ball, and he was sure he could draw them into the theatre. Magnetic! What do you think of him? Why, to tell the truth, Ted, b' gosh, every time Anson walked on the stage it began to snow. I was thinking of having a snow scene painted, to be used when Anse was acting, but he objected. He said it would destroy his magnetism."

Frank McKee joined his partner Hoyt in denigrating Anson: "Anson was such a frappe that every time he entered the theater the steam pipes perspired ice water. He's such a chill that he could put on a linen duster and golf hat and discover the North Pole."

The finger pointing continued unabated. Ex-actor Anson told a reporter that the play was cancelled because it was booked to run until the end of March and he resigned from it so it wouldn't interfere with his spring training preparations. Anson came to New York to January 18, 1896, to make a settlement with Hoyt. He said of the play, "It is a winner. And by a little pruning here and there and some additions to the second and third acts . . . would make this play as successful as any of Hoyt's. . . . We made money in every city we have played except Duluth and one other small place."

Years later Anson mused on the genesis of the play and its fate: "While at a game in Chicago he [Charlie Hoyt] saw me bluff an umpire into changing his decision. After the game he told me that I had more nerve than any man he knew, and proposed to write a play on me. With his ability and my nerve, he said we were sure to succeed. But we didn't. I guess he didn't have enough ability."[14]

Anson also believed it was poor planning by Hoyt that led to failure. He said, "*A Runaway Colt* would have been a success if Hoyt had booked it in the twelve cities of the major leagues. Hoyt made his mistake in taking the show into one-night stands, where they had no interest in Anson. . . . The blame is all thrown on me, and the fact is, I should shoulder none of it."

On the surface Anson's criticism makes perfect sense. Not booking the big-league cities was a major strategic error on Hoyt's part. However, it ignores the fact that the play faltered in Chicago, Anson's hometown. If Anson's fame and magnetism couldn't draw fans to see him there, where could he expect it to happen? Nonetheless, Pop harbored hopes of securing the rights to the play and booking it in all the league cities for the next season.

During the 1896 baseball campaign Anson was frequently and unrelentingly reminded of his failure on stage. Bench jockeys had a field day at Pop's expense. One of the sharpest of these jockeys, Bill "Scrappy" Joyce, tormented Anson unmercifully. During one game he harassed Anson with this patter:

"Hello there, Charley Hoyt. How are all the Harolds and Percys? What news upon the Rialto, mine uncle? I hear you're going to do a song and clog dance. Pretty tough, Pop, when a leading heavy has to do a clog for a living."

Joyce bore down on Anson. On one occasion they were riding on a train as their respective teams traveled together from Chicago to Washington. The two captains were innocently discussing the use of signals. Then Joyce said to Anson, "I notice that when you were playing last winter you didn't use any signals at all." This confused Anson, and he asked Joyce what he meant. Joyce replied, "Why, when you played in *A Runaway Colt*, no one was on the coaching line to signal you when to act."

In the final analysis, there is enough blame to be shared by all parties. *A Runaway Colt* was clearly substandard for Charles Hoyt. He wrote better plays before it, and he wrote better plays after it. Depending upon who was telling the tale, either Hoyt approached Anson with the idea of developing a play about baseball, or it was entirely Anson's idea. We'll probably never know. The essential fact is that the quality of the play was very poor. Anson's popularity as a famous player failed to compensate for his lack of polish as an actor. He was unmistakably out of his element. Making a star baseball player the star of a stage play was a good idea at the time, but Anson simply couldn't carry it off. Very likely the play itself was so bad that no one could have saved it.

Notes

1. *Brooklyn Daily Eagle*, May 15, 1887.
2. *New York Times*, June 27, 1895.
3. *Los Angeles Times*, August 25, 1895.
4. *Chicago Daily Times*, December 24, 1895.
5. *Brooklyn Daily Eagle*, November 24, 1895, and the *Chicago Daily Times*, December 24, 1895.
6. *Washington Post*, August 11, 1907.
7. *Brooklyn Daily Eagle*, November 20, 1895.
8. *Brooklyn Daily Eagle*, November 22 1895.
9. *New York Times*, December 3, 1895.
10. *New York Times*, December 3, 1895.
11. *Chicago Daily Times*, December 24, 1895.
12. *Chicago Daily Times*, January 5, 1896.
13. *The Sporting Life*, February 15, 1896.
14. *The Daily Northwestern*, Oshkosh, WI, January 26, 1911.

Early ERA Titles
A Reexamination of Pre-1951 Qualification Standards

by Dan Levitt

In December 1958 one W. Reich from Sacramento wrote a letter to *The Sporting News* requesting clarification of the minimum playing time criteria for determining the ERA leader.

Recently I was looking over the books I had acquired from The Sporting News, *and I discovered that three pitchers were credited with winning the earned-run-average crown even though they did not throw the required 154-inning minimum.*

I am referring to 1943 in the National League, when Howie Pollet won, pitching 118 innings; 1945, when Hank Borowy won, pitching 122 innings; and 1950, when Jim Hearn won, pitching 134 innings.

Why are these three given credit for the leadership? And if they are legally the leaders, then why wasn't Ferdie Schupp given credit over Grover Cleveland Alexander's 1.55, and why wasn't Tom Zachary, who had a 12-0 record with an ERA of 2.47 in 1929, given the honor over Lefty Grove, who posted a fine mark of 2.82?

The Sporting News responded with an answer that has by now become the conventional wisdom.

The 154-minimum in determining the ERA leader has been in effect only since 1951. Before that the requirement was ten or more compete games. Pollet pitched 12 complete games in 1943, Borowy hurled the route in 11 in 1945, and Hearn also had 11 in 1950. Schupp in 1916 pitched only eight complete games. Alexander hurled 38. When Zachary had his 12-0 record in 1929, he twirled the distance only seven times, while Grove had 21 complete games to his credit.

Unfortunately, the conventional wisdom regarding the pre-1951 criteria—that from the introduction of ERA as an official statistic the minimum criteria for the ERA leadership was 10 complete games—is misleading and not applicable in a surprising number of cases.

The NL introduced ERA as an official statistic in 1912; the AL followed one year later. After the close of the season, each league would release its list of the league's pitchers ordered by ERA, with the lowest ERA heading the list. But the two leagues approached the minimum ERA qualifying standards completely differently. Because the senior circuit consistently used a standard that more closely resembles *The Sporting News* explanation above, I will summarize the history of its minimum criteria first.

From the introduction of ERA as an official statistic, the NL used an objective standard to crown its champion. In 1917 the NL adopted the 10-complete game criteria noted in *The Sporting News* response. In its season-end presentation of the official statistics, the NL listed those pitchers who met the ERA minimum criteria according to ERA from lowest to highest. In a secondary listing, the NL listed those pitchers who failed to meet the minimum. The NL took six years to settle into the 10 complete game minimum; I have outlined the criteria for the first five years below.

1912	15 games pitched
1913	5 complete games
1914	15 games pitched
1915	15 games pitched
1916	12 games pitched

The NL clearly recognized the lowest ERA that topped its list with the ERA title. This includes the three ERA leaders with relatively few innings pitched referenced in Reich's letter: Pollet, Borowy, and Hearn. The only pitcher that met the NL playing time minimum not recognized today as the ERA champion is Ferdie Schupp for his 1916 season (0.90 ERA, 140 IP, 8 CG, 30G).

As I pointed out in an article in the 1996 *Baseball Research Journal*, however, this is a latter-day oversight that should be rectified: Schupp was clearly and widely acknowledged as the leader at the time, a broad recognition that remained in place for many years thereafter. For example, in the *1943 Sporting News Baseball Guide and Record Book*, Schupp was credited with the "Lowest Earned-Run Average, Season, Majors." It was only post-WWII that his ERA title gradually faded from some of the record and reference books because (1) it was forgotten that the criteria was not 10 complete games when first introduced, and (2) there is something unsatisfying about a single-season record that fails to meet present-day minimum playing time requirements.

The AL introduced ERA as an official statistic one year after the NL in 1913 and only sporadically had what could be considered an objective criteria prior to 1946, when it finally adopted the 10 complete game standard as well. While lack of an objective minimum sometimes led to uncertainty and confusion regarding the annual leader, it also had the theoretical advantage of permitting a more reasoned determination of the league leadership.

Until 1919 the AL simply listed its top pitchers by ERA without identifying a minimum standard for inclusion. A check of the record shows that the lists included all pitchers with at least 6 to 15 games pitched depending on the year. Not surprisingly this led to a number of controversies almost immediately—although fewer than one might now assume because the best hurlers all pitched a lot. In 1915 Smokey Joe Wood, currently recognized as the ERA leader, pitched 157 innings and 10 CG to head the AL ERA list at 1.49, edging out Walter Johnson (1.55 ERA, 337 IP, and 35 CG). In their commentary on the league's release of its pitching statistics, *The Sporting News* and the *New York Times* both recognized Wood as the ERA leader. The *Reach Guide*, while recognizing Wood as the leader, also wished to acknowledge Walter Johnson's overall fine season.

DAN LEVITT *is the co-author of* Paths to Glory, *winner of the 2004 Sporting News-SABR Baseball Research Award. He manages capital markets for a commercial real estate firm.*

The American League pitching averages for the 1915 season give the leadership to Joe Wood of the world champion Red Sox, who allowed an average of 1.49 earned runs per game during the season of 1915. The leader was really Walter Johnson, who allowed an average of 1.55 earned runs per game. Wood pitched in 25 games and 157⅓ innings while Johnson participated in 47 games and 336⅔ innings.

Without some objective criteria for listing the pitchers, the *Reach Guide* continued to struggle with how to define the pitching leader. In 1918 when Walter Johnson nominally finished second (39 G, 325 IP, 1.28 ERA) to Red Faber (11G, 81 IP, 1.22 ERA), nearly all sources naturally credited Johnson with the title. A year later, however, when discussing Johnson's 1919 league-leading ERA, the 1920 *Reach Guide* bizarrely credited Faber with the 1918 ERA leadership, noting that in 1918, "he then finished second to Faber."

In 1919 the AL finally introduced an objective criteria for listing its hurlers and began including only those pitchers who met the criteria in its primary listing. Unfortunately, they chose an obviously unsatisfactory standard: 45 innings pitched. The next year they switched to 10 games. In a peculiar decision, the AL switched back to 45 IP for 1921, despite the fact that the 10 game criteria kept Duster Mails (9 G, 63 IP) and his 1.85 ERA from topping charts above Bob Shawkey, rightfully credited with the ERA title. After one year back at the 45 IP minimum, in 1922 the AL finally adopted the 10 CG standard introduced in 1917 by the NL.

Implementation of the 10 CG standard by the AL in 1922 should have ended any confusion. Inexplicably, however, in 1925 the AL reinstated the 45 IP criteria. Again, this is particularly bizarre given that the 10 CG minimum eliminated obviously undeserving pitchers in two of the previous three years. The AL proved fortunate over the next several years, as all the ERA list leaders pitched a substantial number of innings, generating little controversy.

When the annual ERA leaders are displayed in some more recent reference books, a footnote is occasionally attached to Wilcy Moore's 1927 title, remarking that although he did not hurl 10 complete games, an exception was made due to his 213 IP. But this rationale is incorrect; the AL had no such

10 CG standard, so no exception was needed. In fact, a check of the contemporary papers reveals no discussion of any exception for awarding the title to Moore. For example, *The Sporting News* opened its commentary on the official AL pitching averages: "Wilcy Moore, recruit of the New York Yankees, was the most effective pitcher in the American League during 1927." The article made no reference to his complete games.

In 1929 New York Yankee hurler Tom Zachary finished 12-0 with a 2.47 ERA and 7 CG in 120 IP. Zachary bettered Lefty Grove, currently recognized as the ERA leader for his 2.81 ERA in 275 IP. However, contemporary sources all awarded the title to Zachary. *The Sporting News* headline over the release of the official AL pitching statistics read: VETERAN TOM ZACHARY OF YANKEES WAS LEADING A.L. PITCHER OF YEAR. The subtitle continued, LEFTHANDER, WITH BEST EARNED RUN RECORD, WON 12 GAMES AND LOST NONE; GROVE, SECOND. *The Sporting News Record Book for 1930* recognized Zachary under the category "Best earned run average" for the AL. A check of the daily newspaper headlines reveals a similar sentiment. For example, the *New York Times* asserted, "Zachary, with 2.47 Earned-Run Mark, led the American League Pitchers."

Monte Pearson, still today credited with the 1933 ERA leadership, led the AL pitching lists with an ERA of 2.33 in 135 innings pitched. Like Zachary, contemporary sources awarded the title to Pearson despite relatively few innings pitched when compared to the fourth-place Mel Harder with 253 IP (there were two intermediate relievers with over 100 IP). It is significant that in bestowing on Pearson the title, none felt it necessary to emphasize the fact that he completed 10 games; it was simply not a requirement in the AL.

In fact, while Pearson was clearly recognized as the leader, at least some sentiment again leaned toward recognizing the best overall performance as well. "Although younger pitchers came to the fore in earned-run effectiveness in the American League

Monty Pearson

Ernie Bonham

in 1933, it is Robert (Lefty) Grove of the Athletics who appears as the champion hurler of the season, according to the official averages released yesterday [Grove finished fourth in ERA among those who would qualify today with a 24-8 record]," opined the *New York Times* article on the AL pitching averages.

That today Pearson retains his 1933 ERA championship, while Zachary lost his long ago, is only explainable when looked at in light of the fact that as more comprehensive and widely distributed record books were published after World War II, the 10 complete game minimum was retroactively applied, even when not appropriate.

The next few years produced no disagreements as full-time pitchers turned in the lowest ERA's. In 1938 Ivy Andrews technically led the AL list with an ERA of 3.00 but pitched only 48 innings. Lefty Grove, second on the list with an ERA of 3.07 in 164 innings, was not surprisingly awarded the title without any mention of the lightly used Andrews. While there was no mention of a 10 CG minimum, *The Sporting News* invoked a 100-IP benchmark when they declared "second place in the earned-run yield among the hurlers in 100 or more innings went to Joe Krakauskas of the Washington Senators." It is noteworthy that Krakauskas pitched only 121 innings and 5 CG.

The Sporting News found itself in somewhat of a dilemma the next year when the AL pitching statistics put Marius Russo first at an ERA of 2.41 in 116 IP with 9 CG and Grove second at 2.54 in 191 IP. Not unexpectedly, Grove was crowned the champion. *The Sporting News* did not specifically address any criteria, merely noting Russo worked "in only 116 innings as compared to Grove's 191." After conferring the ERA title on Grove, the *Chicago Tribune* simply stated that Russo "really was the leader in the earned run column, but pitched 75 fewer innings than Grove." The *Washington Post* reported, "Russo's earned run average was 2.41, but he was not a regular hurler." Again, no mention of any 10-CG standard.

Reporting of the 1940 AL official pitching statistics

clearly clarifies the lack of any 10 CG minimum in the AL. Ernie Bonham led the AL list with an ERA of 1.91 in 99 innings and 10 CG; Bob Feller finished in second place on the list with an ERA of 2.62 in 320 innings. If a 10 CG minimum existed, then either Bonham would have been given the title or there would have been some explanation as to why an exception was being made. In fact, Feller was awarded the title, and the accounts made no mention of any 10 CG minimum. *The Sporting News* reverted to its 100 IP minimum, stating that Feller "led the league in low earned-run allowance, with 2.62, for hurlers in more than 100 innings."

The 1941 *Spalding-Reach Official Base Ball Guide* discussed the ERA title as well: "Ernie Bonham of the Yankees ranked first on the list in earned runs with 1.91 per game, but he pitched in only a dozen contests, so the real leader, of course, was Feller with his 2.62 record for 43 games."

The *New York Times* summarized the quirky way in which the AL listed its pitchers, again without any reference to a 10 complete game standard:

By reason of a curious method in the American League which lists in its first group of pitchers all hurlers who took place in at least 45 innings, the name of Ernie Bonham of the Yankees actually appears on top with an earned run average of 1.91.

However, the Yankees' crack rookie took place in only twelve games and so, despite this excellent record, top ranking must go to Feller, who appeared in 43 games, winning 27 and losing 11.

While several pitchers tossing less than 100 innings topped the official end-of-season AL lists over the next few years, none led to any ERA title disputes. The leading "regular" pitcher was awarded the title with little or no mention of the titular list leader. In 1944, when two relief pitchers, both with over 100 IP, led the list, they received minimal reference. All reports of the ERA race declared Dizzy Trout and his 2.12 ERA in 352 innings the leader, and they obviously felt no rationalization was necessary. *The Sporting News* dropped any de facto reference to a 100 IP minimum, while others simply referred to regular pitchers, even if not explicitly defined.

In 1946 the AL finally adopted the 10 CG standard, which put the two leagues on the same basis. Five years later in 1951, after three relatively low innings pitched ERA leaders in the NL over the previous eight years, the major leagues finally adopted the modern standard of one inning pitched per team game (for the purists, I will note that the wording—but not the substance—of the criteria has changed a couple of times since).

In awarding the ERA title prior to 1951, contrary to conventional wisdom, the minimum playing time criteria was not 10 complete games in a surprising number of seasons. The NL did not adopt the 10 complete game standard until 1917, five years after the introduction of ERA as an official statistic, but they did have an objective minimum standard during each of those five years. And every pitcher who finished atop the primary list from the introduction of ERA as an official statistic in 1912 until the current standard was adopted in 1951 was regarded by contemporary sources as the league leader.

In contrast, the American League did not permanently introduce an objective standard until 1946, when they finally adopted the 10 complete game minimum. Prior to that (except for a few years in the early 1920s) the AL simply had no objective standard. And in the subjective evaluation, complete games were never more than an ancillary consideration. As is clear from the sources quoted above, innings pitched and games were assigned much more weight. When awarding the title to Moore in the one case and not to Bonham in the other, contemporary sources made no mention of any complete game exception—complete games were simply not part of the AL ERA title award criteria. Furthermore, the subjectively considered playing time minimums fluctuated mildly over time.

All in all, the misapplication of the 10 complete game standard back to all pre-1951 seasons does not much alter the present crowning of the annual ERA leaders. With the obvious exception of Schupp, and the possible exception of Zachary, no clearly recognized ERA leader of that period has lost his title. Nevertheless, for a better and more complete understanding of historical earned run averages, it should be recognized that the minimum qualifications for the ERA title often differed from the current retroactively applied standard.

Photos used by courtesy of the National Baseball Hall of Fame Library, Cooperstown, NY.

Bobby Doerr in 1934
His Reflections on Life in the Pacific Coast League at 16

As told to James D. Smith III

In 2004, a legion of baseball fans celebrated the Boston Red Sox's first World Series title since 1918. Coincidentally, that is also the birth year of their eldest living Hall of Famer, Robert Pershing "Bobby" Doerr. And characteristically—as the post-season headlines bannered Ramirez, Schilling, Lowe, and another second baseman, Mark Bellhorn—his special appearance at Fenway Park was understated and classy. Invited to take part in pregame ceremonies, at age 86 Bob had traveled across the country to honor the game, and the team, he loved.

Bobby Doerr was born and raised in a Los Angeles experiencing its adolescence as a big city, and 70 summers ago—at the age of 16—he began playing professional baseball as second baseman for the Pacific Coast League Hollywood Sheiks. When the franchise shifted to San Diego in 1936, he became an original Padre, and made a lifelong friend in fellow teenager Ted Williams. Doerr played second

for the Red Sox from 1937 through 1951, where he drove in 100 runs six times and set an AL record for consecutive fielding chances without an error. He was elected to baseball's Hall of Fame in 1986.

Respect for Doerr, however, goes deeper than the record books. Williams famously called him "the silent captain of the Red Sox," while a Yankee opponent styled him "one of the very few men who played the game hard and retired with no enemies." Others have quietly honored his 65-year marriage to wife Monica, and his devoted care for her during her many years of facing health issues. A man of deep faith, sharp mind, and striking vitality, our conversation of March 11, 2004 (supplemented by others) offered a memorable glimpse into the story of young "Bobby" as a gifted teenager breaking into pro ball in the mid-1930s.

Bobby Doerr (center) with members of the 1935 Hollywood team.

"My parents, Harold and Frances, were really wonderful people. Dad worked for the phone company, and liked baseball a lot. He never pushed me, but when I showed an interest in the game, there were plenty of opportunities. I learned to play on the Manchester Playground there in Los Angeles, and later enjoyed sandlot ball. Along the way, I made some great friends.

"Our 1932 American Legion team had George McDonald at first, Arnold Owen at shortstop (they later called him "Mickey"), and Steve Messner at third, while I took second base. We almost were the national champions, going to playoffs in Catalina and Ogden, Utah—just missing the big trip to Omaha. That level of competition really helped you grow up and learn the game.

"As a kid I used to shag outfield balls at Wrigley Field, while the Coast League teams were taking batting practice, and then they'd let you watch the game for free. Over time, the Hollywood Sheiks (who were tenants at Wrigley, which was owned by the Angels) became interested in me, and I was invited to work out in the field and take some hitting. In the spring of 1934, they began to talk seriously about signing me.

"The Legion ball officials were upset about this, and even threatened a lawsuit, but it was dropped. My older brother Hal (a catcher) was already in the league. In June, when his Portland team was in town, Dad and Hal picked me up from Fremont High and told me Hollywood was offering a $200 month ironclad contract. Of course I was interested—it was a great opportunity and good money for the time. It was the Depression, you know. My dad insisted on one condition: finishing school at Fremont, which I did with the class of 1935. Of course, when I signed a pro contract, that ended my high school elgibility. So in the summer of 1934—70 years ago, now—it was professional ball.

"There I was at age 16, a Coast League rookie— definitely young, but pretty mature. In L.A., the weather usually allowed us to play ball in the winter, often against pros. So I'd been hitting some good pitching for a while and looked forward to the next

Jim Smith, *a SABR member since 1982, has contributed to* The National Pastime, Baseball Research Journal, *and many other publications. He teaches at Bethel Seminary San Diego and the University of San Diego, and serves as a pastor at College Avenue Baptist Church.*

*Young double-play combination
Bobby Doerr and Geoge Myatt*

level. My friend George McDonald (who still lives in Southern California) signed with the Sheiks too, and that helped. He was a fine fielder (and quite a talker), and enjoyed a long career in the league. It was a great experience!

"My biggest thrill that season was just putting on the uniform and playing in my first professional game. In late June, a matter of days after signing, I was in the lineup as the Sheiks were playing in Sacramento. They assigned me George Myatt as a roommate. He had just turned 20, I think, and was being groomed as a shortstop, so we matched up well on that basis. We also became good friends, and he asked me to be best man when he was married at home plate at Lane Field in San Diego a couple of years later.

"Part of what made it great, too, was the old guys, the veterans on that team. They treated us well. Oscar Vitt was my manager that first season, a seasoned baseball man whose leadership helped get everybody working together. But the one who really struck me—and became our manager in 1935—was Frank Shellenback. He'd been pitching for about 20 years, an old spitballer who'd suck on slippery elm, pick a spot about the size of a quarter to douse the ball, and those pitches would move. Sometimes our infield throws were spitballs! Anyway, he was a real class guy—an active Catholic with a big family who was strict, but just had that makeup you respected.

"Fred Haney was at third, and he helped me with my fielding. Also, he'd been a teammate of Ty Cobb's, and was a great base runner for us. He taught me to slide better and maybe drag a bunt occasionally to keep 'em honest. Our catcher Johnny Bassler, who had been with Detroit, too, was a .300 hitter wherever he went, and taught me some techniques. The greatest hitter, of course, was Smead Jolley. What a slugger, and such a big, nice guy—but, yes, an awful fielder. On shallow flies to the outfield, I could hear the "thump, thump" of his footsteps on the way in. You know, it's the little things that you'd pick up, whether out in the field or on the train trips talking. It was a long season, but I just loved it.

"There were a lot of fine ballplayers in the Coast League in the 1930s, and a real mix of ages. One of the most amazing hitters was Oscar Eckhardt. He beat out Joe DiMaggio for the batting title in 1935—but the most memorable thing was how. A left-handed hitter, he'd whip his bat through the strike zone, drive the ball usually to left field, and before finishing his swing was running like a deer toward first. It was a really unusual stance and stroke, and I played him behind second base. Now that you mention it, that Ichiro who plays for Seattle reminds me a bit of his style.

"Of course in 1934, the Angels won everything. We finished third or so, but the other team was something else. [They won 23 of 26 weekly series and, with a 137-50 record, set PCL marks for wins and percentage.] They had Frank Demaree, Jimmie Reese (who later replaced me in San Diego), Gene Lillard, Fay Thomas . . . strong everywhere. Some have called it the best minor league team ever. We had a pretty good crosstown rivalry, but it was cordial.

"Meanwhile, my folks loved it. Dad kept a scrapbook of my games, stayed away from interfering, and just enjoyed being supportive with Mom. People appreciated them. Two years later, facing economic problems, the owner Bill Lane moved the team down to San Diego, and we became the original Padres. That was the extra seasoning I needed before going up to the Red Sox. And when the Padres

signed Ted Williams, he was still attending Hoover High School—a junior like I had been. So the road was familiar, and from 1936 on we had a wonderful friendship.

"Looking back, I've been blessed in so many ways. In my younger years, I wasn't too much on church. I'd wonder, like everyone else, "What's life about?" When I did pray, it was mostly to be a better ballplayer. What really made an impact on me was the movie *King of Kings*. The scenes and the music moved me to pick up the Bible and read the story of Jesus for myself. When I did, I began to learn and grow—and came to accept Christ as my Savior. There's life beyond baseball, and I'd recommend that to anyone listening."

COURTESY OF BOBBY DOERR

No Stars vs. All-Stars

by Timothy Connaughton

Can there be a star quality team without any All-Stars? Can a team compiled entirely of All-Stars be mediocre? The answer to both questions is a resounding yes, at least theoretically.

Kirk Gibson won an MVP Award, but was never named to a single All-Star roster during his entire career. John Denny won the 1983 National League Cy Young Award, but did not make the NL All-Star team that year, or any other year. What about a player who hit at least .330 four times, drove in 100 runs six years in a row, hit more than 25 home runs four times, and scored more than 100 runs four times? A player such as that would be an All-Star several times over, would he not? No, on the contrary, he never was an All-Star. Surely a pitcher with the eighth-highest winning percentage of all time pitched in a few midsummer classics, right? Wrong.

Findings such as these, along with memories of Atlee Hammaker's performance in the 1983 All-Star game, led me to the following hypothesis: one could formulate an all-time team of players who were never named to an All-Star roster whose talent would be far superior to a roster of actual All-Stars whose careers were, as a whole, mediocre. The goal was not to show that the players who never made an All-Star team should have, or those who did were unworthy of making the team based on a solid half-season performance. Rather, the point was to compare a group of star quality players who were never bestowed All-Star status with a group of players who were named to at least one All-Star team in spite of rather pedestrian careers. The result is a 32-man roster (the current All-Star limit) of players who never made a major league All-Star team that would in all likelihood easily win over 100 games if pitted against

its counterparts—a squad of 32 less than illustrious All-Stars—in a mythical 162 game season.

Players who played any portion of their careers prior to the inception of the All-Star game in 1933 were omitted from consideration. The basis for this is obvious—a player who didn't play after 1933 was never eligible for an All-Star game, so players like Ty Cobb, Honus Wagner, etc., who surely would have been All-Stars, are not included. Likewise, players such as Rogers Hornsby, who continued to play for a few years after the All-Star game came into existence but never made an All-Star team because their best years were pre-1933, were likewise omitted because they, too, likely would have been All-Stars but for the fact that no midsummer game existed at the time. One roster, therefore, will truly be filled with players who were eligible for the All-Star game during every year of their playing careers, but who nevertheless concluded their careers with no All-Star selections.

Players who were still active at the end of the 2004 season were not eligible. Even if they are nearing the end of lengthy careers, the possibility remains that players who are still active may yet be selected to an All-Star roster.

Finally, the fact that a player never *played* in an All-Star game was not enough. There are many instances where players don't make it into the game but are nonetheless on the roster. Similarly, there have been myriad situations involving injured players who don't participate in the game or even attend the contest, but are nonetheless, technically, All-Stars. In order to be eligible, the player must never have been named to an All-Star roster in Major League Baseball.

In the other dugout, the same rules of eligibility apply. The mediocre players who were bestowed All-Star status had to begin their careers after 1932 and retire from the game prior to 2004. There is no

Tim Connaughton *is an attorney who lives in Troy, Michigan with his wife and son.*

requirement that they threw a single pitch, had a plate appearance, or even played in the field. As long as they were named to an All-Star roster, they were eligible. This is the case for the reasons noted above to a certain extent, but also for consistency's sake.

The team of superior talent, but no official All-Stars, will be dubbed the No Stars. Their adversaries will be referred to as the All-Stars.

NO STARS: THE STARTING LINEUP

NO STARS LINEUP	
Hal Trosky	1B
Tony Phillips	2B
Woodie Held	SS
Clete Boyer	3B
Kirk Gibson	OF
Kevin McReynolds	OF
Garry Maddox	OF
Rick Dempsey	C

Hal Trosky

Trosky is the player whose hitting acumen is noted in the opening paragraphs. During his first full season, Trosky batted .330 with 35 home runs, 142 RBI and 117 runs scored. He was not a flash in the pan. He hit at least .330 four times, hammered 25 or more home runs six times, drove in over 100 runs in six consecutive seasons, and scored at least 100 runs four times. He finished the year in the top 10 in the AL in batting average four times, slugging percentage six times, OPS four times and led the league in total bases in 1936. He finished in the top 10 in runs, home runs, and RBI twice, six times, and five times respectively. His 162 RBI in 1936 paced the American League and remained an Indians single-season record until 1999. His 216 home runs with the Indians is fifth on their all-time leader board. Unfortunately for Trosky, he played during a time of outstanding American League first basemen. Lou Gehrig, Jimmie Foxx, and Hank Greenberg were selected over Trosky for the AL All-Star team during his career, as were lesser stars such as George McQuinn and Rudy York. Sadly, Trosky's career was cut short due to unmitigated migraine headaches. While he returned to baseball in the mid-1940s, his career effectively ended in 1941 at the age of 28, when most players are in their prime.

Tony Phillips

The spirited and much-traveled Phillips played a variety of positions during his career, but spent more time at second base than anywhere else. Unlike most players who are traded twice before they reach the majors, Phillips' career was extremely successful. He could hit for power (160 home runs), steal bases (177) and score runs (1,300). In fact, he led the AL in runs scored in 1992 and finished in the top 10 six times during that decade. Phillips was also prolific at getting on base. His lofty on-base average was due in large part to his ability to draw walks. He led the league in that department in 1993 and 1996, and finished in the top five in the American League in bases on balls seven times in the 1990s. While Phillips moved around a lot, playing eight stints with six different franchises in his career, his bat kept him employed for almost two full decades. In 18 years in the big leagues, however, it never resulted in an All-Star selection.

Woodie Held

Although not terribly impressive with the glove, in six seasons with the Indians Held averaged 21 home runs, finishing his career with 179. While the premier shortstops of today routinely hit 20 or more round trippers per year, it was not nearly as commonplace in Held's day. Luis Aparicio was Held's contemporary, and Pee Wee Reese and Phil Rizzuto played near the same time. All three are Hall of Famers. Aparicio and Rizzuto combined for 121 home runs, and Reese hit 126, fewer than Held. While he is obviously not a Hall of Famer, he had more power than even the best shortstops of his era.

Clete Boyer

Boyer won his only Gold Glove with the Braves and showed more power while in the National League, but he spent the majority of his career in the American League, and contributed greatly to the success of the Yankees during his years with the club. Playing the hot corner for one of the strongest defensive infields of all time, Boyer helped the Yankees to five consecutive pennants and back-to-back World Series titles in 1961 and 1962. In spite of the success of his teams, often a significant factor in All-Star selections, Boyer never made a single All-Star roster. While the Orioles third sacker, Brooks Robinson, explains not only why Boyer wasn't winning Gold Gloves but also why he wasn't *starting* midsummer classics, it's interesting to note who was backing up Robinson at the All-Star games in those days. Other third basemen invited to participate during Boyer's tenure in the AL include

Max Alvis, Dick Howser, and Rich Rollins, but no Clete Boyer, one of the finest fielding third basemen of all time. Boyer also had some power, clouting double-digit round trippers in nine of ten seasons in which he had more than 350 at-bats, while most of the time hitting seventh or eighth in the order, with no protection behind him.

Kirk Gibson

While Gibson's most famous moment occurred while a member of the Dodgers, he had long before ingratiated himself to AL fans as a member of the Tigers. Although he never quite lived up to Tiger manager Sparky Anderson's proclamation as the next Mickey Mantle, Gibson's aggressive play and athleticism helped Detroit to great success during the 1980s. His post-season exploits are well documented, beginning with the 1984 world champion Tigers. He was the 1984 ALCS MVP and clouted two home runs in game five of the World Series in which Detroit closed out the overmatched Padres. Gibson drove in seven runs in the 1984 World Series and stole three bases as well. In the 1988 NLCS, as a member of the Dodgers, Gibson continued his clutch play with a 12th-inning game winning home run in game four, a three-run homer in game five and the game-winning RBI in game seven. While he managed only one at-bat in the World Series that year due to injury, it was one of the most replayed at-bats in the history of the game. Gibson's home run in the bottom of the ninth won the game, and in some people's opinion, the Series. As Gibson had done to Goose Gossage in the 1984 World Series, he beat another of the game's great closers, the Athletics' Dennis Eckersley. In all, Gibson finished his career with seven home runs and 21 RBI in 21 post-season games.

Gibson truly had a power/speed combination. He ranks tenth all-time in Tiger home runs, and sixth in the club's history in stolen bases. He finished in the league top 10 in home runs three times, slugging four times, and stolen bases four times. He won the National League MVP in 1988, and remains the only MVP never to be named to an All-Star roster. Although Anderson, and later Dodger manager Tommy Lasorda, reportedly asked Gibson if he would like to play in the game (invitations he obviously declined), the fact remains that he was never on a single All-Star roster in either league.

Kevin McReynolds

Rob Neyer, in his *Big Book of Baseball Lineups*, calls McReynolds the best left fielder in Mets history, and the second-best center fielder in Padres history. His best season was 1988, when he finished third in MVP balloting as a Met. McReynolds batted .288 that summer, with 27 home runs, 99 RBI and was a perfect 21 for 21 on the base paths, culminating a two-season string that saw McReynolds caught stealing only once in 36 attempts. McReynolds ranks in the top 10 all-time in Mets history in most major offensive categories. McReynolds was also a fine defensive outfielder.

Garry Maddox

The "Secretary of Defense" is widely regarded as one of the best defensive outfielders of all time. His defensive skills were so highly regarded that broadcaster Ralph Kiner is often quoted as having said, "Two-thirds of the earth is covered by water. The other third is covered by Garry Maddox." The only outfielders in NL history with more Gold Gloves than Maddox's eight are Willie Mays and Roberto Clemente. Maddox contributed with his bat as well. He was a lifetime .285 hitter, and finished third in the NL in batting average twice. His 1976 season earned him fifth place in MVP voting. He finished his career with 248 stolen bases and was among the top 10 in the NL in stolen bases, doubles, and triples three times each. Maddox recorded the series-winning hit against Houston in the 1980 NLCS in extra innings, culminating one of the most exciting post-season series in NL history.

Rick Dempsey

Dempsey caught in four different decades and did so with great success. He caught more games than any other player in Oriole franchise history. During his career, he played in 25 post-season games and earned MVP honors in the 1983 World Series. The Orioles acquired him midway through the 1976 season in a trade with the Yankees. Dempsey did not hit much, but was an excellent defensive catcher. Bill James rates him as the 43rd best catcher of all time. On this mythical team, he handles a staff peppered with Royals and Cardinals.

THE ROTATION

John Tudor

Tudor never had a losing record during any season in the 1980s. The high point of the decade was 1985, Tudor's first season with St. Louis, when he was a runner-up for the NL Cy Young. Although he started the season 1-7, he finished 20-1. The slow start deprived him of an All-Star berth. His 21 wins tied for second most in the NL. He finished the year with a 1.93 ERA, 14 complete games, and 10 shutouts, all good for either best or second best in the league. Tudor has a lifetime winning percentage of .619, and ranks first in that category in Cardinal history. He also owns the second lowest career ERA among Cardinal hurlers.

Dennis Leonard

Shockingly, Leonard never made an All-Star roster in spite of the fact that he won more games than any other pitcher in the junior circuit from 1975 to 1981. His 120 wins during that span paced several strong Royals teams, including a pennant winner in 1980. He ranks first all-time in Royals complete games and shutouts, second in wins, and third in strikeouts and games started. He is the only Royals pitcher to post three 20-win seasons and finished fourth and tied for seventh in Cy Young voting in 1977 and 1978 respectively. He tied for the league lead in wins in 1977 and shutouts in 1979. He had multiple other league top 10 finishes during his career, including five top 10 finishes in strikeouts, five in wins, and six in shutouts.

Paul Splittorff

Leonard's teammate, Splittorff, was likewise snubbed by All-Star managers. He has more wins in a Royals uniform than any pitcher in franchise history with 166. He also ranks at the top of the franchise list in games started, second to Leonard in complete games and shutouts, and fifth in strikeouts. He garnered enough recognition in 1978 to tie for seventh in Cy Young voting, but not enough to win a place on the All-Star team.

Charlie Leibrandt

The third former Royal on the staff began his career with the Reds. His success, however, came primarily in Kansas City, where he ranks eighth all-time in wins and tenth in ERA and strikeouts. He finished fifth in Cy Young voting in 1985, but was overshadowed by two teammates who finished first and fourth—Bret Saberhagen and Dan Quisenberry. Although Saberhagen is largely considered the ace of the Royals staffs of the mid and late 1980s, Leibrandt won 60 games from 1985 to 1988, while Saberhagen posted 59 victories during that span. Leibrandt finished in the league top 10 in wins three times, ERA three times, and shutouts four times.

Bob Forsch

Forsch, another Cardinal hurler, made hitters earn their way on base. He finished in the top 10 in the league in fewest walks per nine innings five times during his career. He led the league in that department in 1980. He ranks third all-time in Cardinal wins, behind only Bob Gibson and Jesse Haines. He also ranks third in Cardinal history in strikeouts and ninth in shutouts. Forsch also helped himself, handling the bat well.

THE BENCH

Lyman Bostock

Bostock was murdered on September 23, 1978, in the waning days of his fourth big-league season. Bostock, a member of the California Angels at the time of his murder, had finished a game against the White Sox in Chicago earlier that day, and traveled to Gary, Indiana, to visit his uncle. The two men were riding through the streets of Gary with two ladies, one of whom was the estranged wife of Leonard Smith. Smith drove up beside the vehicle and shot into the car, striking Bostock in the head. Bostock died later that evening. Smith was acquitted of the crime, a jury finding him insane. He spent less than two years in an asylum and was released in the midst of the 1980 season, which would have been Bostock's sixth.

Bostock, the son of a former Negro League player, was only 27 years old when he was killed, and was undoubtedly entering the prime of his career. He hit .323 in 1976, his first full season in the majors. That was the fourth-best average in the American League. The following year, he hit .336, second best in the American League. 1977 was Bostock's breakout season. He finished in the top seven in the American League in seven major offensive categories, including second in average, fourth in runs scored, and seventh in on-base percentage. During the season he tied a major league record for putouts in a nine-inning game by a center fielder, with 12, and set an American League record for putouts in a doubleheader with 17. He helped the Twins set a franchise record for most runs scored in a season. In short, he had become a star, and was arguably the most sought-after player in the free agent market between the 1977 and 1978 seasons.

In 1978, after signing a hefty free agent contract with the California Angels, Bostock started the year miserably, and demanded that Angels owner Gene Autry keep his money until Bostock started earning it. When Autry refused, Bostock gave the money to charity. In June, his bat came alive, and his average for the remainder of the season was well over .300. He finished at .296.

That capped a three-year stretch during which Bostock hit .318, the third highest average in the game during that span, behind only Rod Carew and Dave Parker. Bostock garnered a few points in the MVP voting in both 1977 and 1978. His body of work for the three-year stretch of 1976-78 is impressive in and of itself, but consider that those were his first full major league seasons, and the numbers are even more impressive. Unfortunately, Bostock was murdered before he had a chance to reach more lofty heights, and his career ended without a single trip to a major league All-Star game.

Elmer Valo

Valo, one of only four major leaguers born in Czechoslovakia, and the only native Czech with any success, spent the bulk of his career in Philadelphia. He was noted as a hustling player, not afraid to crash into an outfield wall to make a catch. While

Elmer Valo

not blessed with significant power, Valo was adept at getting on base. His lifetime OBA is 50 points higher than the league average during his career, and he finished in the top 10 in OBA twice, and ranks eighth all-time in Athletics franchise history. He also notched league top-10 finishes in batting average, OPS, doubles (twice), triples (three times), RBI, walks (twice), and stolen bases (seven times). Also contributing to his ability to get on base was his knack for getting hit, finishing in the top 10 in HBP four times. According to baseball historian Bill James, Valo has the third highest on-base percentage of all time among outfielders who played at least 1,500 games and are not in the Hall of Fame. As Barry Bonds and Rickey Henderson are ranked one and two on that list, it is only a matter of time before Valo reaches the top. Evidently, he is already the leader among players who were never All-Stars.

Cesar Tovar

Tovar was a very versatile player, once playing all nine positions in a single game. He struck out Reggie Jackson while on the mound. Tovar finished in the top 10 in the AL in stolen bases six times, and totaled 226 for his career. He hit .311 in 1971 while leading the league in hits. The year before, he hit an even .300 and led the AL in both doubles and triples. He finished in the top 10 in the AL in runs six times, hits four times, doubles four times, and triples four times. He recorded the lone hit in five one-hitters during his career. He did a lot of things well, but didn't dominate any aspect of the game, which is the likely cause of his omission from All-Star rosters.

Dwayne Murphy

One of the finest-fielding center fielders of all time, he won six consecutive Gold Gloves. He displayed power (hitting at least 15 homers in five consecutive seasons) and speed (swiping at least 10 bags in four consecutive campaigns). In his only post-season, he hit .545 in the ALDS, collecting 6 hits in 11 at-bats in a series victory against the Royals in the strike-shortened 1981 campaign. Despite his acumen at the plate, on the base paths, and especially roaming the outfield, he was never recognized as an All-Star.

Dan Driessen

Never a starter with the Big Red Machine during its truly dominant stretch, Driessen moved to first when Tony Perez moved to the Expos. He exhibited a good glove during his seven-year stretch as the Reds starter at first, a period that began in 1977 and ended in 1984, when he, like his predecessor, went to Montreal. He tied for the NL lead in walks in 1980 and throughout his career showed good power and speed, finishing with more than 150 home runs and more than 150 stolen bases lifetime.

Bill Doran

Doran was an integral member of the successful Astros teams of the 1980s with both his glove and his bat. He was a two-time team MVP and ranks in the top 10 in Astros history in OBA, games, at-bats, runs, hits, total bases, triples, walks, and stolen bases. His speed on the base paths was a particular asset to Doran and the Astros. He finished his career with over 200 stolen bases, including 42 for Houston's 1986 division-winning team.

Solly Hemus

Hemus finished his playing career with a phenomenal lifetime on-base average of .390, thanks in large part to a willingness to sacrifice his body. He led the league in times hit by a pitch three times. His propensity to take one for the team also allowed him to score more than 100 runs in both 1952 and 1953.

Richie Hebner

Hebner was seemingly in the post-season constantly, although most often for teams that lost once they got there. He was, however, a big reason why many of those teams made it as far as they did. He was a lifetime .276 hitter with 203 home runs, 890 RBI and 865 runs scored. He ranks in the top 25 in the illustrious history of the Pirates in multiple offensive categories, including home runs, slugging, total bases, RBI, walks, extra-base hits, and times hit by a pitch.

Bill Bruton

Bruton was the table-setting leadoff man for the strong Braves teams of the 1950s. He led the NL in stolen bases his first three seasons in the majors, 1953-1955. In all, he placed in his league's top 10 in swipes eight times. His speed also manifested itself in triples, a category in which he led the league twice and finished in the top 5 six times. Bruton led the National League with 112 runs scored in 1960, and had three other top 10 finishes in that department. While he would have made a fabulous leadoff hitter in front of Mays, Clemente, Aaron and other perennial NL All-Stars of the 1950s and '60s, he was never a member of an All-Star team.

Don Slaught

Although not regarded as one of the best defensive catchers in the league, Slaught's offensive contributions were noteworthy. He hit over .300 six times in his career, including a .345 clip in 1992 with the Pirates.

Doug Rader

Rader's defense is too impressive to ignore. He won every NL Gold Glove at third base from 1970 to 1974. Rader could handle the bat as well, hitting 155 career home runs. Rob Neyer calls him the best third baseman in Astros history.

Jim Gantner

Gantner played more games at second base than anyone in Brewers history, and it isn't even close. In fact, other than Robin Yount and Paul Molitor, Gantner has more games played and at-bats than anyone in franchise history at any position. His consistency over the course of his career resulted in his place among the top eight in Brewers history in hits, runs, doubles, triples, RBI, walks, stolen bases, and sacrifices. He is the club's leader in sacrifices.

THE BULLPEN

Alex Fernandez

Alex Fernandez's career was short-circuited by injuries, but while he played, he was among the game's most successful pitchers. His best years were 1993-1997, when he recorded a mark of 74-46, for a .616 winning percentage. He tied for sixth in the American League Cy Young voting in 1996, only to leave for the Marlins the following year, where he led the World Series champs in victories. During his short career he finished in his league's top 10 in wins four times, strikeouts four times, shutouts five times, complete games three times, and ERA twice.

Bill Hands

Hands finished in the league top 10 in wins, complete games, and fewest walks per nine innings three times each. He never walked more than 76 batters in a season.

Don Gullett

Gullett was the unheralded ace of the Big Red Machine. His career winning percentage of .686 ranks eighth in the history of the game. While some may attribute that solely to the offense that supported him in Cincinnati, he had a lifetime ERA of 3.11, and finished sixth in the league in 1971 with a 2.65 mark. He was seventh in Cy Young voting in 1974 and fifth in 1975, yet never made an All-Star squad. He was a member of two world championship teams in Cincinnati and one in New York, with the Yankees.

John Denny

While Kirk Gibson is the only MVP in the All-Star era without an All-Star game on his resume, Denny is the only NL Cy Young winner never to play in a midsummer classic. (Pete Vuckovich, a near miss for this roster, won the 1982 AL Cy Young without a career All-Star appearance.) Denny won the award in 1983 after leading the league in wins (19-6), and compiling seven complete games and an ERA of 2.37. Denny walked only 53 batters in over 240 innings that season. Seven years earlier, Denny led the league with a 2.52 ERA.

Ellis Kinder

"Old Folks," as he was affectionately dubbed, did not pitch in a major league game until his 30s. Once he started, he flourished. Kinder finished fifth in the AL MVP race in 1949 and seventh in 1951. He was a versatile pitcher, compiling a league-leading six shutouts and winning 23 games in 1949 (second in the American League), while at the end of games showing his worth by leading the league in saves twice and finishing in the top 10 six times. He ranks third on the Red Sox all-time saves list.

Gene Garber

His 218 saves ranks 29th all-time. While he never led the league in saves, he finished in the top 10 six times, and is second only to John Smoltz in saves as a Brave. He finished seventh in Cy Young voting in 1982, when he saved 30 games and posted a 2.34 ERA.

Ron Perranoski

Perranoski split his time between the leagues. His best season came as a member of the Dodgers in 1963. He was 16-3 with 21 saves and a 1.67 ERA. He was fourth in MVP voting that year. He saved 179 games in his career, leading the American League twice. He finished in the top 10 in saves seven times and is 43rd all-time. He's fifth in Dodgers history and seventh in Twins history in saves.

ALL STARS: THE STARTING LINEUP

Ron Coomer

Coomer was a decent hitter and a good fielder, but never finished in the top 10 in any season in any offensive category and never hit .300. He never hit more than 16 home runs, while playing a position that is typically associated with power. Coomer also grounded into a lot of double plays. That said, Coomer is one of the better hitters on this team, but would not make the No Stars team.

Emil Verban

Verban made three All-Star teams in three consecutive seasons, 1945-47. He is evidently considered, or at least was, a fine fielder. Although that may be true, his career fielding percentage was basically league average. He hit a grand total of one home run in his entire big-league career, and never had a batting average higher than .289 or an on-base percentage higher than .316. Although he was nicknamed "The Antelope," he stole only 21 bases in his major league career, and never more than five in a season.

Rocky Bridges

Bridges made the American League All-Star team as a member of the Senators in 1958. He had little power, hitting 16 career home runs and driving in 187 in parts of 11 major league seasons. He struck out more than he walked and was caught stealing more often than not.

Eddie Kazak

Kazak's short career reached its apex in the summer of 1949, when he was the starting third baseman for the NL All-Star team. He had a solid season in 1949, but in his entire career had only 165 hits. Speed was not his game either, as he was never credited with a single stolen base. Kazak's career was that of a part-time player, evidenced by the fact that he had only two seasons with more than 33 at-bats.

Richie Scheinblum

1972 was a good year for Scheinblum, who was rewarded with an All-Star selection that summer. Other years were not as productive. Scheinblum recorded single-season batting averages of .218 (1968), .186 (1969), .143 (1971), and .183 (1974). He homered only 13 times and drove in only 127 runs during his entire career. He was never successful in attempting to steal a base, a feat he attempted to accomplish on only six occasions.

Dave Engle

The Twins had to have an All-Star representative in 1984, and Engle was the man. He was a part-time outfielder/catcher who also played designated hitter. He was below average defensively, and although he had some power, he played so infrequently that he hit only 31 career home runs. Engle was part of a trade for Rod Carew while in the minors.

Oris Hockett

Hockett homered every 166 at-bats or so, not exactly Ruthian numbers. His career on-base percentage was .329 even though he played most of his career during World War II, against somewhat lesser competition.

Don Leppert

Ken Retzer caught more games for the Senators in 1963 than Leppert, yet Leppert made the AL All-Star team. In other words, he wasn't even the starting catcher on his own team. Leppert's lifetime batting average was .229 and lifetime on-base average was .289. He clobbered 15 major-league home runs, drove in 59 runs, and scored 46 times. He never played in more than 73 games during any major league season.

THE ROTATION

ALL STARS ROTATION	
JERRY WALKER	RHP
ATLEE HAMMAKER	LHP
JACK ARMSTRONG	RHP
HAL GREGG	RHP
WAYNE SIMPSON	RHP

Jerry Walker

Walker finished his career with a record of 37-44 and a 4.36 ERA, playing for the Orioles before they hit their stride in the 1960s. He never finished a season more than one game over .500 as a pitcher, and he accomplished that feat only twice.

Atlee Hammaker

Hammaker, truth be told, was not a bad pitcher. The 1983 All-Star game may have been the worst thing that ever happened to him. He gave up six hits and seven runs in the midsummer classic, retiring only two batters and giving up a home run to Jim Rice and the first All-Star grand slam ever to Fred Lynn. After leading the National League in ERA in 1983, his career was never the same.

Jack Armstrong

As a Red in 1990, Armstrong started the season 11-3 with a 2.28 ERA and was rewarded with a starting assignment in the All-Star game as the NL's hurler. The rest of the season, Armstrong was 1-6 with a 5.96 ERA. 1990 proved to be Armstrong's only winning season in the major leagues. He finished his career having only one full-season ERA under 4.49. In spite of his early success for the Reds in 1990, he did not pitch in the NLCS and logged only three innings in the World Series.

Hal Gregg

An All-Star in 1945, Gregg won 18 games that season. He won only 22 in every other season of his career combined. His lifetime ERA was 4.54. Gregg was not a control freak. He walked more batters during the course of his career than he struck out, and led NL pitchers in walks in 1944 and in 1945, his All-Star season. In 1944, he also led the league in earned runs allowed, wild pitches, and hit batsmen.

Wayne Simpson

Largely due to arm trouble, Simpson was 14-3 with an ERA of 3.02 in 1970, and achieved much of that success in the first half of his rookie season, resulting in his only All-Star selection. The rest of his career was not as impressive. He was 22-28 with a 4.89 ERA between 1971 and 1977.

THE BENCH

```
┌─────────────────────────────────────┐
│       NO STARS BENCH                 │
│                                      │
│  MIKE HEGAN . . . . . . . . 1B       │
│  RAY MACK . . . . . . . . . . 2B     │
│  EDDIE KASKO . . . . . . . . SS      │
│  FRANKIE ZAK . . . . . . . . SS      │
│  BILLY HUNTER . . . . . . . . SS     │
│  BILLY GRABARKEWITZ  3B              │
│  JIM FINIGAN . . . . . . . . . 3B    │
│  MORRIE ARNOVICH . . . OF            │
│  LEE WALLS . . . . . . . . . . OF    │
│  GINO CIMOLI . . . . . . . . OF      │
│  STEVE SWISHER . . . . . . . . C     │
│  JERRY MOSES . . . . . . . . . C     │
└─────────────────────────────────────┘
```

Ray Mack

With the exception of the 1940 season, his All-Star campaign, Mack never hit higher than .232 in a season in which he had substantial playing time. His career on-base average was only .301, but he was a solid defensive player.

Eddie Kasko

Kasko did not get on base often (career on-base average of .317) and was caught stealing as often as he was successful. He averaged a bit more than two home runs per season.

Frankie Zak

This 1944 NL All-Star never hit a home run and drove in a mere 14 runs during a career which spanned only three seasons and 208 at-bats.

Billy Hunter

Hunter finished his career with the following percentages: batting average .219, on base average .264, slugging .294.

Billy Grabarkewitz

During a career hampered by injuries, Grabarkewitz had a fine season in 1970. A comparison of that season to the rest of his career is mind-boggling. He hit 17 home runs in 1970, but only 11 the rest of his career. He drove in 84 runs in 1970, but only 57 during all his other seasons combined. He stole 33 bases in his career, 57% (19) of those in 1970. He never hit higher than .226 in any single season the rest of his career, and 153 of his lifetime 274 hits came during his All-Star summer of 1970.

Jim Finigan

Finigan was an All-Star his first two seasons. In a six-year career he hit only 19 home runs and drove in 168 runs. Only three of those home runs and 49 RBI came after his second major league season.

Morrie Arnovich

Ten of Arnovich's 22 career homers came in 1937. He was an All-Star, however, in 1939, when he hit .324, by far the highest average of his career.

Lee Walls

Walls struck out almost twice as often as he walked during his career. With the exception of the 1958 season, he never generated more than 11 home runs or 54 RBI. His All-Star season of 1958 was excellent.

Gino Cimoli

Cimoli never reached .300 or hit more than 10 home runs in any single season. He struck out more than twice as often as he walked.

Mike Hegan

The son of catcher Jim Hegan, Mike was a good-fielding first baseman with a .242 lifetime average. He led the Pilots in 1969 with a .292 mark, and represented the team at the All-Star Game. Mike drove in more than 50 runs only once, and stroked 53 home runs in 12 big-league seasons.

Steve Swisher

Like Cimoli, Swisher struck out more than twice as often as he walked. He was a career .216 hitter with an on-base average of only .279. A former first-round draft pick, he had season batting averages of .214, .213, .236, .190, .151, .143, and .172. He was selected as an All-Star in 1976, ahead of such players as Ted Simmons and Manny Sanguillen.

Jerry Moses

Moses was a career .251 hitter with an on-base average under .300. He had only one season with more than 200 at-bats, his All-Star campaign of 1970. He scored a total of 89 runs in his entire major league career, which spanned almost a decade. He struck out nearly three times as often as he walked.

THE BULLPEN

NO STARS BULLPEN	
MATT KEOUGH	RHP
DAVE STENHOUSE	RHP
TYLER GREEN	RHP
JASON DICKSON	RHP
ED FARMER	RHP
JOHN O'DONOGHUE	LHP
DEAN STONE	LHP

Matt Keough

Although Keough posted a 3.24 ERA in his All-Star season of 1978, he finished the year with a record of 8-15. That season marked one of four campaigns in which he lost at least 13 games. He won that many only once. He finished three different seasons with an ERA over 5.00, and in 1982 he walked 26 more batters than he struck out, and led the league in home runs allowed, earned runs allowed, and losses.

Dave Stenhouse

Stenhouse started one of the two major league All-Star games played in 1962. He won 10 games by the All-Star break during that, his rookie, season. He won six the rest of his career. (He was 10-4 by the All-Star break and 6-24 from that point until the end of his career in 1964.) He never had a winning season.

Tyler Green

Green's career record was 18-25 and he finished with a 5.16 ERA. Although he was an All-Star in 1995, his lowest single-season ERA came in 1997, when he posted a 4.93 earned run average.

Jason Dickson

Dickson suffered from arm injuries during his short career. He posted an ERA above 6.00 in both 1998 and 2000, and finished his career with a record of 26-25 with a 4.99 ERA.

Ed Farmer

The well-traveled Farmer achieved his most success with the White Sox, for which he saved 30 games in 1980. He finished seven of his 11 seasons, however, with an ERA over 4.00, and had a career ERA of 4.28. He won 30 games and suffered 43 defeats during his nomadic tenure in the big leagues.

John O'Donoghue

Oddly, O'Donoghue led the American League in losses during his All-Star season of 1965. His only winning season was 1970, when he was an unspectacular 4-3 and posted a 5.12 ERA. His career record was 39-55.

Dean Stone

Stone won more than six games only once and finished only one season with an ERA under 4.00. Lifetime, Stone was 29-39 with an ERA of 4.47.

The No Stars feature speed and power throughout the batting order. Phillips is the likely leadoff hitter followed by Maddox. The best hitter of the bunch, Trosky, hits in the third spot, although he could bat cleanup as well. McReynolds, Gibson, and Boyer bat fourth through sixth, with Held and Dempsey hitting before the pitcher. If a designated hitter were allowed, a manager would love to have the ability to insert Bostock, Hebner, Murphy, Driessen, Doran, etc. The bench is deep and has speed, power, and defensive prowess. Their All-Star counterparts cannot field a starting lineup that competes with the bench of the No Stars.

Likewise, the No Stars have eight or nine starting pitchers who are arguably superior to anyone the All-Stars can send to the mound. The No Stars bullpen has three legitimate closers to finish games.

For the most part, the All-Stars roster consists of players who had a good half season. If these rosters were pitted against one another, all players in their prime, for a mythical 162-game season, the All-Stars would have difficulty winning 40 games against the opposing team, devoid of a single All-Star.

Jackie Robinson in Film

His Significance in *Do the Right Thing* and *Bringing Down the House*

by Frank Ardolino

Perhaps the most revered number and jersey in baseball history belongs to Jackie Robinson, who wore number 42 throughout his 10-year career with the Dodgers.

As John Odell has said, "Robinson wore number 42 throughout his major league career; for baseball fans and American historians, the number . . . is . . . associated with no other player, and likely never will be."[1] On April 15, 1997, the 50th anniversary of Jackie's debut, his number was permanently retired, with only Yankee pitcher Mariano Rivera allowed to continue to wear it. Odell concludes, "Robinson's jersey certainly signifies his tremendous playing career. Ultimately, however, what no jersey can ever show are the marks of insults and slurs hurled at Robinson while playing, the injustices he endured on and off the field, and the character he showed throughout his life. It remains our responsibility to collect artifacts like this jersey to pass on larger stories to succeeding generations."[2] Odell is correct that although the jersey can not convey literally the hostility Robinson overcame in his pioneering debut in 1947 and career, it can represent figuratively his story and subsequent mystique. The two films to be discussed use Robinson's number and jersey to memorialize the baseball star and civil rights pioneer as a cultural artifact, a repository of meanings which can continue to represent and address social, personal, and racial problems.[3]

Spike Lee's *Do the Right Thing* (1989) concerns the riot that occurs in a Bedford-Stuyvesant neighborhood when police choke a young black man to death. Lee plays the central character Mookie, the pizza delivery boy, who wears a Robinson jersey for much of the movie until he discards it when the riot

occurs. Lee also includes a number of other athletic jerseys, posters, and pictures to signal the power of iconic images to help form ethnic cultural identity.[4] Clifton, the white yuppie who owns a brownstone in the neighborhood, wears a Larry Bird jersey; a black youth wears a Magic Johnson jersey; Mookie appears at the beginning of the movie wearing a Jordan jersey; a huge sign advertising Mike Tyson as Brooklyn's favorite is prominently posted on the side of a building; and, finally, a photo of the Marciano-Walcott fight is shown burning on the "wall of fame" in Sal's pizzeria during the riot. Mitchell has observed that these signs "are commercial objects *and* vehicles for the propagation of public statements about personal identity."[5] It is the Robinson jersey that creates the most important public image for the film's themes and motifs of personal identity and racial conflict.

Lee has indicated why he had Mookie wear Jackie's Dodger jersey with the number 42 on the front and back: "The jersey was a good choice. I don't think Jackie Robinson has gotten his due from Black people. There are young people today, even Black athletes, who don't know what Jackie Robinson did. They might know he was the first Black major leaguer, but they don't know what he had to bear to make it easier for those who came after him."[6] But Mookie, the mercurial messenger, is not heroic in any sense like Robinson. He is a man stuck uneasily in the middle, a bridge between Sal's Famous Pizzeria and the black community. As Nelson observes, "The Jackie Robinson jersey that Mookie wears does not suggest that he's a racial pioneer but that he's a man watched closely by interested parties on both sides of the racial divide. Both sides think that he's loyal to them—that's how he survives."[7] Moreover, McKelly has argued cogently that the film is based on conflicting ideas instilled in Mookie by different

FRANK ARDOLINO *is a professor of English at the University of Hawaii at Manoa, where he teaches Shakespeare and modern drama. He is currently working on* Reversing the Curse in Literature and Film.

characters and cultural forces: "Mookie . . . becomes . . . an entire 'sociology of consciousness,' a cacophony of autonomous, irreconcilable significations in conflict, each reflecting the persistence of 'double consciousness': Sal/Buggin Out, Pino/Vito, Da Mayor/ Mother Sister, Jade/Tina, 'whiteness'/'blackness', 'King'/'X,' cool/heat, 'LOVE /'HATE,' 'right thing'/ wrong thing."[8] The most important of these binaries are the black/white and love/hate dichotomies, which are represented respectively by the Robinson jersey and the picture of Malcolm X and Martin Luther King, which Smiley sells and illustrates by the words *love* and *hate* inscribed on his knuckle rings.

The movie consists of a series of attempted integrations resulting in racial conflicts. Buggin' Out, the neighborhood radical, is upset at Mookie being friendly with Sal's son Vito, but Mookie tells him to shut up. "Vito is down." Clifton spills juice on Buggin' Out's new Air Jordan shoes, and when some angry neighborhood people tell him to move to Massachusetts, he says, "I was born in Brooklyn." Pino, Sal's racist son, declares that his favorite great black athletes and entertainers transcend their color. When Mookie retorts that Pino harbors a secret desire to be black, he is incensed. Then in separate scenes, Pino and Mookie exchange choice ethnic insults in rapid fashion. Pino wants whites and blacks to be segregated in their own neighborhoods and tells his brother that blacks can not be trusted. Mookie, in turn, tells Vito to disavow his brother's racism.

The precipitating factor in the ensuing disturbance occurs when Buggin' Out, the neighborhood radical, wants to integrate Sal's wall of fame, which sounds like the Hall of Fame, by including pictures of black stars, not just Italian Americans. Sal menaces him with a baseball bat and declares that since it's his pizzeria he can put on the wall the heroes he chooses. The wall of fame is important to Sal because he owns the store and wants a public declaration of the fame of certain Italian Americans as proof that Italians have entered American life. However, the wall is also important for Buggin' Out because it graphically represents the exclusion of blacks from American society.[9] Integrating the wall would not solve the major problems of the neighborhood, but it would be a token of public acceptance by its major white business establishment: "Spike Lee's film articulates the desperation of a minority . . . calling on the majority to open the doors to the public sphere promised by its official rhetoric."[10]

Sal's policy parallels the lack of integration in baseball, which claimed to be the national pastime but excluded black players until Robinson played for the Dodgers in 1947. He refuses to integrate the wall with African American heroes despite the fact that the Bedford-Stuyvesant community is the source of his business. For Sal, Mookie represents the unity and progress which he thinks his family pizzeria has fostered in the neighborhood. But he will not expand this recognition to the community at large by allowing black heroes on the wall of fame.[11]

After Buggin' Out organizes a boycott of the pizzeria, Mookie discards the Robinson jersey and wears a Sal's Famous Pizzeria jersey in the Italian national colors of red, white, and green. When he wore this shirt earlier, it signified, like the Robinson jersey, that Mookie was the link between the pizzeria and his community. However, Sal's livery now represents the servile position he will rebel against. The riot begins with Sal crushing Raheem's boom box with a baseball bat and exchanging racial epithets with Buggin' Out. When the police choke Radio, his knuckles show the words *love* and *hate*. After he dies, Mookie smashes the garbage can through the window, and the crowd sets fire to the pizzeria. As it burns, Smiley finally integrates the wall by posting a photo of Malcolm X and King on it.

The movie ends with two quotations, one on nonviolence from King and the other on the necessity for taking action against violence (self-defense) by Malcolm. In his final statement on the movie's ending, Lee seems to declare his allegiance to Malcom X: "Both men died for the love of their people, but had different strategies for realizing freedom . . . [and] justice. . . . The way of King, or the way of Malcolm. . . . I know who I am down with."[12] Similarly, by his participation in the riot, Mookie seems to have disavowed King's as well as Robinson's policies of non-violence and integration, but within the complex and ambiguous context of Mookie's behavior, Lee has both revered and dismissed Robinson's nonviolent legacy as a viable policy for black advancement.

Bringing Down the House (2003) stars Steve Martin as a yuppie lawyer who learns to incorporate elements of stereotypical ghetto language and behavior to win a case for a black woman who has been framed by her boyfriend.[13] The plot is in some sense a comic take on the motifs of black/white integration in *Do the Right Thing*. Like Mookie, Peter Sanderson wears Robinson's number 42 as the representation of his ability to go between the two communities. But in the comedy, the wearing of Robinson's number results in a successful integration.

The movie begins with the Internet blind dating communication between divorced tax lawyer Peter Sanderson and Charlene, who represents herself as "lawyer girl," but actually is a black woman charged with an armed robbery she claims she didn't commit. When they meet, he doesn't understand her ghetto language and gets rid of her quickly. But when he is at work, she throws a party in his house for a black charity and infuriates him and his all-white neighborhood. She also infiltrates his country club in full ghetto power dress and beats up Ashley, his ex-wife's sister, who insists on treating her as a waitress. Charlene reveals that she is "bilingual" in white and black language and culture. She keeps showing up in Peter's white sanctuaries and manages to defeat any attempts to eject her. She teaches Peter to be less uptight, to dance instinctively, and to be more aggressively romantic by using black "styling."

Widow, Charlene's tough ex-boyfriend who framed her, hangs out at the Down Low, a club where a white man can't go. But to prove Charlene's innocence, Peter buys a rapper outfit from two home boys, replete with stocking cap, chains, Air Jordans, and a sweatshirt with 42 stitched on the back. He explodes on the scene uttering rapper lingo and shaking his booty on the dance floor, with 42 visible throughout his maneuvers. Peter offers to launder Widow's money and records proof that Charlene was framed. During the ensuing struggle, Charlene is shot by Widow, but is saved when the bullet hits Peter's cell phone, which she had been carrying. At the end, he returns to his wife and quits the firm to go off on his own, declaring to his boss, "Kiss my natural black ass." Charlene says, "You ain't black," to which he responds, " Well, I'm off white."

Peter has learned to function in two worlds as the result of his contact with Charlene. When he dons the ghetto outfit with 42 on the back, he becomes a latter-day comic white parallel to Robinson's integration of the formerly segregated major leagues. Similarly, Charlene has taken on white characteristics, as represented by his protective cell phone, which she had earlier denounced as a symbol of his uptight white lawyer's world. Together, they have brought down the house, destroying Widow's place and earning our applause. Unlike *Do the Right Thing*, *Bringing Down the House* has used Robinson's mystique as the means of representing a successful reduction of racial conflicts.

Notes

1. John Odell. "On the Road with *Baseball as America.*" *Memories and Dreams*, 26, 2004:31.
2. Odell, 31.
3. Jackie Robinson has been the subject of four movies: *The Jackie Robinson Story* (1950), *A Homerun for Love* (1978), *Court-Martial of Jackie Robinson* (1990), and *Soul of the Game* (1996). In addition, *Rhubarb* (1951), which ostensibly concerns a cat's inheritance of a baseball team, is actually about Robinson's integration of baseball. See my articles, "Breaking the Color Line: Five Film Representations of Jackie Robinson 1950-1992," *Aethlon* 13.2, 1996, 49-60; "Tearing Up the Pea Patch at Ebbets Field: Rickey, Robinson, and Rhubarb," *Aethlon*, 1992, 133-43.
4. Douglas Kellner. "Aesthetics, Ethics, and Politics in the Films of Spike Lee," Spike Lee's *Do the Right Thing*. Mark A. Reid, ed. (Cambridge: Cambridge University Press, 1997), 80.
5. W.J.T. Mitchell, "The Violence of Public Art," Spike Lee's *Do the Right Thing*, 124.
6. Spike Lee with Lisa Jones. *Do the Right Thing: A Spike Lee Joint* (New York: Simon & Schuster, 1989), 110.
7. George Nelson, "Do the Right Thing." *Five for Five: The Films of Spike Lee*," Terry McMillan, ed. (New York: Stewart, Tabori & Chang, 1991), 80.
8. James McKelly. "The Double Truth: *Do the Right Thing* and the Culture of Ambiguity," *African American Review* 32, 1998, 223-24.
9. Mitchell, 110-12.
10. Mitchell, 123.
11. McKelly, 221-22.
12. Lee, 282.
13. *Bringing Down the House*. Adam Shankman, director; 2003.

The Joy of Foul Balls
The Inside Story of Baseball's Holy Grail

by Tim Wiles

"Even at my age, I'd still like to catch a foul ball, if only to give it to Miguel," said a random fan one day as I was walking into Yankee Stadium. The sentiment is universal; every true baseball fan daydreams about the ball they will one day catch, perfecting the link between that fan and the game that he or she loves. The foul ball is our connection to the players on the field, and it is a thrill unique to baseball. Having a basketball land in one's lap is not only extremely rare, but somehow not as exciting as catching a baseball. Plus, you would probably have to return it.

The foul ball is baseball's trickster, leaving the perfect geometry and symmetry of the baseball field and taking off into the great masses of fans, where it can bring joy or wreak havoc, often on the same play. The foul ball truly makes the fans part of the game, if only for a brief moment.

While the vast majority of fouls bring a thrill for one or two folks who may touch them fleetingly before they career off into another pair of waiting hands, some foul balls leave a mark of humor or coincidence that gets written into the annals of baseball forever.

Consider the case of Norm Zauchin, a first baseman for the Red Sox and the Senators in the 1950s. One hot summer afternoon in 1950, the year before he made the show, Zauchin went tearing toward the stands in pursuit of a foul pop-up. Diving over the front railing, he snared the foul backhanded and tumbled into the stands. When he got his bearings, he found he'd fallen head over heels into the lap of pretty young Janet Mooney, attending the game with her parents. "Hi" was all he could manage to say, but that led to a dinner invitation from the family after

the game, and the following season, after he'd gotten the call from the Red Sox, Norm and Janet were married. Talk about a great catch.

Not all foul balls are so romantic. Some are just plain crazy. On August 11, 1903, the A's were visiting the Red Sox, then playing in the old Huntington Avenue Grounds. At the plate in the seventh inning was Rube Waddell, the colorful southpaw pitcher for the A's, who was known to run off the mound to chase after passing fire trucks, and to be mesmerized whenever an opposing team brought a puppy onto their bench to distract him. Waddell lifted a foul ball over the right field bleachers that landed on the roof of a baked bean cannery next door.

The ball came to rest in the steam whistle of the factory, which began to go off. As it was not quitting time, workers thought there was an emergency and abandoned their posts. A short while later, a giant caldron containing a ton of beans boiled over and exploded, showering the Boston ballpark with scalding beans. It is probably safe to say that this was the most dramatic foul of all time.

Still, a foul ball hit by the aptly named George Burns of the Tigers in 1915 is worth mentioning in the same breath. His "scorching" foul liner struck an unlucky fan in the area of his chest pocket, where he was carrying a box of matches. The ball ignited the matches, and a soda vendor had to come to the rescue, dousing the flaming fan with bubbly to put out the fire.

One of baseball's most ironic foul ball incidents happened on Mother's Day, 1939, when Lena Feller traveled from Iowa to see her son Bob pitch against the White Sox in Comiskey Park. In the third inning, Feller delivered a pitch which Marv Owen fouled into the stands, striking Mrs. Feller above her right eye and breaking her glasses. Young Bob ran into the stands to assist his mom, but watched helplessly as

TIM WILES *has been director of research at the National Baseball Hall of Fame Library since 1995. He is co-editor of* Line Drives: 100 Comtemporary Baseball Poems (*Southern Illinois University Press, 2002*).

Richie Ashburn

she was led off to the hospital, where stitches were required. "There wasn't anything I could do," Feller said, "so I went on pitching." The incident shook him up, but after settling down, he won the game en route to leading the league with 24 victories that season.

Richie Ashburn figures in many of the best foul ball stories in baseball lore. A contact hitter, Ashburn had the ability to foul off many consecutive pitches till he found one he liked. On one occasion, he fouled off fourteen consecutive pitches against Corky Valentine of the Reds. Another time, he victimized Sal "The Barber" Maglie for "18 or 19" fouls in one at-bat. "After a while," said Ashburn, "he just started laughing. That was the only time I ever saw Maglie laugh on a baseball field." Ashburn's bat control was such that one day he asked teammates to pinpoint a particularly offensive heckler seated five or six rows back. The next time up, Ashburn nailed the fan in the chest.

On another occasion, Ashburn unintentionally injured a female fan who was the wife of a Philadelphia newspaper sports editor. Play stopped as she was given medical aid. Action resumed as the stretcher wheeled her down the main concourse, and, unbelievably, Ashburn's next foul hit her again. Thankfully, she escaped with minor injuries.

Another notable foul ball hitter was Luke Appling, the Hall of Fame shortstop with a career batting average of .310. As the story goes, Appling once asked White Sox management for a couple of dozen baseballs, so he could autograph them and donate them to charity. Management balked, citing a cost of several dollars per baseball. Appling bought the balls from his team, then went out that day and fouled off a couple dozen balls, after which he tipped his hat toward the owner's box. He never had to pay for charity balls again, the legend goes.

Another great foul ball story involves Pepper Martin and Joe Medwick of the St. Louis Cardinals famous Gas House Gang teams of the mid 1930s. With Martin at bat, Medwick took off from first base, intending to take third on the hit-and-run. Martin fouled the ball into the stands, and Reds catcher Gilly Campbell reflexively reached back to home plate umpire Ziggy Sears for a new ball. Then, just for fun, Campbell launched the ball down to third, where Sears, forgetting that a foul had just been hit *and* that he had given Campbell a new ball, called Medwick out. The Cardinals were furious, but, not wanting to admit his error, Sears refused to reverse his call, and Medwick was thrown out—on a foul ball!

The great Cal Ripken Jr. made life imitate art with

a foul ball in 1998. In the movie *The Natural*, Roy Hobbs lofts a foul ball at sportswriter Max Mercy, as Mercy sits in the stands drawing a critical cartoon of the slumping Hobbs. *Baltimore Sun* columnist Ken Rosenthal faced a similar wrath of the baseball gods after he wrote a column in 1998 suggesting that it might be time for Ripken to voluntarily end his streak—at that point several hundred games beyond Lou Gehrig's old record—for the good of the team. Ripken responded by hitting a foul ball into the press box which smashed Rosenthal's laptop computer, ending its career. When told of his foul ball's trajectory, Ripken responded with one word: "Sweet."

Another sweet story involves a father and son combination. In 1999, Bill Donovan was watching his son Todd play center field for the Idaho Falls Braves of the Pioneer League. Todd made a nice diving catch and threw the ball back into the second baseman, who returned it to the pitcher. On the next pitch, a foul ball sailed into the outstretched hands of the elder Donovan. "I was like a kid when I caught it," said the proud papa. "It made me wonder when was the last time that a father and son caught the same ball on consecutive pitches."

Had he made his catch a few generations earlier, Mr. Donovan might not have been allowed to keep his treasured souvenir. In the game's early years, balls were comparatively very expensive, and fans were encouraged, even occasionally forced, to throw them back. In 1901, in fact, the National League rules committee suggested disciplining batsmen who fouled off good pitches, as a way of cutting costs. In 1904, a rule change allowed the teams to post special employees in the stands to retrieve the fouls caught by the fans.

However, fans already had a sense of magic and luck concerning fouls, and they wanted to keep them. They would often hide them from the "goons" sent to retrieve them, or engage in games of keep-away from the same hapless employees.

A solitary voice among the owners, however, was Charles Weeghman of the Chicago Cubs, who saw the public relations value in a free, but rare, souvenir. In 1916, Weeghman went against the grain and announced that Cub fans would be allowed to keep foul balls. He was immediately supported in an editorial in the influential *Baseball Magazine*, which said, "The love of souvenirs is firmly implanted in the blood," and also chastised the other owners by saying "it isn't always good business to be penny wise." The other owners failed to follow suit immediately, however.

About the same time, a 1915 article in *The Sporting Life*, a major baseball newspaper of the day, complained of the excessive cost of foul balls, saying, ". . . some fans are indignant and abusive when special police make attempts to recover balls hit into the crowd. The practice of concealing balls fouled into grandstand or bleachers has reached disgusting proportions in New York, where it is far more common than anywhere else."

There was a short truce in this developing war between the fans and the owners over fouls in the late teens, as both sides agreed to donate all fouls hit into the stands to servicemen, who would need the balls for on-base recreation during World War One. After the war ended, though, the foul ball dispute was rekindled.

One day in 1921, New York Giants fan Reuben Berman had the good fortune to catch a foul ball, or so he thought. When the ushers arrived moments later to retrieve the ball, Reuben refused to give it up, instead tossing it several rows back to another group of fans. The angered usher removed Berman from his seat, took him to the Giants offices, and verbally chastised him, before depositing him in the street outside the Polo Grounds.

An angry and humiliated Berman sued the Giants for mental and physical distress and won, leading the Giants, and eventually other teams, to change their policy of demanding foul balls be returned. The decision has come to be known as "Reuben's Rule."

While Berman's case was influential, the influence had not spread as far as Philadelphia by 1922, when 11-year-old fan Robert Cotter was nabbed by security guards after refusing to return a foul ball at a Phillies game. The guards turned him over to police, who put the little tyke in jail overnight. When he faced a judge the next day, young Cotter was granted his freedom, the judge ruling, "Such an act on the part of a boy is merely proof that he is following his most natural impulses. It is a thing I would do myself."

The tide eventually changed for good, and the practice of fans keeping foul balls became entrenched. World War II was another time when patriotic fans and owners worked together to funnel the fouls off to servicemen. A ball in the Hall of Fame's collection is even stamped "From a Polo Grounds Baseball Fan," one of the more than 80,000 pieces of baseball equipment donated to the war effort by baseball by June 1942.

One of those baseballs may well have been involved in one of the strangest of all foul ball stories. In a military communiqué datelined "somewhere in the South Pacific," the story is told of a foul ball hit by Marine Private First Class George Benson Jr. which eventually traveled 15 miles. Benson's batting practice foul looped up about 40 feet in the air, where it smashed through the windshield of a landing plane. The ball hit the pilot in the face, fracturing his jaw and knocking him unconscious.

A passenger, Marine Corporal Robert J. Holm, muttering a prayer, pulled back on the throttle and prevented the plane from crashing, though he had never flown before. The pilot recovered momentarily, and brought the plane to a landing at the next airstrip, 15 miles away.

In 1996, at the age of 71, former President Jimmy Carter made a barehanded catch of a foul ball hit by San Diego's Ken Caminiti, while attending a Braves game. "He showed good hands," said Braves catcher Javy Lopez.

With foul balls by this time an undeniable right for fans at the ballpark, what are your actual chances of catching a foul ball at a game? Well, to start with, the average baseball is in play for six pitches these days, which makes it sound as though there will be many chances to catch a foul ball in each game. While comprehensive statistics are not available, various newspapers have sponsored studies which, uncannily, seem quite often to come down to 22 or 23 fouls into the stands per game.

That seems like a healthy number until you look at average major league attendance at games. In the year 2000, the average game was attended by 29,938 fans. With 23 fouls per game, that works out to a 1 in 1,302 chance of catching a foul ball. With numbers like that, no wonder it feels so special to catch a foul ball.

Nevertheless, those who yearn to catch a foul ball *can* improve their chances. I have listed some tips to help you bring home that elusive foul ball. Good luck!

TIPS FOR CATCHING FOUL BALLS

1. Wear a glove. Catching balls is a lot easier—and far less painful—with a glove.

2. Watch for ricochets—most fouls are caught after their initial impact.

3. However, don't try to play them on the bounce. A ballpark is not a baseball field, and there is a great chance a bouncing ball will career off at a crazy angle. If you have a chance to catch it on the fly, do so.

4. Sit in the lower decks, along the baselines. In the upper deck, try to sit in the front row. As they say in the real estate business, there are three important things, location, location, and location.

5. Arrive early for batting practice. This more than doubles your chances.

6. Pay attention. Fastball pitchers generate more fouls than finesse guys. Two-strike counts produce more fouls as hitters swing more often to protect the plate.

7. Remember that lefties are likely to hit more fouls down the third base line, and righties more likely to hit fouls toward first. As there are more righties than lefties, consider sitting on the first base line more valuable than the third base line.

8. Don't eat or drink during game action. You could be caught flat-footed.

9. Sit on an aisle when possible. You'll have far more room in which to operate.

Reuben Berman's Foul Ball

by David Mandell

You may be trampled and bruised, but if you catch a foul ball at a major league baseball game, it's yours. Thanks to the actions of a 31-year-old stockbroker, Reuben Berman, baseball fans can now keep foul balls, which have become the game's ultimate souvenir.

The story begins on May 16, 1921, in New York's Polo Grounds. Berman, a Hartford, Connecticut, native living in New York City, went to watch his favorite team, the New York Giants, battle the Cincinnati Reds. The Giants were managed by Hall of Famer John McGraw, and its lineup included two more Hall of Famers, first baseman George "Highpockets" Kelly and second baseman Frankie Frisch, the Fordham Flash. 1921 was an eventful year for the Giants. On February 15, team president Charles A. Stoneham arrived in New York from Cuba, where he and manager John McGraw owned a stable of racehorses. Stoneham was so confident of his team's chances that he printed programs of an all-Manhattan world series featuring the Giants and the Yankees. An exhibition game against the Washington Senators on April 4 in Jackson, Tennessee, ended when the Senators refused to continue play as a protest against umpire Bill Brennan. On May 3, Stoneham had the Giants autograph baseballs to benefit the army hospital in New York.

Given the excitement of the new season, few fans paid attention to Giants' policy that fans must "conduct themselves in a gentlemanly and orderly manner and comply with all reasonable and proper requests, rules and regulations of the Giants." To Charles Stoneham, that meant foul balls hit into the stands belonged to the Giants, not to lucky spectators.

DAVID MANDELL *practices law in New London County, Connecticut and is a lifelong Giants fan. He has caught one foul ball, at a Yankees minor league game.*

In 1921 major league baseball teams maintained the right to set their own policies on foul balls, and most agreed with the Giants. Chicago Cubs spectators began keeping foul balls in 1916 after a brawl broke out between fans and security staff over a ball during a game with the St. Louis Cardinals. Owner Charles H. Weeghman, who had owned a team in the defunct Federal League, decided it was better business to let fans keep the balls. Charles Stoneham and the other owners did not share that sentiment.

During the game a foul ball sailed Berman's way and he caught it. Ushers spotted Berman and demanded that he give them the ball or toss it on the field for reuse. Berman refused. As the ushers approached him, Berman tossed the ball backward, where it disappeared into baseball lore. The Giants weren't amused. Security men took Berman to team offices, where he was interrogated and threatened with arrest. After his questioning Berman was expelled from the ballpark, although his ticket price was refunded.

Giants management thought they had proven their point. Fans would not dare try to keep foul balls again. They did not know Reuben Berman. His grandson, New York City teacher Steven Kronovet, recalls that his grandfather had an independent streak and a keen sense of humor. Berman wasn't going to tolerate being abused for keeping a foul ball. On August 11, 1921, his attorney, S. Michael Cohen, served Giants secretary Joseph D. O'Brien with legal papers. The next day Cohen filed them in New York's Supreme Court, its trial division despite its grandiose name, charging that the team, officially called the National Exhibition Company, had unlawfully detained, imprisoned, and threatened Berman. He sought $20,000 for humiliation, suffering mental and bodily distress, and loss of reputation. Court records don't reveal why, but team attorneys failed to respond properly. On December 11, 1922 Justice Edward Gavegan gave them 10 days to answer or face default. Their attorney, William Butler, did so, going to the heart of the dispute. He pointed to the ticket language stating that the team reserved the right to revoke the license granted by the ticket by refunding the purchase price. In his view, so long as the Giants refunded the price, they were free to treat fans any way they chose.

The Giants put a benevolent spin on the incident. Giants ushers had merely asked Berman to throw the ball to them and requested that he leave his box and appear at their offices. Following his interrogation, they again requested that he leave the premises. As a parting shot they charged that if Berman suffered any damages, it was due to his own fault, act, and misconduct. The case was tried and Berman was awarded $100 for his treatment at the Polo Grounds. Court records don't reveal details of the trial, but Berman told his grandson Steven Kronovet about collecting the $100. Although the monetary judgment was small, Reuben Berman had proven his point. The Giants soon changed their policy and the remaining holdouts followed.

Reuben Berman continued to follow baseball after the incident. Like many Americans he was hit hard by the stock market crash of 1929, but he went on to build the U.S. Ribbon Company and worked well into his final years. His sense of humor remained strong. In the early days of television Maxwell House advertised its coffee as good to the last drop. Berman called the station and asked, what's wrong with the last drop? With many New York baseball fans he lamented the move of the Giants and Dodgers to California in 1958. Reuben Berman died in 1975. Although he was never officially recognized by major league baseball, his gift to baseball fans endures. The National Baseball Hall of Fame maintains his court records and has contemplated an exhibit if space can be found. Perhaps the ultimate tribute to Reuben Berman came on May 28, 2003. The Milwaukee Brewers offered fans a foul ball night, guaranteeing all spectators a baseball used in the game. Baseball had come a long way from John McGraw's era.

Berman's tradition also runs in the family. One night at Boston's Fenway Park, Reuben Berman's great-grandson, a Yankees fan no less, caught a foul ball and kept it.

JACK "OF ALL TRADES" ROTHROCK: Best remembered for playing all nine field positions in one season are Bert Campaneris and Cesar Tovar, who each performed this feat in a single game, Campaneris in 1965 and Tovar in 1968. Before them there was Jack Rothrock, who played all nine positions for the Boston Red Sox during the 1928 season. He not only played all nine field positions at some point during the season, but also pinch-hit and pinch-ran several times. Rothrock was a true jack-of-all-trades on the ball field for the last-place Red Sox in 1928. Rothrock played complete games at six of the nine positions—first base, shortstop, third base, left field, center field, and right field—at least six times each in 1928. He subbed at second base twice, on July 7 and August 4. Late in the season, after the Red Sox had clinched last place with a loss to Detroit on September 23, Rothrock pitched one inning on September 24 and then caught one inning on September 29, the next-to-last game of the season, to complete the nine-positions-in-one-season achievement. He was no slouch on the mound. Moving from the shortstop position, Rothrock pitched in a mop-up role in the eighth inning of an 8–0 Detroit shutout of the Red Sox, yielding no hits and no runs. Behind the plate in a game at Cleveland, Rothrock committed no errors before moving to left field to replace a pitcher playing that position, Danny MacFayden.　　　　　—CHARLIE BEVIS

Old Hoss
The Greatest of the 19th-Century Tobacco Hurlers

by Jim Foglio

Rarely can an athlete lay claim to having been both the most colorful and productive in a respective time period. Ali and Ruth were two colossal examples, but for the underrepresented enigma of nineteenth-century baseball, Charlie "Old Hoss" Radbourn provides a fascinating fusion of personality and achievement. In the days when mounds were only fifty feet away, the tang of whiskey on Radbourn's breath presented as much an inconvenience for rival batters as his rising underhand fastball.

Radbourn is widely recognized as the greatest of all 19th-century pitchers, as reads his plaque in Cooperstown, where he was inducted in 1939. His 1884 season alone was astonishing. That year Radbourn led Harry Wright's Providence Grays to the National League pennant and ultimately the first "World Series" championship over the American Association's New York Metropolitans in a three-game sweep, where he tossed three complete games, including a shutout. Radbourn led the league that season with 60 wins, a 1.38 ERA, 441 strikeouts, and 678 innings pitched.[1] At one point he pitched 30 of 32 games and 27 straight, winning 26.[2] His career totals include 308 wins, 1,767 strikeouts, and an incredible 473 complete games. In five years during his prime with Providence, Radbourn tallied 26 shutouts, 158 complete games, and more than a three-and-a-half to one strikeout/walk ratio.[3] Other career highlights include a no-hitter on July 25, 1883, against Cleveland and 51 complete games in 1882. Additionally, in 1881, his first full season with Providence, Radbourn shared mound duties with legendary John Montgomery Ward, replacing

JIM FOGLIO *is a freelance writer based in Wray, CO. He has a M.A. in Sport History and has most recently published articles in* Beckett's Monthly, Nevada Magazine, *and* American History. *He is currently working on a travel memoir.*

Ward as the club's ace the following year. While it is impractical to juxtapose Radbourn's statistics with contemporary numbers, he truly stands as the original iron man. Before Lou Gehrig, Cal Ripken Jr., and Brett Favre, "Old Hoss" set the standard for durability and consistency.

Part of Radbourn's success was due to his innovative delivery. In fact, the rules were changed after the 1884 season and pitchers were not allowed to jump toward the plate as they delivered the ball. While it cannot be verified officially, the timing of the rule change suggests that baseball brass had Radbourn's 1884 dominance in mind, much the same way NBA officials widened the key because of Wilt Chamberlain's ascendancy. After 1884, whether it was the stress on his arm or the rule changes, his stats declined. Providence folded in 1885, replaced by the Washington Senators, and in four seasons with Boston, he went 27-12, and including his swan song year with Cincinnati, Old Hoss finished 181 of his final 185 starts.

Radbourn was a pioneer of the curveball. According to former manager Ted Sullivan he had a "drop ball he did not have to spit on, a perplexing slow ball that was never duplicated . . . [and was] the master of curves and deliveries." Radbourn's curve has been compared to a French restaurant where the customer would order the same dish every day with a new name, but it was equally appealing.[4] One contemporary boasted there was "not a curve that he was not the master of, and to invent new deliveries was the constant occupation of his mind." Journalist Sam Crane noted the variety of curves as the primary reason for Radbourn's inclusion as number 16 on his 1912 list of the top 50 players in baseball history.

But it was not only Radbourn's hook and intimidating delivery that quieted opponent's bats; he could toss the heat with the best of them. According to one former teammate, "Rad had plenty of speed but never let it loose 'til it was absolutely necessary . . . that is why his arm lasted for so many years." At one point in a game against Cap Anson's Chicago club, Radbourn struck out Hall of Famer King Kelly, Ned Williamson, and George Gore in succession with the bases loaded. One former manager noted that Radbourn could deliver the ball with the "speed of a catapult."

Radbourn is often listed in box scores as a right fielder, and according to reports he certainly was a well-rounded player. But like most existing major league pitchers, his batting statistics declined when he started to pitch regularly. Sullivan wrote that Radbourn was a "natural ballplayer . . . and batter at all times." He also praised him in the clutch. "The closer the game," Sullivan noted, "the better he could hit." Radbourn was certainly a serviceable position player, with a .238 lifetime average, 585 hits, and 259 RBI. His best season at the plate was in 1883, the year prior to taking over the full-time pitching duties from Ward. Radbourn batted .283 with an OPB of .308, and racked up 17 extra-base hits along with 48 RBI. After 1883, his average season was only .220, while prior to concentrating primarily on pitching the number was nearly 30 points higher. In the Deadball Era, this was certainly sound production for a pitcher.

But the right field slot has modern significance. When Radbourn did not start on the mound, he was inserted into right field, like many of his contemporary hurlers. In 19th-century ball, non-injury substitutions were prohibited. The potential relief, or "exchange" pitcher, was almost always placed in right, hence the bad knock that right fielders have received all the way down to the little league game. Ironically, however, in today's game, left field is often the position where managers "hide" a player in order to get his bat into the lineup, and right field remains the spot for a power-hitting superstar. Still, allocating pitchers almost exclusively to right field surely had its origins in their arm strength, given the distance of the throws when compared to center and left. It is no coincidence that today's right fielders have the top arms; this is merely an extension of the 19th-century game.

One of Radbourn's accomplishments involved helping to bankrupt an entire league. According to accounts, in 1879 Sullivan tricked rival manager James McKee, who led a popular Rockford, Illinois, team, into thinking that Radbourn was no more than an average player. Sullivan managed a Dubuque, Iowa, club in a four-team league that included squads from Omaha, Nebraska, and Davenport, Iowa. The crafty manager had seen Radbourn play on a Peoria, Illinois, nine from an independent league the previous spring, and assured the other managers at the league meeting that Charles Comiskey had "hit him over the canvas" and another had blasted him "over a haystack." After the gathering, Sullivan admits the "train could not come fast enough" to Radbourn's home in Bloomington, Illinois, and he hired the pitcher on his front doorstep for a monthly salary of 75 dollars.[5] That season the Dubuque club blasted Rockford for six straight games, setting the tone with their fresh stud pitcher. According to Sullivan, "Radbourn won so many games that the league lost heart and busted in August."

But it was more than Radbourn's stellar play that fueled changes in the baseball landscape; it was actually his sharp tongue that might have indirectly landed him in Cooperstown. When teammate and fellow pitcher Charles Sweeney was banished from the team at a pivotal point in the 1884 season, Radbourn's antics were to blame. Sweeney had been tearing through opponents that year and had set the single-season strikeout record at 19. But the record lasted only a month before Hugh Daly, a one-armed hurler from Chicago, equaled the mark. One night a slurring Radbourn poked fun at the unpredictable Sweeney, who was nine years his junior, referring to the fact that a man with one arm had tied his record. The two nearly came to blows; in fact, Radbourn is said to have hurled a can of tobacco juice at Sweeney. Providence management initially sided with Sweeney, but after two consecutive errors in a game and consistently serving up lobs to opponents, manager Frank Bancroft yanked him and suspended the young gun without pay.[6] Sweeney signed with St. Louis of Henry Lucas' Union League in only mild controversy against the reserve clause, and despite Providence considering disbandment, they agreed to ride "Old Hoss" to the finish.

Providence went on to win it all, but more intriguingly still, management had assured Radbourn his release after the season if he "piled up a lot of wins." This curious move seems to have been the product of practical thinking on both sides. Radbourn had been offered more money from other clubs prior to the season, so after a productive stretch run, he knew he could command a raise. Management seems to have also foreshadowed the long-term strain on an overworked arm, and wanted to get what they could out of Radbourn and send him on his way. If they were lucky, they would get a pennant, which they did; either way Old Hoss would get paid. But in a legendary moment of victory euphoria, management presented him with two sheets of paper, his release and a blank contract. Radbourn stared at the ground, spit some tobacco in deliberation, then tore up the release, and gave himself a $2000 raise to remain in Rhode Island.[7] Without a dose of whiskey-infused sarcasm toward Sweeney, however, Radbourn would have never signed this contract, nor enjoyed his mythological 1884 campaign, which catapulted him into the Hall of Fame. In the end, while Old Hoss landed in Cooperstown, Sweeney, who eventually pitched St. Louis to a pennant, ended up in a California prison for murder.

═══

Radbourn was born on December 11, 1854, in Rochester, New York. His only education was in a grammar school just outside Bloomington, Illinois, where he moved with his parents as an infant. Like most early ballplayers, Radbourn sought refuge from working-class labor; his father, Charles, an English immigrant, was a butcher who required his son to work in the slaughterhouse. There is little mention of this relationship anywhere in the record, so it would be poor scholarship to speculate on how this might have impacted his baseball career. But by the time he was 24, Radbourn was barnstorming and had little contact with his family. He married Carrie Clark Stanhope in Chicago in 1887, adopting her son.[8] In 1891 Radbourn retired from baseball and spent most of his time at a pool hall and saloon that he opened in Bloomington four years prior. Radbourn's Place was advertised as having the "best of everything in wet goods and cigars." In 1894 he lost his right eye after an unlucky hunting accident on Friday the 13th. In his reduced state, Radbourn's proclivity for liquor and loose women increased, and ironically his cherished right arm became paralyzed from syphilis. He died from complications less than three years later, and was buried in Evergreen Memorial Cemetery in Bloomington.

Much of Radbourn's life outside baseball is pierced with enigma. An 1891 New York Times article identifies him with the Illinois regiment of the Civil War, and given his location during that time, this seems plausible. But Old Hoss is omitted from a plaque in Cooperstown that commemorates Hall of Famers who served in the U.S. Armed Forces. This could represent a glaring slight if the Times is accurate. There is also the question of whether or not his last name ends in an "e." One Bloomington city directory listed the correct spelling of his name to be Radbourn. His father also once spelled his name without an "e" on a hunting license. To add to the mystery, Old Hoss's last will and testament disappeared in 1988, initiating a police investigation. In the pre-eBay world, this signed document was still estimated to have been worth in excess of $8,000.

Chemical dependency seems to have contributed to an unpredictability and obstinacy that was at times severe; Radbourn would drink a quart of whiskey each day and constantly chew tobacco. After allegedly defeating his two brothers in a hunting contest, ties with them were severed for several years. Radbourn explained this conflict without emotion to friends as a "family weakness." One instance, after purchasing a pair of Canadian hunting dogs for $500, he immediately shot them when they failed to obey his initial commands. It was later found that the dogs were trained to respond only to French. In one comical flash in 1876, a few of his independent league teammates were suspected of fixing a game. Radbourn was exonerated of any guilt—well, at least culpability as related to gambling—and was charged with "being drunk." One might speculate whether or not Radbourn used his high as a cover in this instance, but there were never any other allegations against him, and all accounts praise his character and integrity. Still, when the bottle is involved, values are often compromised, so the possibility of his involvement needs to be at least considered.

At a stocky 5'9" and 165 lbs., Old Hoss represented endurance, resourcefulness, and loyalty. While some of his record outside baseball remains clouded with amber, his contribution to the game is less ambiguous. The original workhorse of pitchers, Radbourn set the standard for baseball's working-class commitment. His 1884 season is one of the most impressive feats in the history of sport, with a record 60 wins that will stand forever. He was an uncommon recipe of mental and physical prowess with a kicker, the propensity for revelry. Radbourn's plaque in Cooperstown appropriately flanks that of the morally principled Gehrig, with a hint of irony that must bring a smile beneath that tobacco-stained curved mustache.

Notes

1. Radbourn's 1884 strikeout and innings pitched totals were fourth and second highest of all-time, respectively.
2. During the 1884 stretch, Radbourn struggled to even roll out of bed. Reports indicate he could barely raise his arm to brush his mustache or hair. Each day he would arrive at the ballpark hours early, rub down his arm, and start tossing the ball underhand from only a few feet away, gradually extending the distance. When teammates realized that he could reach his partner, who was standing at home plate, all the way from center field, they breathed a sigh of relief and were confident they had a chance to win that day.
3. It is important to note that walks equaled six balls in Radbourn's playing days, but batters could also call for a pitch in their desired hitting zone.
4. Chances are, this French metaphor also had something to do with French food being "heavy," a word also often used to describe drop balls in baseball.
5. Radbourn negotiated this number up from an initial offer. This was the first of two instances in his career when Radbourn bargained himself a better salary, something not always common in an era where owners enjoyed much of the clout. Remember, the White Sox were referred to as the "Black Sox" because their owner, Comiskey, refused to clean their uniforms, one of the reasons for the 1919 scandal.
6. Because of the substitution rule, Providence was forced to cover the outfield with only two men. They lost to Philadelphia on eight unearned runs in the ninth inning.
7. There are conflicting sources on the amount of the raise. One letter cites it as $2,000, while another maintains that it was $1,000.
8. Records indicate that Radbourn's stepson, Charles, "inherited" a fondness for whiskey from his stepfather.

Works Cited

Bancroft, Frank C. "Old Hoss Radbourne," *Baseball Magazine 1*, July 1908, pp. 12-14.

Charles Radbourn file, Bart Giamatti Research Library, Cooperstown, New York.

Daily Bulletin (Bloomington, Illinois), July 20, 1892, p.1.

Daily Pantagraph (Bloomington, Illinois), February 6, 1897.

Letter from Red Ringeiser to Lee Allen, February 3, 1963.

Letter from Red Ringeiser to Lee Allen, April 23, 1967.

Sullivan, Ted. "Ted's Tribute: Radbourne was master of Curves and Speed," *The Sporting News*, February 27, 1997.

Sullivan, Ted. "Crooked and Spun: Mr. Sullivan Narrates Tale of Radbourn's Skill," *The Sporting News*, January 10, 1887.

IN 1905, THE UNITED STATES' NORTH ATLANTIC FLEET spent the summer conducting gunnery exercises in the Cape Cod area. Many of the ships stayed in the port at Provincetown, MA, and when the sailors were given leave they spent time in town. There wasn't much for a sailor to do in Provincetown on a Sunday in 1905, so they played baseball. This did not go over well with a small, but vocal, segment of the public. They appealed to the Secretary of the Navy Charles Bonaparte in the hope he would issue orders that the sailors could not partake in sports on the Sabbath. His compromise was to tell the men that they should wait until after church services had ended. Secretary Bonaparte also received a request from Provincetown business people expressing the opposite sentiment. They felt the ballgames were enjoyed by many and kept the sailors out of mischief. The issue was raised again in the spring of 1906. Rear Admiral Robley Evans wrote a letter to the selectmen of Provincetown explaining why it was necessary for the sailors to participate in baseball and other games while they were off duty. The selectmen replied to the Admiral with an invitation to make their harbor the home of the fleet during the exercises. Playing baseball would be fine. This didn't sit well with some of the preachers in the area who felt the selectmen were giving in too easily to the Navy's wishes. After hearing of the latest objections being raised by the clergy, Admiral Evans decided he had heard enough. He announced the Atlantic Fleet would spend the summer in Rockport instead. Raising a stink about playing baseball cost Provincetown the business of the 10,000 sailors who would have visited on leave. This upset most of the business people, who said that regular vacationers made more of a ruckus than the sailors did. There were even rumors that leaders of the baseball ban were threatened with tarring and feathering.

—SCOTT FIESTHUMEL

Dubuque–Chicago, 1879

by Brian Cooper

Picture this: The 2005 Chicago Cubs using a day off in their National League schedule to play an exhibition game in Dubuque, Iowa. It's improbable today, but an event of that order occurred—twice—more than 125 years ago. In the summer of 1879, Dubuque's professional team, the eventual champion of the start-up Northwestern League, split two exhibitions with the National Leaguers from Chicago. The visitors were the White Stockings; today, the franchise is the Chicago Cubs.

In-season exhibitions were common in the first 75 years of pro baseball. Dubuque's games against the White Stockings were noteworthy because the rosters featured so many future Hall of Famers, major league managers, and among the Dubuque nine, future big-league players. And there was an acrobat.

The Hall of Famers were Adrian "Cap" Anson, the White Stockings player-manager; Dubuque player Charles Comiskey, who changed the way first base is played and became a powerhouse owner in the American League; and Dubuque pitcher Charles "Old Hoss" Radbourn, whose dominance as an "ironman" remains legendary. Coincidentally, each was enshrined in Cooperstown in 1939—60 years after the Dubuque exhibitions.

The records of the Hall of Famers have been extensively documented elsewhere, so only an abbreviated review is necessary.

Anson joined the White Stockings in 1876 and became their player-manager in 1879, the year of the Dubuque exhibitions. He managed the team to five NL pennants and hit at least .300 in 19 of his 22 seasons as a player. Anson was the first manager to move preseason training to a warm locale in the South, one of the first to rotate pitchers, and an early advocate of base stealing and the hit-and-run. Not all his contributions to the game were as positive. Anson was tempestuous and bigoted. He enforced team rules with his fists, baited opponents and umpires, and refused to take the field against any team with a black player.

Dubuque's star pitcher in 1879, Radbourn joined Providence (National League) in 1881 and started piling up astounding statistics for effectiveness and endurance. Throwing "submarine" style even after the rules permitted overhand deliveries, Radbourn completed more than 97 percent of his starts. His best season was 1884, when he went 59-12, pitched 678⅔ innings, struck out 441, and posted an earned-run average of just 1.28. Over 11 major league seasons (including one in the Players League), his career record was 309-195 with a 2.67 ERA.

Comiskey is best known as a founder of the American League and the charter owner of the Chicago White Sox. (Chicago's National League team abandoned its White Stockings nickname in 1890. Comiskey appropriated it for his new team in 1901, the inaugural season of the American League. The name was soon condensed to "White Sox.") A Chicago native, Comiskey first made his mark on the game as a player. He developed a new way of playing first base. Instead of standing with a foot on the bag as each pitch was delivered, as was then the practice, he experimented with playing away from the base. He snared more batted balls but could still run to the bag in time to receive an infielder's throw.

Comiskey's leadership, innovative defense, and solid offense earned "The Old Roman" the job of player, captain and, later, manager of the St. Louis Browns, then of the American Association but today known as the St. Louis Cardinals of the National League. (Comiskey's St. Louis Browns are not to be

BRIAN COOPER *is executive editor of the* Telegraph Herald, *Dubuque, Iowa. He is writing a biography of Hall of Fame pitcher Urban "Red" Faber, a native of Dubuque County.*

confused with the American League team that used the nickname from 1902 through 1953.) Except for one season (1890) with the short-lived Players League, Comiskey played in St. Louis from 1882 until 1891. He then became player-manager of the Cincinnati Reds (1892-94)

Including Comiskey, three members of Dubuque's 1879 team went on to manage at the major league level and helped form and stabilize minor leagues. The others were "Ted" Sullivan and Tom Loftus.

Born in Ireland in 1851, Timothy Paul Sullivan came to the United States when he was about 10. He got the baseball bug while studying at St. Mary's College in Kansas, where Comiskey was his roommate. Thus began a lifelong personal and professional friendship between Sullivan and "The Old Roman." A few years later, the friends married sisters from Dubuque.

For most of 1883, Sullivan managed the St. Louis Browns, who lost the American Association title to the Philadelphia Athletics by just one game. (Comiskey managed 19 games that season.) The next year, Sullivan won 35 of 39 games with the St. Louis Maroons of the Union Association before taking over the lowly Kansas City Unions (13-46). After a couple of years managing in the Texas League, which he helped create, Sullivan in 1888 managed the Washington Senators, then of the National League.

Sullivan's greatest contributions to the game were as a scout and an administrator. He briefly owned the minor league franchise in Clinton, Iowa (Northern Association). In addition to serving as Comiskey's confidante and aide, he helped establish several minor leagues, including the Northwestern, Southern, Atlantic Association, and Texas.

An outfielder and captain of the 1879 Dubuque team, Tom Loftus became highly regarded in baseball circles. "Always of sunny disposition and the soul of good humor," the *Chicago Tribune* said of Loftus, "he probably possessed more friends both in baseball and business than almost any one else connected with the game." When he arrived in Dubuque, Loftus had three games of National League experience, in his native St. Louis (1877). In 1883, he joined his pals Comiskey and Sullivan on St. Louis' American Association team, but it was a brief reunion—Loftus saw action in only a half-dozen games.

Though the game placed him in various cities during the season, after 1879 Loftus made his home in Dubuque, where he entered the saloon business.

His big-league managing experience included the Milwaukee Grays (Union League, 1884), Cleveland Spiders (1888-89), Cincinnati Reds (1890-91), and the Chicago Orphans (NL, 1900-01). He was part owner and manager of Washington's American League franchise (1902-03). Loftus also owned or managed teams in Columbus and Grand Rapids. He came out of baseball retirement in 1908 when he was drafted to serve one year as president of the Three-I League, which was wracked by political division. Working from Dubuque, Loftus provided the leadership that kept the league intact.

Loftus died of throat cancer in 1910. At the funeral in Dubuque, his honorary pallbearers included Comiskey, Sullivan, and American League president Ban Johnson. Other members of the 1879 Dubuque squad included:

Bill Gleason, a shortstop, played eight seasons in the American Association, including St. Louis' string of four championships. He and teammate Arlie Latham are credited with the idea that resulted in designated coaches' boxes along the first- and third-base lines. Upon retirement, he joined the St. Louis Fire Department and rose to the rank of captain. On a fire call, he suffered a serious injury when he came into contact with an electrical wire.

Jack Gleason, Bill's older brother, played most of his top professional games in the AA. He also became a St. Louis firefighter and was hurt in the same incident as his brother.

Laurie Reis, pitcher and outfielder, who had played a handful of games for the Chicago White Stockings the previous two seasons before joining Dubuque.

Catcher **Tom Sullivan** (no relation to Ted) went on to play a few years for Buffalo and the St. Louis Browns before landing a political job affiliated with the St. Louis Police Department.

The acrobat was **Al Alveretta**, an outfielder for Dubuque. He scored the only run of the second game against the White Stockings, Alveretta was also known as a cross-country runner. When he left baseball, he joined his brothers in an acrobatic troupe. Later, he managed a Philadelphia theater.

This was the group that would take on the White Stockings.

The 1879 season was the first for Northwestern League and the first for a professional team in Dubuque. The team's local backers included U.S. Senator William Allison and D. B. Henderson, a future Speaker of the U.S. House. During the off-season of 1878-79, league member Rockford (IL) swooped in to sign the entire Milwaukee team after it lost its National League franchise. However, Ted Sullivan, who helped found the league and agreed to run the Dubuque team, responded by signing a batch of players from Peoria, including Loftus and Radbourn, and recruiting his friend Comiskey. As the season got under way, Loftus recalled years later, "We were a lot of youngsters who looked good only to ourselves and our manager." However, Dubuque started winning—and often.

Sullivan arranged for Anson to bring his White Stockings to Dubuque for an exhibition on July 29, 1879. Local anticipation ran high. Railroads serving the region offered excursion rates for parties of at least 20 fans departing for Dubuque from the same town.

Some 2,000 fans jammed Base Ball Park, on the north edge of Dubuque, for the event. Sullivan hiked ticket prices to 35¢ for general admission, 50¢ for "amphitheater" seats and a quarter for children under 14. Curiously, he did not charge extra for reserved seats.

Pre-game entertainment included a 100-yard race between two White Stockings. Outfielder George "Orator" Shaffer won $20 by crossing the line a few feet ahead of pitcher Terry Larkin.

Larkin might not have yet caught his breath at 3:45 P.M., when Dubuque leadoff hitter Jack Gleason stepped to the plate. (In those days a coin toss usually determined which team batted first.) Dubuque slapped out a couple of first-inning hits, but Larkin recovered to hold his hosts scoreless.

The Old Roman, playing outfield instead of first base, sparkled at defense. "Comiskey distinguished himself in the field by his remarkably fine catching of difficult flies," the *Dubuque Herald* reported, "one of which he held after running over one hundred feet and rolling over and over, but holding to the ball with a death grip."

However, Comiskey's outstanding defense could not offset his teammates' repeated blunders. The White Stockings received an unearned run in the first inning after an Anson single. The score was still 1-0 in the Chicago half of the sixth inning when Dubuque turned especially generous. It handed Chicago four unearned runs on no hits.

"It seemed as though they were playing to see who would make the largest record in the error column," the *Herald* observed. "W(illiam) Gleason carried off that prize and especially distinguished himself by his remarkable fumbles."

Exactly 100 minutes after the first pitch, umpire Robert F. Ross signaled the game's last out. The final score: Chicago 8, Dubuque 1.

The *Herald*'s game report, tucked next to community briefs and an obituary on an inside page, carried the headline "A Comedy of Errors" and opened, "The Chicagos departed for home . . . well pleased with their first visit to the Key City." Apparently so. They agreed to return to Dubuque within the week. Dubuque fans, who saw their team collapse under major league pressure, were less enthusiastic about the rematch on August 4, 1879. Ticket sales dipped.

However, in the second game Dubuque went with its best pitcher: Radbourn. Three years earlier, while playing for Bloomington, IL, one of the best amateur teams around, Radbourn had beaten the White Stockings.

"Radbourn kept the audience roaring by his deceptive down shoot, which the Chicagos would vainly strike at and saw wind magnificently," the *Herald* reported. He shut out the White Stockings on four hits. The Dubuque defense was still shaky, but it held firm at critical moments.

Shortstop Will Gleason, the defensive goat in the previous game, redeemed himself by making a spectacular running catch and connecting for three of Dubuque's four hits against Chicago's Frank Hankinson.

Dubuque scored the game's only run in the sixth inning. Alveretta, the acrobat, reached first on an error. He advanced to second while Comiskey was caught in a rundown between third and home. After stealing third, Alveretta scampered home when a Chicago infielder made a wild throw to first.

The hosts had some other breaks go their way. Anson did not play and Chicago's starting catcher, Frank "Silver" Flint, suffered a dislocated finger on his throwing hand in the second inning and finished the game in the outfield. (Flint's injury contributed to the collapse of the 1879 White Stockings, who fell from first to fourth with a 14-21 conclusion to the season.)

"When the third man on the Chicago side was put out in the last inning," the Dubuque newspaper reported, "the audience with one impulse sprang to their feet and tossed up their hats and hurrahed and hurrahed again on the assured victory of the Dubuques." Final score: Dubuque 1, Chicago 0.

Historical references in Dubuque make much of the second game, but little or no mention of the first. Some articles elevated the White Stockings to defending National League champions and made the case that Dubuque, therefore, was the best team in baseball. The White Stockings did win the title in 1876, but they had placed no better than fourth the next two campaigns.

There was talk of squeezing in a third and deciding game to the series, but it was not to be. Within two years all the Dubuque stars were gone, soon to make their mark on the major leagues.

References
Baseball Magazine
Chicago Tribune
Dubuque Daily Herald
Dubuque Daily Times
Dubuque Telegraph Herald
Elfers, James E. *The Tour to End All Tours.* Lincoln: University of Nebraska Press. In addition, personal correspondence with author.
National Baseball Hall of Fame
Retrosheet. Some information in this article was obtained free of charge from, and is copyrighted by, Retrosheet, 20 Sunset Road, Newark, DE 19711.
The Sporting News
Washington Post

Captain Eddie Grant by Damon Runyon
Philadelphia North American, October 23, 1918

With the American First Army, October 22—Harvard Eddie Grant, the old Phillies' and Giants' third baseman, sleeps in the forest of Argonne, only a few yards from where he fell. His grave is marked by some stones and a rude little cross tenderly reared by his men.

Eddie died leading his battalion in a desperate fight to relieve Whittesley's beleaguered men two weeks ago. He was commanding a company of the Three Hundred and Seventh Infantry, from Camp Upton, when the battle began.

For four days and four nights his company was part of the command which was trying to get to Whittesley. On the morning of the day that relief was effected, Eddie was so worn out he could scarcely move. Some of his brother officers noticed him sitting on a stump with a cup of coffee in front of him.

Two or three times, they say, he tried to lift the cup. But he was so weak he couldn't do it. Finally, with a terrific effort, he gulped down the coffee when the command came to move.

He stepped off at the head of his company as briskly as ever. On the way thru the forest, fighting at every step, Grant came upon stretcher-bearers carrying back the major commanding the battalion, who had been wounded. The major called to Grant, "Take command of the battalion."

Eddie Grant was then one of the few officers left. The major had hardly spoken when a shell came thru the trees, dropping two lieutenants in Grant's company. Eddie shouted, "Everybody down" to his men, but without hunting cover for himself.

He called for more stretcher-bearers for the two lieutenants.

He was calling and waving his hands when a shell struck him. It was a direct hit.

Officers and men say that Eddie's conduct during the fight was marvelous. He never slept while the drive for Whittesley's position was on.

The writer yesterday saw Christy Mathewson, Grant's old teammate and his roommate while Eddie was with the Giants. Matty was greatly saddened by the news. He is a captain in the gas corps.

Point Men

by Larry DeFillipo

Major league baseball relies on a steady infusion of fresh talent in order to retain its vitality and popularity. Young players of each generation make their mark on the sport and then move on, replaced by the next. The point men of each generation, the very first to reach the major leagues, have often carried great expectations and met with mixed results. Using each decade to represent discrete generations, these point men can be identified and their stories told. While selecting other generational markers would produce a different set of point men, the careers of these players offer a fascinating look into the events and personalities of each generation.

THE ROSTER

Table 1 lists the first player born within each decade of the 20th century to play in a major league game.[1] Of course no player born in the 1990s has yet graced a major league roster. The list is a mix of modestly accomplished players, short-timers with names unrecognizable to even contemporary fans, and perhaps the most talented young hitter of today—Albert Pujols.

As expected, these point men began their careers at a very young age. Only Albert Pujols began his major league career after his 20th birthday, with the youngest, Dave Skaugstad, appearing in his first game well shy of his 18th birthday. The birthplaces of these players reflect the shift in where the typical major leaguer originates—the Mid-Atlantic States in the first third of the 20th century, Midwest/western states in the middle of the century and Latin America in the past two decades.

THE 1900s

The first player born in the 1900s to appear in a major league game was John Cavanaugh, born in Scranton, PA, in the spring of 1900. Cavanaugh played in only one major league contest, for the 1919 Phillies. Substituting at third base in the late innings of a July 7 contest at the Polo Grounds, Cavanaugh struck out in his only at-bat against Giant ace Jesse Barnes, the NL's winningest pitcher in 1919. The Phillies were swept in a doubleheader that day, enabling the Giants to briefly regain first place in their National League pennant race with Cincinnati. The Redlegs would go on to win the NL crown and face the Chicago "Black" Sox in the World Series.

While Cavanaugh was to play only this single game for the Phillies, it was notable for a record set that day that has not been equaled since. In the bottom of the ninth, trailing by eight runs, the Phillies mounted a valiant comeback against Giant reliever Pol Perritt. The comeback fell short as the Phils managed only three runs but in one stretch, four consecutive Phillie batters reached base on three hits and a walk. Each of those base runners (Luderus, Sicking, Cady, and Cravath) in turn stole both second base and third base—stealing a total of eight bases in a single inning. Newspaper accounts describe the Giants as indifferent to the base-running antics of the Phillies, suggesting that modern rules would not award a single stolen base in a similar situation today. Nonetheless, on the day the first player born in the 20th century participated in a regular season major league game, the 1919 Phillies broke the NL record (and tied the major league record) for stolen bases in an inning.

LARRY DEFILLIPO *is a wannabe Mets statistician masquerading as an aerospace engineer in his newly adopted home of Ashburn, VA. This is his first article published by SABR.*

Table 1. First MLB Player from Each Decade in the 20th Century

	Name	DoB	Location	MLB Debut	Pos.	Age
1900s	John Cavanaugh	6/5/1900	PA	7/7/1919	3B	19y, 33d
1910s	Joe Cicero	11/18/1910	NJ	9/20/1929	PH	18y, 306d
1920s	Walt Masterson	6/22/1920	PA	5/8/1939	P	18y, 317d
1930s	Johnny Antonelli	4/12/1930	NY	7/4/1948	P	18y, 83d
1940s	Dave Skaugstad	1/10/1940	IA	9/25/1957	P	17y, 258d
1950s	Lloyd Allen	5/8/1950	CA	9/1/1969	P	19y, 116d
1960s	Tim Conroy	4/3/1960	PA	6/23/1978	P	18y, 81d
1970s	Wilson Alvarez	3/24/1970	Venezuela	7/24/1989	P	19y, 122d
1980s	Albert Pujols	7/21/1980	Dominican Rep.	4/2/2001	LF	20y, 255d

What exactly happened to Cavanaugh after his debut has not been documented. That very evening, with an ugly 18-43 record and having lost 11 consecutive games, Phillie manager Jack Coombs was fired by owner William F. Baker.[2] Coombs was replaced by outfield star Gavvy Cravath, who immediately announced his desire to upgrade the team's talent level, kicking off a wave of trades and player releases.[3] John Cavanaugh may well have been caught up in Cravath's whirlwind effort to return to the glory of Philadelphia's 1915 NL Championship season. Cavanaugh resurfaced with a Scranton semi-pro team later that year (the "Uniques"), while the Phillies finished securely in last place, not to win another title for 31 years.

THE 1910s

Joe Cicero was both a cousin of actor Clark Gable and the first player born in the 1910s to reach the majors. The Atlantic City, NJ, native joined the Red Sox squad in the spring of 1928 as a 17-year-old shortstop. He began the season with the club but was optioned to Salem of the New England League on June 1 without playing in a single game. The following year Cicero was promoted from Pittsfield to the Red Sox in mid-September, making his major league debut on September 20, 1929. Cicero delivered a pinch-hit single in a 4-2 loss to the Cleveland Indians, followed up nine days later by a three-hit, three-RBI performance in a 10-0 whitewashing of Lefty Grove and the AL champion Philadelphia Athletics. This was to be Joe Cicero's most prodigious major league performance. Used sporadically in the 1930 season, he was sold to the Indianapolis Indians and resumed what was to be a lengthy minor league career.

Joe Cicero did not return to the baseball limelight until 14 years later, when he made headlines as a wartime member of the famed Newark Bears. In the 1944 opening day contest against the Montreal Royals, left fielder Cicero drilled three home runs, including two grand slams and delivered 10 RBI in a 17-8 victory. This game was a likely springboard to the next, and most improbable, chapter in Cicero's career. Faced with wartime shortages of baseball talent, Connie Mack invited Cicero to spring training in 1945 with his Athletics squad. Cicero was the "hit" of the A's camp, "with his booming drives over the leftfield fence."[4] And so the bespectacled Cicero began the 1945 season as the Philadelphia A's starting left fielder—15 years after last appearing in a major league game. He did not hit well against regular-season pitching though, batting only .158 in a dozen games for the last-place A's. Joe Cicero played his last game in May 1945, a few weeks after VE Day, as ballplayers began returning from military service around the globe.

THE 1920s

Walt Masterson, first player born in the 1920s to reach the majors, was impressive in spring training outings for the 1939 Washington Senators as a reliever for manager Bucky Harris. The 18-year-old Philadelphia native impressed AL President William Harridge enough to be included in an article he authored on the eve of opening day in which he previewed the upcoming season. Masterson was listed alongside Ted Williams, Charlie "King Kong" Keller, and Bill Rigney as the class of 1939's most promising rookies.[5] Masterson opened the season at Charlotte but was quickly called up to the Senators in late April, making his first appearance on May 8 in relief against the

Cleveland Indians. The young right-hander pitched a shaky eighth inning, allowing two walks and one hit but no runs in a 6-2 loss.

After another brief outing in relief, Masterson was given his first major league start on May 18 against the Detroit Tigers. Masterson's mound opponent was veteran Buck "Bobo" Newsom, acquired days earlier from the St. Louis Browns in a 10-player deal. Winner of 20 games for the seventh-place Browns in 1938, Newsom would go on to again win 20 games in 1939 and then post a brilliant 21-5, 2.83 ERA season as a workhorse for the AL champion Tigers in 1940. But Masterson spoiled Newsom's Tiger debut, throwing a 4-1 complete-game victory for the Washington Senators in Griffith Stadium. Masterson scattered six hits while walking six and striking out seven, the only Tiger run set up by a wild throw by Masterson himself on a ball hit by Newsom. The rookie held Tiger stars Charlie Gehringer and Hank Greenberg hitless, striking out Greenberg on three straight curveballs with two men on in the ninth to secure the win. Walt Masterson would pitch for 14 years with the Senators, Red Sox, and Tigers, compiling a 78-100 record. He was selected to start in the 1948 All-Star game in what was surely the highlight of his career, but was unlucky enough to be a part of two record hitting streaks during his career. On June 29, 1941, Joe DiMaggio collected a seventh-inning single off Masterson to break George Sisler's 41-game AL consecutive-game hitting streak record. In July 1952 the Red Sox's Walt Dropo went 4-for-4 against Masterson in the first game of a doubleheader with the Senators. Before the second game was over Dropo had collected 12 consecutive hits, setting a new major league record.

THE 1930s

John August (Johnny) Antonelli, one of the first "bonus babies," was also the first major leaguer born in the 1930s. The 18-year-old left hander signed with the Boston Braves for $65,000 on June 30, 1948, reputedly the largest bonus paid to that point for any player. A week later Antonelli made his debut for Boston on the road against the Philadelphia Phillies in the first half of a July 4 doubleheader. Relieving in the eighth inning, Antonelli allowed one run on two hits (to Richie Ashburn and Del Ennis) in one inning

of a 7-2 loss to the Phils. The nightcap of the holiday doubleheader featured the fourth career start and third lifetime win for Phillie rookie and fellow bonus baby hurler Robin Roberts.

Antonelli pitched only three more games in 1948 for the NL champion Braves, earning a save while allowing no hits and no runs. He did not appear in Boston's World Series loss to Lou Boudreau's Cleveland Indians but was awarded a partial share ($571.34) of the World Series losers' bonus money. Antonelli's portion was decreed by baseball commissioner Happy Chandler[6]—overriding his teammates' decision not to award him a cut of the money.

After three years with the Braves as an occasional starter, Johnny Antonelli joined the military for two years, serving in Korea. Prior to the 1954 season he was traded to the New York Giants in a controversial deal for center fielder Bobby Thomson, hero of the 1951 Miracle at Coogan's Bluff. Antonelli would go on to a 21-7 record in 1954, leading the NL in ERA (2.30) and the Giants to a World Series sweep over the Cleveland Indians. He started and won game two over tribe ace Early Wynn and delivered a game four save in relief. Antonelli earned a full $10,795.36 winners' share for his efforts.

In a game remembered by many New Yorkers as vividly as his World Series performances, Johnny Antonelli started and lost the final game played by the Giants in the Polo Grounds on

Walt Masterson

September 29, 1957. He suffered a 9-1 shellacking by the Pittsburgh Pirates, after which Giant fans poured on the field in search of souvenirs, stealing home plate, the bases, and even a center-field monument to Giant infielder Eddie Grant, killed in action during World War I. After four All-Star appearances and winning 108 games for the NY/SF Giants, Antonelli split his final season in 1961 between the Indians and Braves—opponents in the 1948 World Series. Following the end of the season, Milwaukee sold his contract to the expansion New York Mets. Johnny Antonelli elected to retire rather than report, ending his career with the team that first signed him as an 18-year-old phenom.

Johnny Antonelli

THE 1940s

David Wendell Skaugstad was a 17-year-old left-handed pitcher from Compton High School in Compton, CA, when he signed with the Cincinnati Redlegs in September 1957. Skaugstad debuted for the Redlegs in relief against the Chicago Cubs on September 25, 1957. He surrendered three hits and three walks but allowed no runs in a four-inning no-decision, finishing the last game of the year at Crosley Field, a 7-5 loss to the Cubs. Skaugstad was the third of three fledgling pitchers to throw that day for Cincinnati.[7] along with first-time starter and 20-year-old bonus baby Jay Hook (later the first pitcher to win a game for the expansion 1962 Mets) and 18-year-old Claude Osteen.

Despite his fine initial outing, Dave Skaugstad was to appear in only one more major league game. On September 29, the last day of the 1957 season, the Redlegs were in Milwaukee playing the NL champion Braves. On the day after breaking the NL single-season record for attendance, 45,000 hometown fans were treated to a pitching duel between Redlegs starter Jay Hook and Braves starter Bob Buhl, with both throwing no-hitters after five innings. Before the start of the sixth inning Reds manager Birdie Tebbetts remarked, "He's too young to throw a no-hitter,"[8] and lifted Hook, replacing him with Dave Skaugstad. Skaugstad retired pinch-hitter Andy Pafko, second-basemen Red Schoendienst in search of his 200th hit of the season, and shortstop Johnny Logan to preserve the no-hitter. In the seventh inning of the still scoreless game, Skaugstad retired future

Hall of Famers Eddie Mathews and Hank Aaron, but then walked Wes Covington and allowed the first hit of the game to Brave first baseman Joe Adcock. Skaugstad's inexperience got the better of him as he walked the next two batters to force in a run. After pitching 1⅔ innings, he was removed for veteran Hersh Freeman, leaving to a hail of boos from the partisan crowd. Cincinnati rallied to take the lead in the top of the ninth, but eventually lost the game 4-3 in the bottom of the ninth.

Dave Skaugstad enjoyed a minor league career that extended from 1958 through 1965, wrapped around a three-year stint in the Army. A good-hitting pitcher, in 1959 he played first base and outfield between starts for the PCL Seattle Rainiers and lobbied the Redlegs' organization to be converted into an everyday player. His "conversion" ended after he struck out 18 batters in a game during 1960 for Class D Geneva. Back problems caused Skaugstad to take the next year off, during which he enlisted. Pitching for the V Corps Guardians baseball team in Europe, he developed a forkball and a goal of returning to the majors by

Dave Skaugstad, Cincinnati Reds, Wrigley Field, Chicago, 1957. Man in dugout wearing suit is young Skaugstad's father.

1965. After a strong early season showing with Class AA Knoxville in 1965, Skaugstad was called up by Cincinnati to pitch in an exhibition game with the Chicago White Sox. He warmed up in the bullpen once but never appeared in the game. Sent back to Knoxville, he pitched poorly in the second half of the season and a lingering rotator cuff problem caused him to retire at the ripe old age of 25.

THE 1950s

The first major leaguers born in the 1950s were a pair of 19-year-olds—Californian Lloyd Allen and Connecticut native and future Mets manager Bobby Valentine, both of whom debuted in early September 1969 as late season call-ups (Allen with the California

Angels and Valentine for the Dodgers). Allen, the Angels' first selection in the 1968 amateur draft, was the first of the two to appear in a game, pitching an effective inning of relief in the front half of a doubleheader with the Senators on September 1 in a shutout loss to Joe Coleman. A newspaper account of the game mentions that David and Julie Eisenhower attended the game, the newlywed grandson of former President Dwight Eisenhower and daughter of then President Richard Nixon.[9]

Allen's strong showing earned him a start his next time out from manager Lefty Phillips. Allen started the penultimate game of the season for the Angels against the Kansas City Royals on October 1, 1969. In a rain-shortened five-inning game, Allen walked eight batters, including filling the bases by walks twice and lost a 6-0 shutout to Royals' rookie Bill Butler. This was Butler's fourth shutout of the year, helping secure for the Royals the best record by an expansion team in the then 100-year history of the major leagues.

Lloyd Allen played for several more seasons, principally as a reliever for the Angels, Rangers, and White Sox. In 1971, he led the Angels with 15 saves, including a game on July 16, 1971 in which he completed the rare combination of both hitting a home run and earning a save. Allen's career won-lost record was unsightly at 8-25, with 22 saves and a 4.69 ERA. He lost his last 10 decisions between 1972 and 1975, including his final appearance, a ⅔–inning start against the Oakland Athletics in which he allowed a two-run HR to future Hall of Famer Reggie Jackson.

THE 1960s

Tim Conroy was the first player born in the 1960s to reach the majors. Selected by the Oakland Athletics in the first round of the 1978 June amateur draft (the 20th overall pick), Conroy was less than a month out of high school when he was added to manager Jack McKeon's A's squad. Just prior to his arrival, owner Charlie Finley claimed that Tim Conroy had "more poise than Catfish Hunter . . . when I brought [him] up as [a] kid."[10] Conroy joined fellow 18-year-old hurler Mike Morgan on the roster, who had also jumped from high school to the big leagues that same month.[11] Prep catcher Brian Milner, a seventh-round draft choice, also jumped from high school to the majors, debuting the same day as Conroy.

Conroy debuted as the starting pitcher in the second game of a doubleheader with the Kansas City Royals on June 23, 1978. In front of the second largest crowd of the year at Royals Stadium, Conroy pitched 3⅓ innings, allowing only one run and two hits while walking five Royals in a game won by the A's. The second and final major league appearance for Conroy that year was another start in which he did not fare as well—allowing five runs on only one hit in 1⅓ innings at home against the Texas Rangers. A first-inning error by Conroy on a Bert Campaneris sacrifice bunt, four walks, and two stolen bases earned him a quick shower but not a loss as Oakland eventually won in 10 innings.

Reassigned to the minors, Tim Conroy toiled for four years before returning to Oakland in 1982. Ultimately, after a lackluster 10-19 career record with Oakland, Conroy was traded to the St. Louis Cardinals in December 1985 along with catcher Mike Heath for 21-game winner Joaquin Andujar. The trade occurred just two months after Andujar's meltdown in game seven of the 1985 World Series where he charged home plate umpire (and game six "villain") Don Denkinger following two disputed pitches in an 11-0 loss to Bret Saberhagen and the Kansas City Royals. Andujar's Series antics made him a pariah in St. Louis, leading to the quick trade for seemingly unequal talent.

the Chicago White Sox for veteran outfielder Harold Baines. Accompanying him to the Windy City was a young outfielder from the Rangers' Triple A Oklahoma City roster, Sammy Sosa, who a few weeks earlier had drilled his first major league home run. Alvarez was assigned to a ChiSox minor league affiliate, not to appear in another major league game for two years. As a result he carries an ERA of infinity for his 1989 major league season.

Alvarez returned to the major leagues with a bang. Called up by the White Sox from Double A Birmingham in the summer of 1991 after posting a 10-6, 1.83 ERA record, Alvarez was immediately given an opportunity to start. On August 11, in his first outing for the ChiSox and only the second game of his major league career, Alvarez tossed a no-hitter against the Baltimore Orioles. Striking out seven Orioles en route to a 7-0 victory, Wilson Alvarez became the most inexperienced major league pitcher to throw a no-hitter since the St. Louis Browns' Bobo Holloman blanked the Philadelphia A's in his 1953 major league debut.

Later in his career, Wilson Alvarez earned the distinction of starting the first regular season game for the Tampa Bay Devil Rays on March 31, 1998. More recently with the Los Angeles Dodgers, Alvarez suffered the indignity of serving up the 2004 NLDS–clinching home run in the eight inning of game four to St. Louis Cardinal slugger Albert Pujols.

THE 1970s

Venezuelan-born Wilson Alvarez, first major leaguer born in the 1970s, bears the distinction of being one of the few major leaguers to play in the Little League World Series, appearing in the 1982 LLWS with the Coquivacoa Little League of Maracaibo. Alvarez debuted for the Texas Rangers on July 24, 1989, appearing as the starting pitcher against the eventual AL East champion Toronto Blue Jays. Called up from Class AA Tulsa to fill in for an injured Charlie Hough, the 19-year-old left hander was rudely welcomed into the fraternity, as many rookie pitchers are—allowing first inning home runs to Tony Fernandez and Fred McGriff, facing five batters in all without recording a single out.

Alvarez returned to the Tulsa team and five days later was bundled by the Rangers in a trade with

THE 1980s

The preseason rosters for 2001 included quite a few young players born in 1980, including future World Series MVP Josh Beckett, current Indians ace C. C. Sabathia and Dodger shortstop Cesar Izturis. But the very first player born in the 1980s to appear in a major league game was Albert Pujols. The Dominican Republic native was a 13th-round selection by the St. Louis Cardinals in the 1999 amateur draft, turning down the Cards' initial contract offer, but eventually signing for a $60K bonus in the summer of 1999. Pujols earned league MVP honors for Class A Peoria of the Midwest League in 2000, finishing the year with Class AAA Memphis. Taking advantage of a roster spot made available by a spring training injury to Bobby Bonilla, Pujols was the 2001 opening day left fielder for the Cardinals. He went 1-for-3 and was caught stealing in his debut against Mike Hampton and the Colorado Rockies in an 8-0 loss on April 2, 2001. Pujols hit his first major league home run, along with a double and three RBI, on April 6 in the Cardinals first win of the season, against the eventual World Series champion Arizona Diamondbacks.

Albert Pujols went on to earn NL Rookie of the Month honors for May 2001 and was the first Cardinal rookie selected to the All-Star team since Luis Arroyo in 1955. He finished the year batting .329 with 37 HR and 130 RBI, leading the Cardinals to a wild card berth and unanimously winning NL Rookie of the Year honors. Pujols has continued to dominate NL pitching in his four seasons with the Cardinals. He was runner-up to Barry Bonds in the NL 2002 and 2003 MVP voting, leading the NL in 2003 in batting average (.359), hits (212), runs (137), and doubles (51). With another stellar season in 2004, he has joined Joe DiMaggio and Ted Williams as the only players to collect 500 RBI in their first four seasons. Pujols earned the NL 2004 LCS MVP award and, despite his lackluster performance in the 2004 World Series, has emerged as arguably the best young hitter in the game today.

Today there are no major leaguers born in the 1990s, but in four, five, or maybe six years some lucky youngster will be given the opportunity. The tantalizing question is whether his career will follow the course of a John Cavanaugh, ending as soon as it began—or that of an Albert Pujols, challenging the record books with the very real prospect of enshrinement in the Hall of Fame one day.

Notes

1. Technically speaking, 1901 was the first year of the 20th century, and so Phillip "Lefty" Weinert was the first player born in the 20th century to appear in a major league game. Born in Philadelphia, PA, on April 4, 1902, Weinert debuted as a relief pitcher with the hometown Phillies on September 24, 1919, not yet 17½ years old. Though not at the same time, he was a teammate of 1900's firstborn John Cavanaugh, who was also born in southeastern PA. For consistency with the other decades, I've elected to explore the career of Cavanaugh rather than Weinert.
2. *Chicago Tribune*, July 9, 1919, p. 19.
3. Several of the Philly players objected to Coombs' removal and staged a "strike," sitting in street clothes and getting drunk in the bleachers at Baker Field during the July 8 contest with the Cubs. The apparent ringleader, pitcher Gene Packard, was fined $200 by William F. Baker and soon released. As detailed in *Babe Ruth and the 1918 Red Sox*, Packard was implicated by Harry Grabiner, secretary to White Sox owner Charles Comiskey, of fixing the 1918 World Series—won by the Boston Red Sox over the Chicago Cubs, for whom Packard played in 1916 and 1917. AL President Ban Johnson had apparently suspected the 1918 Series was fixed, but neither he nor Commissioner Kennesaw Landis ever launched an official investigation.
4. *Washington Post*, March 16, 1945, p. 12.
5. *New York Times*, April 16, 1939, p. 34. Harridge's article also announced the planned June 12 enshrinement of the inaugural "Hall of Fame" members on the 100th anniversary of baseball in Cooperstown, NY.
6. *New York Times*, October 20, 1948, p. 41.
7. *Los Angeles Times*, September 26, 1957, p. C5.
8. Letters from David W. Skaugstad to the author, November 29 and December 21, 2004.
9. *Washington Post*, September 2, 1969, p. D1.
10. *Washington Post*, June 18, 1978, p. D3.
11. Morgan's debut in early June 1978 was an inauspicious one, lasting less than an inning after he tripped and severely sprained his ankle while backing up third base on a hit to the second batter he faced.

Bibliography
Wood, Allan. *Babe Ruth and the 1918 Red Sox*. Lincoln, NE: Writer's Club Press, 2000.
www.baseballlibrary.com
www.baseball-reference.com
www.retrosheet.org
en.wikipedia.org
www.williamsportonline.com

Sisler Confronts the Evil Empire

by Roger Godin

George Sisler returned to action in 1924 after solving the eye problem that had kept him out of the 1923 season. He would not only return to holding down first base in his usual superb manner while resuming his customary .300+ hitting, he would now be the Browns' manager. After losing an exciting pennant race in 1922 to the Yankees, the Browns had fallen to fifth place in 1923 as Sisler's absence was severely felt. Owner Phil Ball removed Leo Fohl as manager in mid-August and replaced him with longtime coach Jimmy Austin for the balance of the season.

Ball then hired Sisler as manager on October 21, 1923. It was a position he had turned down three years earlier, but with his playing future somewhat in doubt, he was now quite willing to take on the challenge. His contract was for one year with pay contingent upon his ability to play as well as manage. If playing was now out of the question, Sisler was content to manage only. As things played out, he was able to perform at a level well beyond the average player, but not at the level that had seen him hit .407 in 1920 and .420 in 1922.

Sisler had essentially inherited a team that came close to winning in 1922. Rick Huhn in his splendid biography *The Sizzler: George Sisler, Baseball's Forgotten Great*, projected the 1924 Browns:

The regular lineup could certainly hit with the best, but in fairness no longer could be called youthful. The outfield of Jacobson, Tobin, and Williams . . . showed their ages to be 33, 32, and 34 respectively. Sis was now 31, [Catcher Hank] Severeid 33, and shortstop Wally Gerber 32. Only

24-year-old second baseman Marty McManus was a youngster who played regularly from the start. Gene Robertson, 25, eventually took over at third base . . . the pitching . . . was essentially unchanged . . . Shocker was around . . . and in 1923 he had once again delivered 20 wins.

The Browns assembled for spring training in Mobile, Alabama, for the third straight year in 1924, and Sisler soon resumed his comfort zone at the plate. By the time the team reached St. Louis, he was hitting .324 in 16 exhibition games. After a slow start, the Browns were 16-11 and in second place on May 22 while the new player-manager was hitting at a .315 clip by mid-June. That would be as high as they would go, but they were still in the race in late August only three and a half games from first despite being lodged in fourth place. It would be where they would finish the season as a devastating 1-9 run at season's end left them at 74-78, 17½ games from the top as the Yankees took the American League flag. A highlight of the season was Urban Shocker's ironman performance on September 6, when he pitched two complete-game 6-2 victories over the White Sox. One wonders who was doing the pitch count that day.

Sisler himself finished with a .305 average with nine home runs and 74 RBI. These would be great numbers for almost anyone but Sisler. He was no longer the force to be reckoned with that he once was, and Bob Shawkey, Yankee pitcher, in Donald Honig's *The Greatest First Baseman of All Time*, told why:

When he was up at the plate, he could watch you for only so long, and then he'd have to look down to get his eyes focused again. So we'd keep him waiting up there until he'd have to look down and then pitch. He was never the same hitter again after that.

ROGER GODIN *lives in St. Paul, Minnesota, and is the team curator for the Minnesota Wild. He is the author of* The 1922 St. Louis Browns: The Best of the American League's Worst.

True, but he would nonetheless raise his average to close to .350 in 1925 while guiding the Browns to a third-place finish behind the eventual pennant-winning Washington Nationals (Senators). Sisler would be the first major league player to make the cover of *Time* magazine when he appeared there in the March 30 issue. The magazine asked: "Will he, fans wonder, regain his former prowess?" The above number would seem to indicate an answer of: "Yes, but not quite."

The 1925 Browns changed spring training sites, moving from Mobile to Tarpon Springs, Florida. The new site would enable them to be closer to major league opposition for exhibition play. The team had made a major trade over the off-season, giving up the veteran Shocker to the Yankees for right handers Joe Bush and Milt Gaston and lefty Joe Giard. While Bush was past his prime, the three acquisitions would win 39 games between them. Notable newcomers among the position players were outfielder Harry Rice, shortstop Bobby LaMotte, and catchers Leo Dixon and Pinky Hargrave.

The Browns opened the season at home against Cleveland, and Sisler sent Bush to the mound. The initial results were not encouraging as the Indians scored 12 runs in the eighth inning on their way to a 21-14 victory. In the history of the American League in only one other game have both both teams scored as many runs. Sisler himself committed a career-high four errors, and the team then dropped the next three games before finally beating the White Sox. But better things were ahead for both the team and their playing manager.

On May 21 with the team in fifth place, Sisler failed to hit in a game for the first time since the season opened. The 34-game hitting streak still stands as an American League record from the start of a season. By June 5 the club was in the first division at fourth place with a 24-24 record.

Weak pitching would plague the 1925 Browns, and by the time the Yankees arrived at Sportsman's Park for a series on July 8 they had slipped back to fifth at 38-40. That still put them two places above the Evil Empire, which was suffering through a rare bad year. For New York, the season was characterized by Babe Ruth's "tummy ache heard 'round the world" in spring training and his subsequent $5,000 fine for missing two games in a later series with the Browns. Still, there was optimism in New York as the second half of the season began. Harry Cross, *New York Times*, July 6, 1925:

> *These Yanks know as well as any one else that they belong in the first division. . . . As the Yankee excursion whirled from Washington to this city [St. Louis] there was a general and hopeful feeling among the players that the second half of the season of 1925 could not possibly be as depressing for them as the first.*

But it would be. Sisler started the two former Yankee hurlers in the opening doubleheader on July 7. Gaston limited the visitors to two runs while scattering 11 hits in the opener. The Browns got five runs in the fifth and four in the seventh en route to a 12-2 romp, which featured triples by the manager and Jacobson among 13 hits. Ruth went 1-for-4 and sat out the second game.

Joe Giard would have only one noteworthy major league season, and 1925 was his brief place in the sun. He would gain one of his 10 wins in the nightcap, matching Gaston's complete-game effort. Jacobson's three-run homer in the sixth inning put the Browns ahead 5-3 until Earl Combs tied it with a two-run blast in the top of the ninth. The home team would have the last laugh, however, as Harry Rice pounced on reliever Herb Pennock's 1-0 delivery for the winning home run in the last of the ninth to make the final 6-5.

The kind of heat for which St. Louis is famous came out in full force for the single game on July 8. Harry Cross, July 9, 1925: "It was so hot in the ball park that the peanuts were badly burned before the fans could eat them. Ice has taken on the same value as uncut diamonds. . . . When one mentions the fact to a native St. Louisan that it is hot, they come right back with that old one about, 'Oh, this isn't hot. We don't take off our coats until the sun starts to blister the paint on the houses.'" The weather was apparently to the visitors' liking. Ruth put New York ahead 2-0 in the top of the third with a two-run shot off Dixie Davis, and the visitors were never headed. The Yankees were aided by three St. Louis errors, two by third baseman Gene Robertson, and led 6-2 in the eighth before the home team added two to make it close at 6-4.

Cooling rains came to St. Louis the next day and they worked very well in the Browns' favor. Trailing 8-5 in the top of the fourth, Harry Cross, July 10, 1925, describes what happened:

In the third it became as dark as doomsday, accompanied by a sky full of lightning flashes and claps of thunder which shook the grand stand. The rain fell in sheets. . . . There have been rainstorms and rainstorms, but never one like this. There were perhaps 6,000 fans in the stands and not one escaped a drenching. . . . The storm followed a day of stifling humidity and roasting heat.

The rains allowed Joe Bush to escape another bad effort. His former teammates had quickly knocked him out in the first inning with a seven-run barrage, but the Browns managed to claw their way back before the downpour came to wipe out everyone's efforts, including Sisler's two-run homer in the bottom of the first.

The teams resumed play on July 10 with a doubleheader, and Yankee manager Miller Huggins sent Shocker against his former team in the first game. He was superb for six innings as the visitors built up a 6-0 lead. The Browns then sent their old teammate to the showers in the seventh with three runs and then added another in the eighth. New York seemingly put the game out of reach with two in the ninth to provide a 8-4 lead. But Bob Shawkey, who had relieved Shocker, couldn't live with success.

Giving up three runs, he was succeeded by Sad Sam Jones, who then gave way to Herb Pennock, who had lost game two of the July 7 doubleheader. Hanging on to a 8-7 lead with Harry Rice at third and Bobby LaMotte on second, Pennock literally threw the game away. As L. A. McMaster wrote in the July 10, 1925 *St. Louis Post Dispatch*:

Sisler laid down a perfect bunt for a safe hit. The ball was near the third-base line and Pennock was the only one who could get near it. The pitcher finally picked up the sphere and trying vainly for Sisler at first, threw to the right field pavilion. Rice and LaMotte crossed the plate and the contest was over.

The second game proved to be another version of the first game of the July 7 doubleheader. Sisler finally got a good nine-inning effort from Joe Bush, as the Brainerd, Minnesota, native gave his former team only three runs on eight hits while the Browns scored in every inning but the first. When the game was called after the eighth because of darkness, the home team had romped to a 13-3 victory. Trailing 2-0 after an inning and a half, two two-run home runs by Pinky Hargrave and Harry Rice set the tone for the rest of the game, which featured three-run innings

JULY 7 DOUBLEHEADER

NEW YORK	0	0	1	0	0	0	0	0	1	–	2	11	1
ST. LOUIS	1	1	0	0	5	1	4	0	x	–	12	13	1

WP–Gaston   LP–Hoyt

NEW YORK	0	1	0	0	2	0	0	0	2	–	5	8	1
ST. LOUIS	1	0	1	0	0	3	0	0	1	–	6	10	0

WP–Giard   LP–Pennock
HR: Jacobson, Combs, Rice

JULY 10 DOUBLEHEADER

NEW YORK	0	0	0	1	0	5	0	0	2	–	8	9	2
ST. LOUIS	0	0	0	0	0	0	3	1	5	–	9	13	2

WP–Vangilder   LP–Jones

NEW YORK	1	1	0	0	0	1	0	0		–	3	8	1
ST. LOUIS	0	4	1	1	1	3	3	x		–	13	20	2

WP–Bush   LP–Hoyt
HR: Rice, Hargrave, E. Johnson

for the Browns in the sixth and seventh. Yankee starter Waite Hoyt lost his second game of the five-game series.

Sisler had managed his team to victories in four of the five games, and New York would depart still in seventh place, a position they would find themselves in at season's end. The teams would split the season series at 11-11, only one of nine occasions over the Browns' 52-year history when they either broke even or won the season series with New York. On only five of those occasions did they actually win the series. 1925 would find Gorgeous George or the Sizzler, take your nickname, finishing with the best mark of his three-year run as manager. On the way there, he would put together another hitting streak, 22 games, and suffer the passing of his mother on July 27.

By late August the team was in fourth place at 66-59. In September they compiled a 16-11 mark, which would put them in third place at season's end, 15 games behind pennant-winning Washington. In the second game of a season-ending doubleheader with Detroit, Sisler held the Tigers scoreless in a two-inning relief stint. Like Ruth, Sisler had first started his career as a pitcher.

As a player Sisler would finish with his best post–eye problem year with a .345 average, 224 hits, 12 home runs, and 105 RBI. Ever the perfectionist, it left him with little sense of accomplishment. Tom Meany, in *Baseball's Greatest Hitters,* quotes him: "Oh, I know I hit .345 and got 228 [sic] hits in 1925, but that never gave me much satisfaction. That wasn't what I call real good hitting."

Not much satisfaction to the man described as "the perfect player," but great satisfaction to St. Louis fans, particularly in this five-game set in early July 1925 when Sisler hit .524 (11-21) as the Browns took four of the games.

References

Huhn, Rick. *The Sizzler: George Sisler, Baseball's Forgotten Great.* Columbia, MO: University of Missouri Press, 2004.

Meany, Tom. *Baseball's Greatest Hitters.* New York: A. S. Barnes & Co., 1950.

New York Times, July 7, 8, 9, 10, 11, 1925.

Sabol, Ken. *Babe Ruth & The American Dream.* New York: Balantine, 1974.

St. Louis Post Dispatch, July 8, 11, 1925.

St. Paul Pioneer Press, July 9, 1925.

The Baseball Encyclopedia, 10th ed. New York: McMillan, 1996.

A BASEBALL NOVEL WANTED:
GALVIN WOULD BE A FINE CENTRAL FIGURE FOR THE STORY TO TURN PAGES
New York Tribune, July 20, 1890

IT'S A WONDER TO ME," says a publisher, "that nobody has yet written a baseball novel. I should think such a venture would meet with a large and ready sale, if it did not become a craze with the horde of admirers of the game in this century. It might be written around some romantic incident and worked up with a clever plot.

Hawley Smart, the English novelist, you will remember, drew on the racecourse for the material he used in his famous romance From Post to Finish. I have heard people who did not care a snap of a finger about horses say they had read it with the utmost pleasure. I am convinced that a well-constructed baseball novel would catch many of the same class of readers, for there is an excitement about popular sports of any description which is not without its effect even upon the uninitiated."

More About the Kansas City Baseball Academy

by Charlie Metro and Tom Altherr

In a recent SABR *National Pastime* article, historian Richard Puerzer analyzed the Kansas City Royals Baseball Academy of the early 1970s. While he got much of the story right, there were quite a few omissions and some questionable interpretations. I was there on the spot at the creation of this experimental academy and witnessed its development for the first two or three years. Moreover I was instrumental in many of the decisions that led to its founding. Puerzer downplayed my role and thus neglected my insider's perspective. I was director of player procurement, directly involved in putting the Royals together in 1968 and 1969. Then I was director of scouts and players. And in 1970, I was the field manager for the Royals, when Joe Gordon didn't want to manage anymore. The details of all this are in Chapter 10 of my book, *Safe by a Mile* (University of Nebraska Press, 2001). The early success of the Royals as an expansion franchise had more to do with who we drafted and who we traded for, rather than who got developed in the Baseball Academy, Frank White notwithstanding.

My original input began with the selection of the site. I had a connection with John Schab—I may have the spelling wrong—who was a majordomo in the Sarasota area and who was a friend of Hall of Famer Al Lopez. I had met Schab when I was a coach for Lopez and the White Sox in the early 1960s. Schab had

Charlie Metro

been interested in getting the Royals to establish their Spring Training facilities in Sarasota, in conjunction with the White Sox. When the subject of a site for the academy came up, Schab located two parcels of land as possibilities. One was a 600-acre one directly east of Sarasota. We considered it, but then thought it was too far away from the city. The other was a 120-acre piece near the outskirts of Sarasota. The price for the second parcel was $120,000 plus a an $8,000 legal fee. A doctor, who was retired and living in Spain, owned that second piece of land. Ewing Kauffman, the Royals owner, agreed to that purchase price, and the deal was done. Kauffman asked me my opinion, because of my experience wiith Tigertown, the Detroit facilities at Lakeland, Florida. I went out and inspected the land and told him that it was suitable and beautiful. The topography with the palm trees and slightly rolling terrain was gorgeous.

Kauffman asked me about matters of design. I had spent several years at Tigertown and had some definite ideas. I suggested a cloverleaf pattern of four fields, each on different elevations with the elevated center structure serving as an observatory, where you could watch all four fields efficiently. I also suggested implementing batting cages and pitching machines. I did the same thing with the Royals at Municipal Stadium, where I had a batting cage installed in a picnic area along the left field line. For the infield on one of the diamonds, I foresaw the increasing use of astroturf and argued that the Royals players should get used to playing on that surface. Again drawing on my Tigertown days, I urged him to have concentrated dormitories, much like elaborate motels, and a cafeteria with a chef, so the players could eat together and the club could oversee their

CHARLIE METRO *played for the Detroit Tigers and Philadelphia A's, managed the Cubs, Royals, and several minor league teams, and scouted for several franchises.* TOM ALTHERR *teaches in the History Department at Metropolitan State College of Denver, including an American Baseball History class. Together they published* Safe by a Mile *(University of Nebraska Press, 2002).*

diet. And I also persuaded the Royals, over some initial objection to cost, to distribute the instructional manual I had developed to all the personnel at the Academy.

When it came time to pick instructors, I suggested Tommy Henrich, Billy Herman, Tom Ferrick, and Steve Korcheck, among others. I recommended a left-hand and right-hand hitting coaches, an infield coach, an outfield coach, pitching coaches, left and right. Kauffman and I discussed these on a regular basis. I particularly recall one trip to Fort Myers, on which we went over a lot of these details. These discussions were on top of my regular job with the Royals, director of players and director of scouts. I was also the one who brought in trackmen Bill Easton and Wes Santee to boost running speed of the players. We paid them for ten days of instruction, and they greatly improved some of the players' speed, especially catcher Fran Healy.

The Baseball Academy was a great idea, but the full potential got wasted by the leadership at that time. Rather than hire the experienced ex-major leaguers, Syd Thrift chose a bunch of amateur and relatively inexperienced coaches at first. Some of this first collection of instruuctors were teaching poor fundamentals, not major-league caliber techniques. For example, they were teaching bunting by holding the bat straight up instead of parallel to the ground! Eventually the Royals saw their mistake and hired some of the guys I recommended, as well as other ex-major leaguers.

From a professional standpoint, I thought the Royals should have gotten more for the money they invested. Most of the Academy players never panned out as major leaguers. Only Frank White was a bona fide star. Bruce Miller played for the Giants, and Ron Washington was a journeyman with the Twins. The major stars who carried the Royals throughout the 1970s and 1980s, George Brett, Dan Quisenberry, John Mayberry, Freddie Patek, Amos Otis, Dennis Leonard, Steve Busby, Al Fitzmorris, and others came by way of the draft, trades (a couple of which I helped facilitate), and free agency.

ON APRIL 6, 1932, in the first professional baseball game ever played in New Mexico, the home Albuquerque Dons defeated the El Paso Longhorns 43-15, setting the all-time one game scoring record. In the first season of the Class C Cactus League, Dons manager Bobby Coltrin with 22 years of experience in organized ball had modest goals:

"I know that we'll lose a lot of ball games this year. . . . Regardless, I think I'll have a bunch of kids who'll be moving up to fast company soon." It took the 1932 Dons all of 160 minutes to fulfill their manager's wildest expectations.

The bloody details of this game have been previously reported—14 triples, 21 walks, 12 errors, five hit batsmen, and one run scored every two minutes, forty-five seconds. However, there is more to the tale than five Dons starters getting four or more hits each.

The game was played in 50+ MPH winds with gusts estimated to be above 70 MPH. And the wind was blowing straight in from center field so that only one ball was hit over the fence. Longhorn starter Lefty Nielsen was roughed up for 11 hits before he could get five outs. The spectators knew immediately that they were a part of baseball history. The *El Paso Times* reported that the game was a "freakish tilt," and "a wilder game of baseball never will be played again in organized circles."

On the following day the Dons won another slugfest, 14-13, with the two teams cutting their error total in half (12 to 6) and playing the game in just 12 minutes fewer than the previous day's game. The teams complied a two-day total of 85 runs on 74 hits! The *El Paso Times* commented on "the vast improvement over yesterday's wild scramble." Whatever criteria one uses to judge these matters, professional baseball in New Mexico had a wild, wooly, and record-setting start.

—JEFFREY M. LAING